Le Fanu's Gothic

Also by Victor Sage

Fiction

DIVIDING LINES

A MIRROR FOR LARKS

BLACK SHAWL

Criticism

HORROR FICTION IN THE PROTESTANT TRADITION

THE GOTHIC NOVEL: A Selection of Critical Essays

MODERN GOTHIC: A Reader (*ed. with Allan Lloyd Smith*)

MELMOTH THE WANDERER: Charles Maturin (*ed. with Introduction and Notes*)

UNCLE SILAS: J. S. Le Fanu (*ed. with Introduction and Notes*)

GOOD AS HER WORD: Lorin Sage, Selected Journalism (*ed. with Sharon Sage*)

Le Fanu's Gothic

The Rhetoric of Darkness

Victor Sage

First published 2004 by
PALGRAVE MACMILLAN
Houndmills, Basingstoke, Hampshire RG21 6XS and
175 Fifth Avenue, New York, N.Y. 10010
Companies and representatives throughout the world

PALGRAVE MACMILLAN is the global academic imprint of the Palgrave Macmillan division of St. Martin's Press, LLC and of Palgrave Macmillan Ltd. Macmillan® is a registered trademark in the United States, United Kingdom and other countries. Palgrave is a registered trademark in the European Union and other countries.

ISBN 0–333–67755–2

This book is printed on paper suitable for recycling and made from fully managed and sustained forest sources.

A catalogue record for this book is available from the British Library.

Library of Congress Cataloging-in-Publication Data

Sage, Victor, 1942–
    Le Fanu's gothic: the rhetoric of darkness / Victor Sage
        p. cm.
    Includes bibliographical references and index.
    ISBN 0–333–67755–2 (cloth)
        1. Le Fanu, Joseph Sheridan, 1814–1873—Criticism and interpretation.
2. Horror tales, English—History and criticism. 3. Gothic revival (Literature)—
Ireland. 4. Ireland—In literature. I. Title
PR4879.L7Z87 2003
823'.8—dc22   2003058075

10 9 8 7 6 5 4 3 2 1
13 12 11 10 09 08 07 06 05 04

Printed and bound in Great Britain by
Antony Rowe Ltd, Chippenham and Eastbourne

To Moyra

Contents

List of Illustrations

Introduction

J.S. Le Fanu has always been known to *aficionados* as one of the masters of the Gothic horror story, but he remained a kind of Barthesian ghost until 1980, when the first real biography of this notoriously elusive, almost fugitive author was published. Nowadays, he is still known mainly for his shorter fiction, which is frequently anthologised, large amounts of which can still be obtained in two fine Dover anthologies, edited by E.F. Bleiler. The other works he is famous for are *Uncle Silas*, his classic frightener of 1864, which is regularly reprinted, his last (overtly) Irish novel, *The House by the Churchyard* (1861), which has an intertextual connection with Joyce's *Finnegans Wake*, and the fine collection of stories *In a Glass Darkly*, which includes the other single work which has caused his reputation to rise and flourish, the later Gothic masterpiece, 'Carmilla', a novella that has slowly built its reputation, first, through cinema adaptations, in the 1930s, and 1960s, and then, through the rise of the Gothic as a subject of academic study since the 1960s. Le Fanu, today, stands at the conjunction of Irish Studies, Gothic Studies and the study of the Victorian Sensation Novel.[1]

The critical results of this rise in interest are uneven. Le Fanu has certainly been politicised by recent work in Irish Studies and we now have no difficulty seeing his Gothic, along with that of Charles Maturin and Bram Stoker, and even Elizabeth Bowen, as articulating the attenuated, hyphenated existence of a dying Protestant Ascendancy caste. In the last two decades or so, the study of the Gothic itself has been feminised and historicised; and the study of the Victorian sensation novelists has been feminised too, and no longer accepts the label 'sensation fiction' as a real description of this type of writing. Wilkie Collins, for example, who for years was Le Fanu's twin 'sensationalist', and was in a similar state of semi-oblivion, has been put back into contention as a leading Victorian novelist. But for Sheridan Le Fanu, these various agendas leave an area of neglect: there is no extended study of his narrative methods. There are accounts of his thematics, his characters, his politics, and some of his occult beliefs, his Victorianism, his relation to other writers, his *recherché* allusions; but there is no recent attempt to draw together the continuities of reading practice invited by this author.

This book seeks to fill that gap; it is, first, a textual study of narrative codes in a selection of Le Fanu's major texts, mixing well-known with lesser known, and working through from his earliest fiction to his later work. I study the hoops and the loops, the steps, and layers of narrative which a reader is obliged to negotiate. Le Fanu's texts are acutely, but deceptively, aware of the act of narration itself, poised in a space between written and spoken language, which from the outset of his career employ their own poetics of interruption and alienation. My basic concern is the positioning of the reader at any given moment in these texts.

This particular area of relative neglect has also had an effect on the value we attribute to the later work of this fascinating writer after *Uncle Silas*, and outside the more obviously accomplished magazine stories. There are two basic prejudices about these books, both of which began among his Victorian reviewers: one, that they are a form of weak, or failed, realism. Terry Eagleton, fairly recently, described them as 'realist novels shot through with macabre intimations'. This is not dismissive, to be sure; but it is a kind of hybridity by genre-default. This analysis presents textual evidence that the hybridity of these romances is more positive – often drawing on the theatrical – and less dependent on notions of novelistic realism.[2]

The second lingering prejudice is that, because Le Fanu was a prolific writer, a newspaper editor, and a journalist, he wrote too hastily and was simply careless. His powers, it is often vaguely assumed, are declining after the early 1860s. But some of his most powerful work is in the two collections he produced at the end of his life, *In a Glass Darkly* (1871) and *Chronicles of Golden Friars*. The fact is that his Victorian reviewers didn't, on the whole, know how to read him. Geraldine Jewsbury at the *Athenaeum* is a case in point: she had to learn, but she did. Others did not: the *Spectator* of 1869, for example, referred to him, loftily, as having declined 'from sculpture to hasty modelling in mud'. This is an example of the two prejudices – lack of craft and lack of mimesis – in one.[3]

So there is still an uneasy sense with the later romances that they are a 'falling off' – that an evaluative prejudice based on the standards of realism still operates – and we are left with a legacy of uncertainty about how to read these texts as narratives. Hybrid forms, they contain narrative codes and conventions that are still sometimes lost to us as readers.

In studying Le Fanu's Gothic, I want to begin by taking a closer look at this formal point; at how Le Fanu's self-conscious habit of holding narrative at bay in the telling, relates to the cultural contexts of his writing: for example, he has a habit of layering and back-dating his texts which sometimes gives them a double or triple sense of time, affecting their reader's point of view. *Uncle Silas* and 'Carmilla' are both cases in point. So the discussions in this book tend to start from formal points – the nature of framing, layering, gaps in the text, angles of narration, the production of seams and fissures – and move out beyond them into the contexts implied by the language.

Le Fanu, like Dickens, with whom he seems to have established a rapport later in life, is a comic writer, drawn to mixed effects: to the violent, the dreamy, the learned, and the grotesque, sometimes all at once. His tone is richly ambiguous, and not always obvious. His symbolism is frequently occult. Despite the fact that he wrote very rapidly, Le Fanu is an artist and a stylist. The language of his texts is distinctive.

There is another reason for looking closely. The critical picture of Le Fanu's career as a writer is often shaped by the (biographical) notion of 'retreat'. There is a retreat from Irish politics, after the Young Ireland rebellion of 1848; there is a retreat from social life, after the tragic death of his wife in the 1850s, when he was allegedly known as 'the Invisible prince' in Dublin; and there is a retreat 'into the Gothic'. Sometimes all three can come together, as this commentator suggests:

> Scott, as we have seen, was inspired by Gothic novels to write his own historical novels. Conversely, Le Fanu shifted in his career from historical to Gothic fiction. In retreating to Gothicism, he abandoned history.[4]

Despite some suggestive recent work on Scott's Gothic, I tend to agree about the opposition between Scott and Le Fanu, but the claim – made only on the basis of Irish historical novels – seems exaggerated.[5] Le Fanu's early work – poised, as it is, between pro-Jacobite 'even-handedness' and anti-Whig satire – is both Gothic and historical; and I look in this book at how this founding political ambiguity relates to the uncanny, and how that founding ambivalence forms the narrative codes of the later romances. Moreover, the other half of the idea of 'retreat' doesn't quite work either. More recent studies have shown that the writings of the Protestant Anglo-Irish are embedded in the history of a dying caste, so we can't simply make an opposition here, even in the English context, between 'Gothic' on the one hand, and 'history' on the other.

My starting-point is the nature of Le Fanu's Gothic. This is conceived, not as a genre, but a rhetoric: a recurring set of designs on readers' security and pride in their own rationality. The rhetoric of darkness in Le Fanu traverses his texts, combining with other forms of language to create a range of different effects, like a free radical in the textual body. This rhetoric is inseparable from embedding and framing effects. Anyone familiar with Shakespeare's tragedies will remember those moments when the hero deviates from the self-conscious management of his own role as an essentially 'modern' individual, and shifts into a rant which is (1) clearly, *all* role; and (2) a more archaic form of language than the textual surface that surrounds it. First time round, I can still remember, how strange it was to hear Hamlet, the sophisticated intellectual, the touchstone of self-consciousness, say:

> 'Tis now the very witching time of night
> When churchyards yawn, and hell itself breathes out
> Contagion to the world. *Now could I drink hot blood …*

Invisible quotation-marks close round these words, almost as soon as they are uttered: almost, but there is a 'lag' at the moment of utterance before the frame sneaks and settles into place around this rhetoric of 'superstition' and darkness. The same kind of shock occurs in *Lear*, when the king rounds on his favourite daughter, and plunges, with his curse, into the dark:

> For, by the scared radiance of the sun,
> The mysteries of Hecat and the night;
> By all the operation of the orbs
> From whom we do exist and cease to be;
> Here I disclaim all my paternal care
> Propinquity and property of blood …
>
> (I.i. 108–13)

These are transgressive moments, epiphanies of darkness, when the past (several layers of it) usurps the present, and an older universe of 'superstition' and barbarity rushes momentarily into the vacuum left by civilised, 'modern', reasonable doubt. They are framed by the play itself.

I do not mention the more obvious case of *Macbeth*, where the rhetoric of darkness, tied explicitly to images of the Stuart dynasty, is in the bones of the play, drawing the broad noisy daylight of Bankside afternoons into its pocket of black silence, and needs no (Victorian) 'atmosphere' of literally dimmed or extinguished limelights for us to be aware of it. *Macbeth* has always been a key reference point for writers in the Gothic tradition.[6]

There is another literary historical motive that drives this discussion. It is a commonplace that the Gothic finished as a genre in the narrow, commercial sense in 1820 with Maturin, when readers moved on to the historical novel after Scott took over. But there is a kind of literary-historical black hole about what happened to it in the 1830s, which still needs some work. Le Fanu is a key figure here, because he reinvents it, just at the point when literary history assumes it was exhausted, and he places it dynamically in the context of Irish cultural nationalism. In fact, after Maturin and Scott, there seems to have been a diffusion of the old genre into discourse, as (pro-Catholic) authors like Ainsworth used the rhetoric of darkness to hybridise the realism of Scott's historical novel.[7] The Gothic mutates everywhere and survives from then on, self-consciously, as an agent of textual hybridity across genres.[8] This hybridity is the technique of Charlotte Brontë in *Jane Eyre*, the source for which is one of those early stories of Le Fanu in the Dublin University Magazine, which I look at closely in Chapter 1. 'Darkness' afflicts his characters, but it is also a readerly condition in Le Fanu, as it is in Maturin. I think we need to see the Gothic in this period as a cultural response, rather than a bounded genre, and this, indeed, is a key to the question of how it comes to flourish in such a diversity of forms in the nineteenth century after its own genre-death. Le Fanu is crucial to that process of transmission and adaptation.

One more aspect of the myth of 'retreat' needs some comment. One of the pleasures of reading Le Fanu's later work is the great flowering of women characters. These 'female-centred novels' have disappointed some commentators who see them as part of a retreat into the domestic.[9] Le Fanu was very affected by the suicide of his cousin, Frances. Later, after the mysterious and harrowing death of his wife, Le Fanu was left to bring up two daughters and a son. He seems to have been very close to his daughters, and the combination of the memories of Susan Le Fanu's death and the task of bringing up these young women seems to give him a new closeness to all things female. The touching nature of the friendship between Milly and Maud which so delicately suggests the passing of time in *Uncle Silas* is a product of this observation. The shift into an *ingénue* first-person narrator, Maud, in *Uncle Silas* contributes a huge amount to that novel's complexity and richness; and, again, his close portrayal of female friendship through the eyes of Laura, another innocent, is vital to the creation of the most believable vampire in literature, in 'Carmilla'. His final novel, *Willing To Die*, also has a female narrator, Ethel Ware. The title of this last book is an allusion to a female 'plot' which evolves throughout these novels. Le Fanu uses the discourse of the old Gothic romance, mediated through German folktale, to defamiliarise the contemporary Victorian plot of romantic love, studying erotic passion as a morbid and perverse condition which leads to death.

The other main 'plot' whose presence and evolution I have traced in these late romances tends to be male, comes from the theatre and tells us something about this writer's methods of characterisation. It is what I have called the the Two Brothers Plot, coming mainly from eighteenth-century comic tradition, and in particular from the masterpiece of Le Fanu's great-uncle, Richard Brinsley Sheridan. And this plot is Gothicised from moral and political satire into the Double: a dark, passionate, and murderous struggle between the Self and the monstrous Other, which is portrayed in various stages of externalisation.[10]

In each of these 'plots', which are structural elements in the late romances, I have been concerned to show how the textual dynamics – particularly those of narrative perversity and indirection – govern the presentation of the material. There is an obvious relation between unreliable narration and the idea of foregrounded testimony in Le Fanu's writing. I'm particularly concerned with the development of witnessing in his narrative techniques, and the game with authority, the epistemology of reading; because it is simultaneously religious and secular. Le Fanu quite consciously contrived an overdetermined 'equilibrium of explanation' for the events in his narratives. In the early work, the notion of testimony is framed as an antiquarian and anthropological necessity. But in the later work, where narrative conventions demand authority, the methods of narration are equally indirect. Where those methods are of omniscience, it seems easy for this to look like 'inconsistency' and an inept form of realism. But the stress on 'evidence' has a particular relationship to the cultural narrative of the Gothic, as Jan Gordon points out:

> Given the radical Protestant faiths, particularly those in the north of England, that inform the spiritual setting for so much Gothic fiction, it is perhaps understandable that language comes to exist as

'evidence' or a clue to some larger presence, whether Divine or Satanic ... . As the Gothic Kingdom often parodies its Divine counterpart, an inverse relationship is established: rather than exhibiting possessions or establishing some sovereignty over authorized texts, as does traditional religious discourse, the text is possessed by something beyond itself resulting in the structural and thematic questioning that creates various versions of the truth while simultaneously de-subjectivizing the Word.[11]

To see the text as 'possessed by something beyond itself' is startlingly accurate in the case of Le Fanu. Gordon's observation strikes me as giving us a flavour of the cultural and formal function of 'testimony' in Le Fanu's writing: the alienation effect of witnessing on 'authority' (i.e. Godlike, novelistic 'omniscience' as a representation of Authority) which comes from his Protestantism, combined with his legal training. The epistemology of reading is a theme throughout this discussion. So Chapters 1, 2, and 3 begin by studying the rhetoric of 'superstition' and 'attestation' in the Irish work. Chapter 4 studies the first 'English' novel and 5 seeks to relate the narrative self-consciousness of *Uncle Silas* to its textual layering and sense of history. Chapters 6 and 7 are case studies in these themes in two of the later, rarer novels, *The Tenants of Malory* and *Haunted Lives*. Chapter 8 ends by studying the textual dynamics of 'Carmilla'.

Chapter 8 was first delivered in another form to staff and students at the University of Thessaloniki, Greece, in Spring 1999; another version of Chapter 1 was given as a lecture to a research seminar in the University of Toulouse, in summer 2001; and, part of Chapter 3 was offered in Spring 2001 as a paper to the PhD research seminar in the School of English and American Studies at the University of East Anglia. I'm deeply grateful to colleagues for inviting me to try out some of this material. Lastly, many thanks to Charmian Hearne at Macmillan Press for commissioning this book, to the patience of the staff at Palgrave Macmillan, and to the generosity of my university for giving me study leave to research and write it.

My warmest thanks also to friends and colleagues for their conversation and their support. The late Lorna Sage read part of Chapter 8 before her untimely death in 2001, and offered valuable critical suggestions: warmest thanks for their support and interest to the following: Pierre Arnaud, Karin Boklund-Lagopoulou, Jon Cook, Anthony Gash, Michael Hollington, William Hughes, Alex Lagopoulos, Paul Magrs, Roger Sales, and Peter Womack (for several talks about Scott). My appreciation to all my graduate students who have shown sustained interest in this project. Any errors are, of course, my own.

Lastly, deepest thanks to Moyra Sidell for her ready ear and stern discrimination.

Part I
Re-Framing the Gothic

1
Two Stories: Chiaroscuro and the Politics of Superstition

Le Fanu's first rhetorical opportunity comes in the context of a political pressure: that of Protestant cultural nationalism in the Dublin of the late 1830s. That pressure is 'reconciliatory': it is the idea that the interests of a ruling class can be best served by the creation of a single national tradition, which can include Protestant and Catholic sides of the Irish sectarian divide. Here is Samuel Ferguson, writing in 1834, in Le Fanu's own magazine, the *Dublin University Magazine* (*DUM*):

> The Protestants of Ireland are wealthy and intelligent beyond most classes of their numbers in the world; but their wealth has been hitherto insecure, because their intelligence has not embraced a thorough knowledge of the genius and disposition of their catholic fellow citizens. The genius of the past is not to be learned by the notes of Sunday tourists. The history of centuries must be gathered, published, studied, and digested, before the Irish people can be known to the world.[1]

Le Fanu's extraordinary first sequence of stories, written between 1838 and 1840 and published in the *DUM*, was nested perfectly within Ferguson's political brief.

Or so it seems. Le Fanu disappears as author: he writes anonymously, inventing a Catholic priest, Father Purcell, an enthusiastic collector of local traditions, as the 'compiler' of these stories. He then introduces an anonymous editor, who places Father Purcell's papers before his Protestant audience, selecting those which he feels will be of most interest to them. So we read through several layers. The pre-text of Purcell's papers is often a spoken one, written down by the good Father. His texts are then edited, quite intrusively framed, by his anonymous friend and literary executor, who is implicitly of Protestant sympathy, in touch with the audience of the *DUM*.

There is clearly plenty of opportunity for irony here. This recessive framing, or evidentiary technique, is familiar to us from the Gothic novel, from Walpole to Maturin. The editorial fiction is also something extensively used by Sir Walter Scott, whose updating of the Old Gothic into his 'historical romance' is by far the most powerful model for the aesthetic representation of 'reconciliation' in the late 1830s.[2] Purcell is collecting 'superstitions'. To put it more euphemistically, as the text does, he has a 'love of the whimsical and the marvellous'. Of course, the initial prejudice here against him, as a witness, is that Protestants regard the Catholic faith itself as a form of 'superstition'. Catholic Emancipation was only seven years old, and some of the the *DUM*'s audience were still distinctly uneasy about the loyalty of Catholics.[3]

But the pressure towards 'reconciliation' complicates this ancient prejudice, because it introduces elements of class into the question of religion. Purcell is a priest of the old school, of a Continental education (code for Jacobite, and even Jacobin sympathies), and a literary man. He is unlike the current '*alumni* of Maynooth', says the editor, snobbishly. Here we see the other political pressure: Purcell, a figure from the past, is given credibility as a witness to national tradition, against the negative examples of the modern priests (perhaps the sons of publicans or small tenant farmers) who might well be part of what the *DUM*'s readership regarded as the divisive, politically nationalist, campaign of Daniel O'Connell for repeal of the Union with England.[4]

So Purcell gains relative credibility as a witness, with the help of his editor. But there is ultimately a conflict between his role as a Gothic device and the programme of 'reconciliation' inherited by Le Fanu from writers like Ferguson. The Gothic epiphanies of these stories jump out of their ostensible frames, cut across the lines of 'superstition', and destabilise them. All of them employ the discourse of the supernatural and almost all of them involve suggestions of resurrection and revenancy. The ideological reflex of this material is inseparable from the language of its doctrinal implications – the much-disputed question of the Resurrection of the Body, which is an obsession of the Gothic tradition. The degree of metaphor in these fictional resurrections is something the reader must negotiate, however 'post-Enlightenment' the Protestant audience believe themselves to be.

Darkness: imagination, superstition, resurrection

Let me take an example of the way the framing of the text intersects with its thematics, and disrupts the clear lines of the reader's response, creating rhetorical opportunities for the writer. The story 'A Chapter in the History of a Tyrone Family' begins with a suggestion of another function for the accurate (and therefore legalistic and scientific) presentation of narrative: for Purcell, the preservation of a person's words preserves the teller from that 'extinction' from which, as we have seen, he is concerned to rescue national tradition:

> In the following narrative, I have endeavoured to give as nearly as possible the *ipsissima verba* of the valued friend from whom I received it, conscious that any aberration from *her* mode of telling the tale of her own life would at once impair its accuracy and its effect.[5]

But Purcell's own motives for his 'accuracy' here, as opposed to his editor, are evidently not just scientific or a form of disinterested post-Enlightenment anthropology: they are magical and sublime and they involve evidences of the resurrection from the dead:

> Would that, with her words, I could also bring before you her animated gesture, her expressive countenance, the solemn and thrilling air and accent with which she related the dark passages in her strange story; and above all, that I could communicate the impressive consciousness that the narrator had seen with her own eyes, and personally acted in the scenes which she described; these accompaniments, taken with the additional circumstance that she who told the tale was far too deeply and sadly impressed with religious principle to misrepresent or fabricate what she repeated as fact, gave to the tale a depth of interest which the events recorded could hardly, themselves, have produced.[6]

Here he rhetorically brings her before us, even as he is saying he can't: to imagine her at all, is to resurrect her from oblivion. Imagination itself, enshrined in language about language, is a form of resurrection: it brings back 'the dark passages in her strange story'. What does 'dark' mean here? 'Supernatural' only, implying a world of heaven or hell, or 'superstitious'? The precedent for deciding this is ultimately the Gospels and the (corroborative) witnessing of the resurrection of Christ which needs to be 'read' in the right spirit in order to possess the mind of the reader. The form implicitly hands over responsibility to whoever reads the text.[7]

But Purcell himself is framed, in more senses than one. 'Religious principle' looks like a universal appeal. But how far a 'sceptical' (i.e. a politically suspicious) Protestant audience will disbelieve at this point and treat the appeal as a form of 'superstition' is a variable quantity. The framing encourages such a reaction: that the very accuracy of his 'legatee' brings before us, in all its detail, the 'superstition' of Purcell's 'Old Faith', which we must allow for. The authority of witnessing is undermined, even as it is claimed. After all, the witness is witnessed by his editor and found to be, himself, a form of quaintly amusing 'evidence' of how people used to think: such a structure must, one would think, qualify the reader's assent.

And yet such 'religious principle' might be also be construed as common to all who profess a form of the Christian faith: we seem to be in the territory of Defoe's pamphlet, 'The Apparition of Mrs Veal' here, and the 'No spirit, No God' argument is a unifying pressure on reponses which, in other ways, see themselves as opposed.[8]

Whatever the response, this story consists of two stories. The first is told by Purcell's dead, but partly resurrected narrator, whom our editor renames, in a footnote, 'Miss Richardson':

> I have carefully altered the names as they appear in the original MSS., for the reader will see that some of the circumstances recorded are not of a kind to reflect honour upon those involved in them; and as many are still living, who stand in close relation to the actors of this drama, the reader will see the necessity of the course which we have adopted.[9]

This is close to the documentary fictions of Defoe; but here it has several odd effects. It enhances the fictional status of the story, because there is not a lot of detail about the characters, and it seems unlikely that any one would be tempted to try to identify 'the originals' on the evidence given in the text – unless there is a pre-existent legend, or even written narrative, about a specific Tyrone family, which no commentator has yet identified. So the 'editorial' technique exposes the fiction as a fiction, which is always, even in Defoe, one consequence of the claim that fiction is really concealed fact.

But it does have another effect: it brings the past into the present and we are reminded that the time-scale of the narration, as opposed to the events, is not meant to be the remote, but the fairly recent past. On the other hand, Purcell himself belongs to that past – the effect of the framing device – which makes the reader's position strangely indeterminate.

The text consists of two stories: one introductory and very short – an uncanny incident, the other taking up the whole of the rest of the text. They are linked by the question of 'superstition' and the notion of the 'omen'. Fanny Richardson is established from the outset, along with the rest of her family, as someone with an unusual sensitivity to the supernatural. Perhaps her substitute surname has some literary significance. One night, when they know her sister is on her way from Dublin with her new husband to their residence, Ashtown House, Fanny hears the gate:

> I now heard the shrill screaming of the rusty iron, as the avenue-gate revolved on its hinges; again came the sound of wheels in rapid motion.
>
> 'It is they,' said I, starting up; 'the carriage is in the avenue.'
>
> We all stood for a few moments breathlessly listening. On thundered the vehicle with the speed of a whirlwind; crack went the whip, and clatter went the wheels, as it rattled over the uneven pavement of the court. A general and furious barking from all the dogs about the house, hailed its arrival.[10]

Two things are (lightly) suggested here: one, that what is really going on is that her sister's spirit is trying to 'come home' and it is (metonymically) her screams that Fanny hears, and two, that the dogs are reliable witnesses to the presence of something physical. It is about one o'clock in the morning. The family hurry down in readiness and the scene empties beautifully of all its point:

> We hurried to the hall in time to hear the steps let down with the sharp clanging noise peculiar to the operation, and the hum of voices exerted in the bustle of arrival. The hall-door was now thrown open, and we all stepped forth to greet our visitors.
>
> The court was perfectly empty; the moon was shining broadly and brightly upon all around; nothing was to be seen but the tall trees with their long spectral shadows, now wet with the dews of midnight.
>
> We stood gazing from right to left, as if suddenly awakened from a dream; the dogs walked suspiciously, growling and snuffling about the court, and by totally and suddenly ceasing their former loud barking, expressing the predominance of fear.[11]

The witnesses now corroborate each other's bafflement. For the reader, the scene is delicately balanced between emptiness and fullness. But there is no doubt about the interpretation of this event, or non-event, by the whole family:

> We stared one upon another in perplexity and dismay, and I think I never beheld more pale faces assembled. By my father's direction,

we looked about to find anything which might indicate or account for the noise which we had heard; but no such thing was to be seen – even the mire which lay upon the avenue was undisturbed. We returned to the house, more panic-struck than I can describe.[12]

Why are they instantly 'panic-struck'? Would 'we' be? 'They' are 'super-stitious'. They believe something was there, not that their senses were deceived. The 'explanation' follows:

On the next day, we learned by a messenger, who had ridden hard the greater part of the night, that my sister was dead. On Sunday evening, she had retired to bed rather unwell, and, on Monday, her indisposi-tion declared itself unequivocally to be malignant fever. She became hourly worse, and, on Tuesday night, a little after midnight, she expired.[13]

At the word 'expired', that is, just at the point where this coincidence is implicitly claimed (by the narrator, Fanny, and behind her, Father Purcell) as having explanatory force, we have a footnote which inter-rupts the text and re-asserts the frame. Its effect is, however, by no means straightforward:

The residuary legatee of the late Francis Purcell, who has the honour of selecting such of his lamented friend's manuscripts as may appear fit for publication, in order that the lore which they contain may reach the world before scepticism and utility have robbed our species of the precious gift of credulity, and scornfully kicked before them, or trampled into annihilation those harmless fragments of picturesque superstition which it is our object to preserve, has been subjected to the charge of dealing too largely in the marvellous; and it has been half insinuated that such is his love for *diablerie*, that he is content to wander a mile out of his way, in order to meet a fiend or a goblin, and thus to sacrifice all regard for truth and accuracy to the idle hope of affrighting the imagination, and thus pandering to the bad taste of his reader.[14]

The allusion to Bentham and Mill in 'utility' is a pointed piece of con-temporary observation; the 'English' response, and the 'contemporary' response, are atheistical and have no faith – and it is imminent here, too, in Ireland. In fact, the *DUM* was a repository of adherents to 'Political Economy' who were struggling to customise it – to reconcile it with an intervention into the marketplace on national (and Protestant) grounds; and so this joke is aimed at a certain part of the readership, or at another part who know about them and disapprove. The 'precious gift of credulity' is precisely what this paragraph is offering, and beginning the process of persuading us to accept, as part of a national tradition, an Irish inflection of 'reason'. On the other hand, this is reported to us as 'superstition'.[15]

Rhetorically, this 'footnote' is a pre-emptive strike at the reader's objections to assenting to the uncanny. The hope of affrighting our imagination (though not 'idly') is exactly what the text is full of, and exactly what we respond to with alacrity. But the effect of the 'footnote' is profoundly self-contradictory. It momentarily turns into an informal manifesto for the Gothic, naming the responses (discredited by Sir Walter Scott in numerous reviews of Gothic novels) which the reader may be tempted to acknowledge as a motive for reading these tales, before disclaiming them and sliding away into the rhetoric of documentary truth and evidence:

> He begs leave, then, to take this opportunity of asserting his perfect innocence of all the crimes laid to his charge, and to assure his reader that he never *pandered to his bad taste*, nor went one inch out of his way to introduce witch, fairy, devil, ghost, or any other of the grim fraternity of the redoubted Raw-head-and-bloody-bones. His province, touching these tales, has been attended with no difficulty and little responsibility; indeed, he is accountable for nothing more than an alteration in the names of persons mentioned therein, when such a step seemed necessary, and for an occasional note, whenever he conceived it possible, innocently, to edge in a word. These tales have been *written down*, as the heading of each announces, by the Rev. Francis Purcell, P.P. of Drumcoolagh; and in all the instances, which are many, in which the present writer has had an opportunity of comparing the manuscript of his departed friend with the actual traditions which are current amongst the families whose fortunes they pretend to illustrate, he has uniformly found that whatever of supernatural occurred in the story, so far from having been exaggerated by him, had rather been softened down, and, wherever it could be attempted, accounted for.[16]

'Raw-head-and-bloody-bones' mimicks the language of Scott from his reviews about the excesses of popular Gothic. 'Innocently' is a perfect double-take here. We are watching the reader of a new, updated post-Scott antiquarianism being created by the legalistic frame; while the old satisfactions of the Gothic are resurrected in the guise of their own discredit.[17] Disbelievers can relax into the tale, knowing that the writer is not reponsible for it – 'tradition' is. Irish tradition, family tradition, oral tradition 'written down' (note the emphasis here – the editor's imputation of authority here to his manuscript) recorded as a matter of 'fact'.[18]

Intertextual frames: *Bluebeard* and (the real life of) the madwoman in the attic

The text then doubles up and tells another story. The second part depends on the bridge of 'superstition' to link it with the first. But this time it uses the framing device of 'attestation' to turn the tables on the reader, because the fiction that the text is 'evidence' leaves open the question of final explanation of those narrative events. In fact, in foregrounding 'explanation', it encourages 'gaps' in the text.

The second half of Fanny's story (besides the paratextual apparatus) also employs an intertextual frame: a rewrite of Ann Radcliffe's *Udolpho* and Charles Perrault's *Bluebeard*, on which the plot of *Udolpho* itself is founded. Subject to family pressure Fanny marries Lord Glenfallen and goes out with him to Cahergillagh, his country estate. As they draw near, the language of the text modulates into the picturesque, and then echoes Emily's approach to Udolpho:

'There lies the enchanted castle,' said Lord Glenfallen, pointing ... .[19]

Glenfallen has clearly read his Radcliffe:

'There,' said Montoni, speaking for the first time in several hours, 'is Udolpho'.[20]

But, lightly, jokingly, he has also introduced a fairytale register. When they go inside, the first uncanny event takes place – the descent of 'something like a mass of black tapestry', a black veil *à la* Radcliffe. Stepping back, Fanny turns to the old servant, Martha, who doesn't appear to have noticed:

I turned, smiling and half-ashamed, to the old servant, and I said:
    'You see what a coward I am.'
    The woman looked puzzled, and, without saying any more, I was about to draw aside the curtain and enter the room, when, upon

turning to do so, I was surprised to find that nothing whatever interposed to obstruct the passage.[21]

Again, the 'explanation' of the event is suspended. When Fanny asks the simple question, where is the black curtain that had impeded her passage, Martha suddenly turns pale and exclaims: 'The cross of Christ about us!' The effect is just as it is in *Udolpho*: the comic exaggeration of this (Catholic) superstition of the servant discredits 'superstition'; but Fanny (also Catholic, but upper-class and therefore supposed to be more rational) is secretly unnerved, because there is no other explanation. Apparently, Martha has seen it once before and it is an omen of death in the Glenfallen family; most pointedly for Fanny, the death of the wife.

Glenfallen then puts Fanny to the test, and we realise we are in the rewrite of a folktale:

Now I shall make a test of you … I shall be your *Bluebeard* – tush, why do I trifle thus? … You must promise me, upon your sacred honour, that you will visit *only* that part of the castle which can be reached from the front entrance, leaving the back entrance and the part of the building commmanded immediately by it to the menials, as also the small garden whose high wall you can see yonder; and never at any time to seek to pry or peep into them, not to open the door which communicates from the front part of the house through the corridor with the back.[22]

The moral of Charles Perrault's tale is 'Reproof of Curiosity'. This is Propp's condition for narrative drive in the folktale – transgression. But though we recognise the structure, we are caught by surprise: the twist is that the transgression here comes not from Fanny, who is (unexpectedly) obedient, but from an invasion by her secret, fateful, and monstrous Other:

Upon entering the chamber, I was surprised and somewhat startled to find it occupied. Beside the fireplace, and nearly opposite the door, seated on a large, old-fashioned elbow-chair, was placed the figure of a lady. She appeared to be nearer fifty than forty, and was dressed suitably to her age, in a handsome suit of flowered silk; she had a profusion of trinkets and jewellery about her person, and many rings upon her fingers. But although very rich, her dress was not gaudy or in ill taste. But what was remarkable in the lady was, that though her features were handsome, and upon the whole, pleasing,

> the pupil of each eye was dimmed with the whiteness of cataract, and she was evidently stone-blind. I was for some seconds so surprised at this unaccountable apparition, that I could not find words to address her.[23]

'Apparition' here has the ambiguous force of 'ghost' or 'thing that has appeared'. We can imagine the impact this story made upon the young Charlotte Brontë when she read it in the *DUM*, because this is Flora Van Kemp, the original of Charlotte Brontë's 'madwoman in the attic', Bertha Mason. Brontë also uses the self-consciously layered Bluebeard plot in that novel too. Eventually, Le Fanu in *The Wyvern Mystery* reclaimed Bertha from Charlotte Brontë, keeping her name, in a nod to Brontë, as Bertha Velderkaust and moving her origins from the Caribbean back to Holland. Here the seat of unreason is not the colonial slave islands of the West Indies, but the Irish–Dutch connection.[24]

Flora, who claims to be the first wife, is not silenced, however: she is vociferous, and threatens Fanny's life. She is an impossible object, somewhere between a ghost, a projection of the psyche, and a real live bit of Glenfallen's past. This is like a dream. There is no one to 'explain' her existence. Her ambiguous status emerges between the hypotheses, which Fanny prompts, and we offer, to account for her existence. So when finally Fanny, having tackled her husband and been brushed off by him, retires to bed one night and cannot sleep, something happens which precisely hovers between explanations:

> ... my eyes, in their involuntary wanderings, happened to alight upon the large mirror which was, as I have said, fixed in the wall opposite the foot of the bed. A view of it was commanded from where I lay, through the curtains. As I gazed fixedly upon it, I thought I perceived the broad sheet of glass shifting its position in relation to the bed; I riveted my eyes upon it with intense scrutiny; it was no deception, the mirror, as if acting of its own impulse, moved slowly aside, and disclosed a dark aperture in the wall, nearly as large as an ordinary door; a figure evidently stood in this, but the light was too dim to define it accurately.[25]

The reader is teased, momentarily, with the idea of a supernatural intervention; but, by the time we reach the end of the paragraph, the supernatural has given way almost completely to a naturalistic explanation: almost, but the painterly idea of a 'figure' still hovers mid-way between subjective vision and real event.

This is Flora, 'the Dutch hag', come in earnest to cut Fanny's throat. But the ordeal, though horribly real, still resists explanation, and by the end of the story, when Flora is executed on Glenfallen's testimony after a horrendous court scene, we are still in some doubt as to whether Glenfallen was actually married to Flora, and whether she was put up to Fanny's murder by him, as she claims. Glenfallen goes mad through guilt at Flora's death, and kills himself; Fanny survives, driven into an anchoritic piety, 'never to learn the history in whose termination I had been so deeply and tragically involved'. (135)

'Curiosity' – the parody of the reader's lowest instincts – is left unsatisfied, leaving us to reconstruct the case from what is, paradoxically, a witnessed emptiness at the heart of Purcell's antiquarian frame of attestation. However, what we have learnt is that this uncanny event is Dutch, testified to by a member of an old Catholic family, which is somewhat unexpected to begin with, since the Protestant tradition, which apparently founds the Protestant society, to which this text addresses itself (in its outer frame), is also significantly Dutch.[26]

Chiaroscuro: attestation and the peephole effect

Motifs of 'resurrection' and 'revenancy' make for thematic continuity in all of these stories. They form uncanny interventions, violent, comic, disturbing, acting out a dialectic of demoniac possession and material dispossession. The more Gothic stories are the better-known and the more resonant and complex, and they are also early versions of stories and novels which Le Fanu continued to re-write: 'The Fortunes of Sir Robert Ardagh' is a Faustian bargain story, with a demonic servant, come from Hell to drag off Sir Robert by main force into the other world; 'Passage in the Secret History of an Irish Countess', in this version, is the resurrection of a *murder*; and 'Schalken the Painter' (based on a Dutch folktale, 'Jan Schalken's Three Wishes') is a vision of the devil himself who comes to carry off Rose Velderkaust when she tries to escape him. In 'A Chapter in the History of a Tyrone Family', the 'madwoman' is variously 'dead' and 'resurrected', as the metaphors of the story suggest.

The 'resurrection' motif is equally prominent in the romances and the comic and vernacular texts of the collection:[27] 'The Ghost and the Bone Setter' is the story of a picture of a dead man that gets down out of its frame; 'The Last Heir of Castle Connor' is a story of romantic Catholic martyrdom that turns to horror at the possibility of the death of the soul with the body; 'The Drunkard's Dream' involves a resurrection from drink into sobriety and a final claiming by demons; 'The Bridal of

Carrigvarah' also has a subdued version of the wolfish demonic servant who destroys, for no reason, young O'Mara and his Bride, Ellen Heathcote; 'Jim Sullivan's Adventures' is a traditional comic resurrection story which Synge later recycled in 'The Shadow of the Glen'; 'An Adventure of Hardress Fitzgerald: A Royalist Captain', which is a very Scott-like story, a first version of the two romances Le Fanu wrote in the 1840s, has a grotesque epiphany which calls into question its romance format; 'The Quare Gander' is a comic version of the transmigration of souls in which a man 'comes back' as a gander; and 'Billy Malowney's Taste of Love and Glory' is another traditional tale of the Irish peasant who saves Europe from Bonaparte, and then appears as a revenant to his family and friends.[28] And even the simplest, most 'oral' of these texts are equally part of the four-way split between present and past, and oral and written, which is a split governed by the notion of 'attestation'; a rhetorical device that provokes the gap between superstition and rationality in order to cross it, usually momentarily, in a set of nasty epiphanies.[29]

The other aspect of framing which needs to be added in at this point is the notion of *aesthetic* framing, coming from painting. 'The Ghost and the Bone Setter' is a piece of traditional popular farce, like the scenes with the Horse-Courser in Marlowe's *Dr Faustus*. But this farce is mixed with another popular tradition: the Gothic idea of the painting that gets down out of its frame.

Several commentators have studied this self-conscious reference to painting, but perhaps the most relevant to my theme here is Kel Roop, in a very interesting piece called 'Making Light in the Shadow Box: The Artistry of Le Fanu'.[30] Roop calls our attention in Le Fanu's stories to 'an intricate structuring of light patterned after the technique of the minor Dutch painter Godfrey Schalken'.[31] Schalken was a student of Gerald Dou, who experimented with optics, inventing a number of devices. In particular, Schalken is interested in framing. Roop's account is suggestive:

> As a student of Gerard Dou, a master of *Helldunkelstudien*, Godfrey Schalken received a thorough introduction to the chiaroscuro popular with Dutch painters of the seventeenth century and appears to have adopted many of his mentor's candlelit subjects as his own. But in his combination of light sources (such as the blending of candle, pipe, and ember light in 'A Comely Woman at an Arched Window'), Schalken exceeded Dou's intruction. In order to capture the hybrid gleam most effectively, he often arranged his subjects within a series of frames formed by windows and curtains for which his spots of light provided the focus.[32]

It seems, according to Roop's sources, that Schalken used an optical device, a shadow-box. Roop draws an analogy with Le Fanu's narrative technique of framing:

> Le Fanu seems to have written 'Schalken the Painter' and the four supernatural stories of *In A Glass Darkly* ('Green Tea', 'The Familiar', 'Mr Justice Harbottle', 'Carmilla') in a similar fashion. He leaves only the smallest opening of perception in his layered narrations, yet through this aperture he, the reader, and the characters see and plummet into scenes moulded by flickering candlelight. Le Fanu's careful ordering finally betrays a universe permeated by a malignant glow which usurps human power.[33]

Roop concludes: 'Through a compounding of internal frames, the painting becomes a three-dimensional shadow-box which draws the reader into terror.'[34]

This three-dimensional shadow-box corresponds very closely to the semantic aspects of framing I have been talking about, which create a peephole into a forbidden, or a forgotten world, created dialectically out of its very cancelling rhetoric. The nasty epiphany – an image – which is revealed like a Venn diagram's matrix, through the overlaps between the surrounding legalistic and explanatory frames – springs from those surrounding frames and imposes itself, sometimes subtly and sometimes with grotesque and comic violence, upon the reader's imagination. The point which Kel Roop makes is that the horror is not simply associated with darkness, but that, in 'Ardagh', 'Carmilla', and some of the stories in *In a Glass Darkly*, the gloom is effected by the flickering flame of a candle, an ironic harbinger of the cavern into which man must fall. This allusion to painterly 'chiaroscuro' corresponds on the level of language to the ambiguities of 'superstition'. Roop's final point in this excellent discussion is explicitly both ideological and aesthetic, painterly and theological:

> Although Le Fanu's light-bearers may resemble the participants in certain death rites, such as the old Catholic sacrament of the Extreme Unction, their light does not issue in the grace of God but fiends of unearthly horror. Indeed, through their ignorance they ignite the candle's wick.[35]

Purcell, as we have seen already, is the perfect vehicle for a satire on Catholic 'superstition', which however somehow is allowed to backfire on itself, because he is also the vehicle of a Tory satire on Whig ideas of progress. He is the perfect witness for deathbed scenes, the horror and the comedy of which is a repeated pattern throughout these first stories of Le Fanu. But the texts are excessive, overdetermined: Roop ends recalling McCormack's point about the title 'In a Glass Darkly', that it is a perversion of a quotation from St Paul's Corinthians: 'Through a Glass Darkly', a verbal twist which leaves the individual (characters and sometimes readers) trapped in a 'dark' mirror, a representation, dead, but still on this side of death, without Paul's traditional consolation.[36]

The horrors of this are the horrors of revenancy, but in Le Fanu, the code is, from the outset, that of a peculiarly material resurrection. The 'ghosts' from the past in Le Fanu are always more solid and three-dimensional (square-built), than those wispy or guilty individuals in the narrative present (which may itself be merely a more recent epoch of the past) who see them. In the case of one of the most powerful and resonant early stories, 'A Strange Event in the Life of Schalken the Painter', the demon, a kind of animated corpse, is again Dutch, like Flora Van Kemp, and the 1837 text suggests a particular cultural pattern of revenancy – that Le Fanu sites the threat within the Dutch origins of the invasion of William of Orange and its incursion into the story's present.

The structure of the text is that of a layering of representational forms: it begins with the account of a painting. The painting is the pretext for the story we read: it frames it, starting and finishing it, in that sense. But the fiction purports to tell us of the origin of the painting: it drives us towards what it represents. So the fiction also frames the painting. The painting represents 'one scene' of the story it is a part of, and that scene is an uncanny one. But we may not be able to identify that 'scene' absolutely, particularly the angle from which it is seen, because the story is a corpus of legend, not just a literal rendition of the painting in another medium (i.e. language). The relation between painting and tale is not itself mimetic: so, by the time we get to the end, although we know the story already, the horrible climax is a fresh scene and we don't anticipate it.[37]

The relation between the painting and its original 'scene' also turns out to be a key to the character of Schalken which, it is hinted, is not just a question of the Dutch stereotype:

> There are few forms upon which the mantle of mystery and romance could seem to hang more ungracefully than upon that of the uncouth and clownish Schalken – the Dutch boor – the rude and dogged, but most cunning worker in oils, whose pieces delight the initiated of the present day almost as much as his manner disgusted

the refined of his own; and yet this man, so rude, so dogged, so slovenly, I had almost said so savage, in mien and manner, during his after successes, had been selected by the capricious goddess, in his early life, to figure as the hero of a romance by no means devoid of interest or of mystery.[38]

However, Schalken strays unconsciously into 'superstition'. The narrative concerns a version of the Faustian bargain which is to form an important plot in several of Le Fanu's other stories – some in this collection – notably 'Robert Ardagh', for example – and in his novel, *Uncle Silas*, not to mention later stories in other collections.[39] The bargain often concerns the selling by the older generation of the younger one. Schalken the painter, an apprentice to Douw, and Rose Velderkaust, Douw's ward, fall in love and declare their love for each other, but they have no financial prospects. Hoping to improve and thus gain his independence quicker, Schalken stays late one evening in the studio, 'engaged in composing a group of extremely roguish-looking and grotesque imps and demons, who were inflicting various ingenious torments upon a perspiring and pot-bellied St Anthony ...' (II, 195). Schalken is 'sketching a design, an operation which, unlike that of colouring, might be continued as long as there was light sufficient to distinguish between canvas and charcoal' (II, 194). That moment is reached, in which 'charcoal and canvas' (i.e. reality and representation) cannot be distinguished. It is twilight, and Schalken unwittingly changes the conditions of representation as he contemplates his fading sketch:

> The patience of the young man was exhausted, and he stood before his unfinished production, absorbed in no very pleasing ruminations, one hand buried in the folds of his long dark hair, and the other holding the piece of charcoal which had so ill executed its office, and which he now rubbed, without much regard to the sable streaks which it produced, with irritable pressure upon his ample Flemish inexpressibles.
>
> 'Pshaw!' said the young man aloud, 'would that picture, devils, saint, and all, were where they should be – in hell!'[40]

The detail of the hand in the hair later in Le Fanu becomes a curious private code for the uncanny – in 'Carmilla', for example. The young man rubs sable streaks, inadvertently, on himself, edging himself into the representation. And his curse, which by implication is surely meant to exclude himself, violates the frame of both picture, and narrative, by taking in vain the name of the Devil, whom he has depicted:

> A short, sudden laugh, uttered startlingly close to his ear, instantly responded to the ejaculation.[41]

With this 'instant response', the frame has been altered and a new configuration created. What was inside – the represented devil – is now outside, and what was outside – the painter – inside the frame. The tales of Hoffmann include this motif. But the effect is double: it clearly preserves the level of 'superstition' (the curse), but the prose keeps alive the natural explanation, too, and the figure of the Devil is a parody of a Dutch burgomeister, a realistic figure from Dutch genre painting, who appears merely to have entered the studio while Schalken was not looking:

> The artist turned sharply round, and now for the first time became aware that his labours had been overlooked by a stranger.
>   Within about a yard and a half, and rather behind him, there stood what was, or appeared to be, the figure of an elderly man: he wore a short cloak, and a broad-brimmed hat with a conical crown, and in his hand, which was protected with a heavy, gauntlet-shaped glove, he carried a long ebony walking-stick, surmounted with what appeared, as it glittered dimly in the twilight, to be a massive head of gold, and upon his breast, through the folds of the cloak, there shone what appeared to be the links of a rich chain of the same metal.[42]

The effect is to embed the uncanny into the representation, so that the materiality of the gold is picked out in the twilight, in a painterly manner, as it does on the dark surface of Dutch interiors. But its symbolic significance here heralds that bargain that he will make with Gerard Douw for Rose. Phrases like 'what was, or appeared to be ...' keep the perspective of the set-piece constantly shuttling between appearance and reality.

The next paragraph imitates the last rush of darkness and the failing of the light and becomes more menacing, qualifying the adjective 'elderly', as Schalken takes this person in:

> The room was so obscure that nothing further of the appearance of the figure could be ascertained, and the face was altogether overshadowed by the heavy flap of the beaver which overhung it, so that not a feature could be discerned. A quantity of dark hair escaped from

beneath this sombre hat, a circumstance which, connected with the firm, upright carriage of the intruder, proved that his years could not yet exceed threescore or thereabouts.

There was an air of gravity and importance about the garb of this person, and something indescribably odd, I might say awful, in the perfect, stone-like movelessness of the figure, that eventually checked the testy comment which had at once risen to the lips of the irritated artist.[43]

The figure has started to change already. This changing – almost invariably worsening – appearance, is the code of many of Le Fanu's demons and revenants – square-built, physically powerful, sometimes Dutch, three-dimensional presences, a quantity of dark, or even 'sooty', hair escaping from under their old-fashioned hats. Here the posture of the body, however, is uncannily and unnaturally still, indicating to the reader (but not the character, because, without knowing it, Schalken is now in the same world as this creature) that this is a physical resurrection of the body.

In his 1851 rewrite, often thought of as for an English audience, Le Fanu cleverly toned down the archaic, literary excess of this passage, getting rid of the Shakespearian beaver and allowing the shadow of the hat and the room's obscurity to do the work. Schalken's specificity about 'hell' he also removed in favour of a more generalised 'curse', but the breaking and metamorphosis of the representational frame remains.[44]

Schalken has no idea of what he has set in motion. 'Mynheer Vanderhausen' comes again the following night and, unbeknownst to either Schalken or Rose, 'buys' her in gold ingots from her uncle, Gerard Douw, who signs a contract and even has Schalken sign it too as a witness, the young painter unconscious that he is signing away his love for ever. The contract is colluded in by a Jew, too, who evaluates the ingots, always a bad sign in Le Fanu, whose texts seem to become more and more anti-Semitic as he gets older. By the time Mynheer Vanderhausen arrives to supper to meet his bride, he has changed for the worse. His hair is 'grizzled', though his clothes again are presented in a pastiche of Dutch genre-painting detail. It is when we get to his face that the 1837 text explodes into an epiphany of grotesque and Gothic effects:

So far all was well; but the face! – all the flesh of the face was coloured with the bluish leaden hue which is sometimes produced by the operation of metallic medicines administered in excessive quantities; the eyes were enormous, and the white appeared both above and below the iris, which gave to them an expression of insanity, which was heightened by their glassy fixedness; the nose was well enough, but the mouth was writhed considerably to one side, where it opened to give egress to two long, discoloured fangs, which projected from the upper jaw, far below the lower lip; the hue of the lips themselves bore the usual relation to that of the face, and was consequently nearly black. The character of the face was malignant, even satanic, to the last degree: and, indeed, such a combination of horror could hardly be accounted for, except by supposing the corpse of some atrocious malefactor, which long hung blackening upon the gibbet, to have at length become the habitation of a demon – the frightful sport of Satanic possession. (I, 224–5)[45]

The resurrected body is riddled with syphilis, the 'cure' for which in the seventeenth century was worse than the condition itself, consisting of mercury poisoning, causing the tell-tale symptoms of the leaden hue and the 'dropped mouth' – a standard appearance among seventeenth-century rakes.[46] This is perhaps more Hogarthian than Schalkenesque, but still painterly; and after this, the motif of accuracy and detail switches into full-blown Gothic: from syphilitic aristocrat to 'atrocious malefactor' and the long, discoloured fangs give the touch of the vampire or werewolf. These latter accoutrements went in the 1851 revision, presumably again because of their Gothic excess, as did the corpse and the explicit lines about possession. But the logic is more obvious in 1837: the figure is a set-piece emblem, explicitly, of lust and murder. As far as the politics of 'superstition' go, however, this Gothic epiphany is a surprisingly unreconciliatory combination: the sensual rake, and the criminal murderer, two rotten corpses for one, two excluded ends of a Whig, Protestant, bourgeois social spectrum, lurk horrifically in the garments of a solid, Dutch burgomeister.

2
Gothic and Romance: Retribution and Reconciliation

When we come to the two historical romances which Le Fanu wrote in the 1840s, the rhetorical situation is somewhat different from that of *The Purcell Papers*. The evidentiary mode – the home of dark epiphany – has to go, and plot – the plot of History – must take its place. It was not really possible in the 1840s to write a historical romance that had a 'national' character, without responding to the work of Scott.[1] To emulate Scott, you had to find a way of doing the opposite of what Le Fanu had done so brilliantly in *The Purcell Papers*: you had to imply that two or more different traditions were one. The whole sweep of *Waverley*, the panorama created by its rhetorical fiction of 'centrality', suggests that if you look at history from a certain vantage-point, it all makes sense and leads into the present. And that meant introducing some kind of fictional *détente*, some notion of negotiation, even perhaps of mutual recognition, between hostile, or traditionally opposed, parties, within the parameters of a single language or, at least, a single text. The most striking example of this structure is the way the Jacobite cause is finally dismissed as outmoded by the modern political state in *Redgauntlet*, which is done by giving the violence and the romanticism of Jacobite conspiracy enough room and textual presence to allow it to become an anachronism and give way ('historically', i.e. by the choice of the characters) to the 'modern' (Hanoverian) political state.

But in these romances, although he adopts the overview method, Le Fanu reads Scott as romantic, not realist.[2] And he adopts a number of conventions to produce textual unity, which keep on breaking down and getting threatened. He adopts a sentimental register, which is broken into by the grotesque; and he adopts a historical discourse which exists in tension with very un-Scott-like outbreaks of the Gothic and the uncanny.

This latter point can be illustrated quite succinctly. *The Fortunes of Torlough O'Brien* (1847) recycles several of the stories from *The Purcell Papers*, but in each case, their Gothic or uncanny elements have been removed. For example, Turlogh O'Brien in Chapters 50 and 51, disguised as a pedlar, is captured by the Protestant forces and his enemy, Garrett. This incident is recycled from the short story 'An Adventure of Hardress Fitzgerald' from *The Purcell Papers*. There, it took place with the background of the (first, I take it) siege of Limerick. In the romance, *Torlough O'Brien*, it is transferred to just before the battle of Aghrim (Aughrim), three years later. In each case, the plot is the same: a resentful soldier betrays his Protestant masters, and the prisoner, Fitzgerald in the story (or O'Brien, in the romance) is given a weapon with which he kills his jailor and escapes. Here is the Gothic epiphany of the story, which violates the decorum of the Scott model:

> As I arose and shook the weapon and the bloody cloth from my hand, the moon, which he had foretold I should never see rise, shone bright and broad into the room, and disclosed, with ghastly distinctness, the mangled features of the dead soldier; the mouth, full of clotting blood and broken teeth, lay open; the eye, close by whose lid the fatal wound had been inflicted, was not, as might have been expected, bathed in blood, but had started forth nearly from the socket, and gave to the face, by its fearful unlikeness to the other glazing orb, a leer more hideous and unearthly than fancy ever saw.[3]

This is a moment of revenancy: the 'other world' shows through, here, in a flash of imagination (i.e. 'superstition') beyond mere 'fancy'; so that for the reader the 'leer' is asserted and denied in the same phrase. This is the chiaroscuro effect: attention is paid to the lighting of the scene. The corpse of Captain Oliver is resurrected here for a moment, in a pocket of the uncanny that is most undecorous from the Scott point of view: it exists in tension with the boy's own adventure story of Hardress Fitzgerald.[4]

But the epiphany also harnesses a political point: Captain Oliver is a (power-mad, vengeful) Protestant Williamite and the narrative pursues the adventure of a dauntless Catholic rebel. This incident is recycled in *The Fortunes of Torlough O'Brien*. But in the romance, Torlough O'Brien merely gets back his charger from the rascally Garrett and rides to Aughrim to join Sarsfield's cavalry unit, an engagement in which he is wounded. In the romance version, the Gothic effect – a moment that defies narrative extension – is subdued to sentimental and heroic plot-convention.[5]

Rewriting like this is evidently a response to the dominance of a certain rhetorical mode in the historical romance. There is a struggle to retain and yet occlude, and alter, the language of the grotesque; and the uncanny is also more interestingly evident in a number of places. These examples amount to a much more ambiguous and interestingly personal inflection of a tension between the the legalistic framing devices of the 'old Gothic' (already fully developed and updated by Le Fanu, in a strikingly effective fashion, as we have seen) and the quite different conventions of historical overview in Scott's new historical romance.

The Cock and Anchor (1845): Gothic instabilities

Plot versus rhetoric

The plot of this novel is reconciliatory, crossing the divide between Catholic and Protestant; but the divisions in Irish culture which associate themselves with the overcoded epiphanies of a demonic rhetoric in *The Purcell Papers* are portrayed as fully established in the social system, and seem to have a more powerful and pervasive position in the immediately post-civil War society, in the anti-Whig argument of this first novel, *The Cock and Anchor*. The roots of Le Fanu's Gothic are close to satire.[6]

Here again the plot is a sentimental crossing of the boundaries between Catholic and Protestant traditions. We are now in the early eighteenth centry, about 1710. Edmond O'Connor, the handsome young Milesian, and soldier in exile, has fallen in love with the daughter of the unpleasant Whig baronet, Sir Richard Ashwoode (i.e. wood that is, or has become, unsound). O'Connor has returned to Ireland from the Continent, to ask for Mary Ashwoode's hand. His love is returned by Mary, but Sir Richard Ashwoode, is determined, for economic reasons, that his daughter, Mary, should marry the ancient, foppish Whig peer, Lord Aspenly (even more unsound wood). O'Connor's friend, Mr Audley appeals on his behalf, to Sir Richard, offering a dowry, but is waved aside. Another friend, an old soldier, Major O'Leary, then intervenes and fights a duel with Lord Aspenly, who afterwards rejects the marriage. After a paroxysm of fury, Sir Richard dies. Meanwhile, his son and heir, Mary's brother, Sir Henry, is also deeply in in the hands of moneylenders. O'Connor happens by chance to save his life, which he repays with rank treachery by acting as an agent for his father against O'Connor's interests in the marriage. Reduced by gambling debts to desperation, his own cynical marriage plans having fallen through, Sir Henry falls victim to a plot to ensnare him and forges a cheque in the name of a dastardly villain, Nicholas Blarden, the penalty for which is death. Sir Henry has publicly and savagely beaten Blarden at Smock Alley theatre for daring to approach his sister, and Blarden has sworn revenge; now, he is in Blarden's hands and Blarden's revenge on him is to have Mary in marriage, having hired a rascally clergyman to perform the ceremony, and take over Morley Court, where she is being kept a prisoner. In a long sequence of pastiche-Gothic suspense, Mary (the imprisoned heiress) escapes with her resourceful maid, Flora Guy, and they manage to travel to safety at her uncle, Old Oliver Trench's estate in the country at Ardgillagh. Sir Henry is hanged. O'Connor finally returns and finds Mary, and but too late. She has fallen ill and died.

Rhetoric

We first see O'Connor at the ramshackle inn which gives to the novel its title. This wooden structure (like the Carbrie in *Torlough O'Brien*) acts as a site of 'irregularity', of picturesque, a rambling building vaguely reminiscent of ecclesiastical architecture in the medieval Catholic tradition:

> The front of the building, facing the street, rested upon a row of massive wooden blocks, set endwise, at intervals of some six or eight feet, and running parallel at about the same distance, to the wall of the lower story of the house, thus forming a kind of rude cloister or open corridor, running the whole length of the building.
>
> The spaces between these rude pillars were, by a light frame-work of timber, converted into a succession of arches; and by an application of the same ornamental process, the ceiling of this extended porch was made to carry a clumsy but not unpicturesque imitation of groining. Upon this open-work of timber ... rested the second story of the building; protruding beyond which again, and supported upon projected beams whose projecting ends were carved into the semblance of heads hideous as the fantastic monsters of heraldry, arose the third story, presenting a series of tall and fancifully-shaped gables, decorated, like the rest of the building, with an abundance of grotesque timber-work.[7]

This stretch of picturesque is a mini-allegory: a political set-piece. 'Cloisters', 'groining', 'fantastic monsters' and 'grotesque timber-work' all suggest the anti-utilitarian past, an earlier tradition of (Catholic) cathedral-building in stone. This building is a part of this book's subdued, but insistent allegory about the unsound forests – the rottenness of the 'present' (i.e. 1710; 1845 is a discreetly silent layer here), Whig-dominated, house – of Ireland, to which it acts as a counterpoint.[8] It has been left behind, 'narrowing the street with a most aristocratic indifference to the comforts of the pedestrian public' (4) and the luxury and fancy of its charming old woodwork may suggest a lost tradition of benign patrician rule: sound aristocracy and religious tolerance – which opposes itself to the brutal and ruinous combination of commercial exploitation and penal law which claim to be 'modern'.

It is in this inn that the Jacobite plot is first developed; we witness an encounter between Edmond O'Connor and a stranger, Captain O'Hanlon, who turns out to be an old friend of O'Connor's father. O'Hanlon gives two speeches in O'Connor's room, the first of which is addressed to the spirit of his deceased old friend and comrade-in-arms, Richard O'Connor:

'Nevertheless – over-ridden, and despised, and scattered as we are, mercenaries and beggars abroad, and landless at home – still something whispers in my ear that there will come at last a retribution, and such a one as will make this perjured, corrupt, and robbing ascendancy a warning and a wonder to all after times. Is it a common thing, think you, that all the gentlemen, all the chivalry of a whole country – the natural leaders and protectors of the people – should be stripped of their birthright, ay, even of the poor privilege of seeing in this their native country, strangers possessing the inheritances which are in *all* right their own; cast abroad upon the world; soldiers of fortune, selling their blood for a bare subsistence; many of them dying of want; and all because for honour and conscience' sake they refused to break the oath which bound them to a ruined prince. Is it a slight thing, think you, to visit with pains and penalties such as these, men guilty of no crimes beyond those of fidelity and honour!'[9]

This ominous speech suggests the more retributive context of this romance, in this early eighteenth-century period. After the Civil War of the 1690s and the Williamite settlement, Ireland is now a betrayed house, the flower of whose Catholic aristocracy, or even middle class, have been driven from their land by the new interest, a cold-hearted company of rulers emblemised, and, briefly, led, by Lord Wharton. It turns out that O'Hanlon was one of the highwaymen who set about young O'Connor, on the road to the inn, mistaking his identity for that of a Whig messenger:

I took you for one who we were informed would pass that way, and about the same hour – one who carried letters from a pretended friend – one whom I have long suspected, a half-faced, cold-hearted friend, carried letters, I say, from such a one to the castle here; to that malignant, perjured reprobate and apostate, the so-called Lord Wharton – as meet an ornament for a gibbet as ever yet made feast for the ravens.[10]

Catholic reviewers objected to the way this plot is handled, and the bloodthirstiness of one of the conspirators, a Catholic priest, when they capture O'Connor who has strayed innocently into the grounds of Finiskea House in Phoenix Park, a house they are occupying, and threaten to execute him as a spy.[11] But it is not only Captain O'Hanlon's prejudice, as a Catholic exile, that represents Wharton as corrupt. Later in the novel, there is an interesting scene inside Dublin Castle, in which the text dramatises a conversation between Swift, Addison and Wharton. The text allows us to witness the way in which a patter of double-talk and blackmail is operating at the top of the social system. Swift is casually blackmailed by Wharton:

He paused, but Swift remained silent. The lord lieutenant well knew that an English preferment was the nearest object of the young churchman's ambition.

He therefore continued –

'On my soul, we want you in England – this is no stage for you. By——you cannot hope to serve either yourself or your friends in this place.'

'Very few thrive here but scoundrels, my lord,' rejoined Swift.

'Even so,' replied Wharton with perfect equanimity – 'it is a nation of scoundrels – dissent on the one side and popery on the other. The upper order harpies, and the lower a mere prey – and all equally liars, rogues, rebels, slaves, and robbers. By——some fine day the devil will carry off the island bodily. For very safety you must get out of it. By——he'll have it.'[12]

We catch a glimpse of the Gothic irony about 'superstition' here, and the retributive plot rears its head briefly. In his cynical frankness, Wharton jokes in the language of 'superstition', describing with ironical accuracy the culture he has himself created. It is the Devil's work. Wharton has Swift in his power here, and the process of corruption and cynicism in Ireland, in which the good and heroic are preyed upon by the merely manipulative, is portrayed as beginning at the top of the political system. Wharton is described ironically as 'a steady and uncompromising Whig, upon whom, throughout a long and active life, the stain of inconsistency had never rested ...'.[13] By contrast, when a country prebendary at a gathering Dublin castle looks upon Swift's face, he finds a 'countenance, full, as it seemed, of a scornful, merciless energy and decision, something told him that he looked upon one born to lead and command the people ...' (I, 267).[14]

The text suggests that noble and natural (i.e. patrician) leaders, everywhere in this Whig-dominated Ireland, both Catholic and Protestant, are in thrall to mercenary and manipulative interests. What price now the old oak of the 'Cock and Anchor' which has lasted so long? The Williamite Settlement led to a drastic reduction in the numbers of old estates that were in Catholic hands. The bitter conditions created by the penal code partly explain this romance's tone and its code of 'unsound timber'. The novel's most recent editor, Jan Jedrejewski, sees the Wharton scene in Dublin Castle as a rather weak piece of historical realism, judging it by the standards of Scott, because Le Fanu had simply based it on a pamphlet by Swift.[15] But Joseph Spence argues, rightly, I think, that this scene is crucial to the intellectual structure of the novel because Le Fanu's anti-Whig polemic does not commit itself to being anti-Hanoverian. Le Fanu is careful not to praise, blame, or even mention, Wharton's successor, Ormonde, when he could have done. Seen in this light, the novel's 'even-handedness' is in tension with its rhetorical energy, a conflict which follows on from the ironical connection between 'superstition' and the theme of Williamite guilt in *The Purcell Papers*. This tension associates itself in the text with undercurrents of the Gothic – the grotesque and uncanny.

These are strange times, the text argues, which generate an exotic undergrowth of shabby blackmailers, grotesque money-lenders, and rascally parasitic lawyers, low types who creep into the lowest rungs of professions to leech off foolish or desperate Whig aristocrats and their wastrel offspring. The villain of the novel, Nicholas Blarden, is a kind of Gothic echo of Wharton's joke about the devil ('old Nick', as his friends refer to him) who drives the second-half of this plot in his relentless squeezing of young Sir Henry Ashwoode and pursuit of his sister, Mary. Old Sir Richard, likewise, has his creepy shadow, Mr Craven, who is a mixture of stereotypes:

The bell pealed and the knocker thundered, and in a moment a servant entered, and announced Mr Craven – a spare built man, of low stature, wearing his own long, grizzled hair instead of a wig – having a florid complexion, hooked nose, beetle brows, and long-cut, Jewish, black eyes, set close under the bridge of his nose – who stepped with a velvet tread into the room. An unvarying smile sate upon his lips, and about his whole air and manner there was a certain indescribable sanctimoniousness, which was rather enhanced by the puritan plainness of his attire.[16]

The demonising rhetoric of this figure is made up of two Dickensian stereotypes: the old-fashioned theatrical figure of the Puritan hypocrite, and the almost immemorial figure of the Jewish usurer. 'Craven' means coward, principally, but it also connotes 'pleading' (cf. Miles Garrett's 'I crave your pardon' in *Torlough O'Brien*) and Mr Craven is a lawyer, a professional pleader. It is implied that his 'lowness' is a combination of low church, low class, and low race. This anti-puritan, anti-Semitic caricature is the beginning of a long line of figures associated with the Whiggification of society in Le Fanu's later romances. Indeed this anti-Whig novel is really a template for many of those later texts, whose anti-Semitism reaches its apotheosis in *The Tenants of Malory*.[17]

I have no space here to scrutinise the nuances of the rhetoric, constantly shading into darkness, the grotesque and the uncanny, in which a number of minor characters (servants and hangers-on) are encased in this text.[18] But there is also another concealed Gothic story which deserves comment, because it simply looks an excrescence at first sight. In a characteristically roundabout and backhanded way, it again sets Catholic 'credulity' (superstition) against Whig rationalism. This is the curious rewrite of the 'Locked Room Mystery' in II, v, which is inset into Sir Richard Ashwoode's death. The retributive Gothic is mediated through the 'superstitious' witness, the Italian, forger and hanger-on, Parucci. Whole passages here are recycled from *The Purcell Papers*. Parucci pushes open the door of the baronet's dressing-room and encounters 'A candle, wasted to the very socket ...' but still burning on the table beside the 'huge hearse-like bed ...' (II, 53). Parucci seems to have heard Sir Richard speaking, in the next room, and he asks himself who could possibly have been with the baronet:

'What made him speak; nothing was with him – pshaw, nothing could come to him here – no, no, nothing.'
    As he thus spoke, the wind swept vehemently upon the windows with a sound as if some great thing had rushed against them, and was pressing for admission, and the gust blew out the candle; the blast died

away in an lengthened wail, and then again came howling and rushing up to the windows, as if the very prince of the powers of the air himself were thundering at the casement; then again the blue dazzling lightning glared into the room and gave place to deeper darkness.

Pah! that lightning smells like brimstone. Sangue d'un dua, I hear something in the room.

Yielding to his terrors, Parrucci stumbled to the door opening upon the great lobby, and with cold and trembling fingers drawing the bolt, sprang to the stairs and shouted for assistance in a tone which speedily assembled half the household in the chamber of death.[19]

This is a flash of Gothic. This wind was used to very good effect later by M.R. James. The undermining of the witness's full credibility yields the required ambiguity between natural and supernatural explanations. But this is not just a detached 'formal' property of the Gothic genre here, incongrously and perhaps wilfully thrust into a historical romance about the Williamite Settlement. There is a retributive logic: Parucci is a conventional materialist – hence his expressions of contempt – but here the irrational has taken him back to his Catholic roots and stimulated his imagination, and the supernatural ambiguities of the shorter fiction are left for the reader to respond to as an equilibrium of competing explanations.[20]

Coda: readerly darkness: *The Fortunes of Torlough O'Brien* (1847)

Plot

We must go back to the summer of 1689. King James II has left the throne of England and removed himself to France, and the Prince of Orange has entered London and occupied the throne of England. Ireland is in a state of anarchy, under the violently discriminatory rule of James's deputy, the Earl of Tyrconnel, who (in the eyes of many) has set about creating a Catholic state. The Irish Parliament has been disbanded. The countryside is full of 'rapparees', armed bandits who tend to be discharged soldiers from James's armies.

Old Sir Hugh Willoughby, a Protestant peer and the current occupant, when the novel opens in 1689, of Glindarragh Castle, a large rambling fortified house in County Limerick, is accused on a charge of treason, trumped up by his cousin, Miles Garrett of Lisnamoe. The time-serving Garrett who is a justice of the peace, is an apostate from Protestantism to Catholicism and his main concern in life is simple: to acquire

Glindarragh for himself. He tries what he thinks of as the honourable way – by asking for the hand of Grace Willoughby, Sir Hugh's beautiful daughter, but the old man violently rejects him. Garrett, however, has acquired influence with Tyrconnel himself: it appears that Old Sir Hugh's wife, Lady Willoughby, who is now half-imprisoned in obscurity somewhere in Dublin, has had an affair with Tyrconnel, a fact which allows Garrett to blackmail him into accepting the charge of treason, despite its evident flimsiness.

Garrett calls on 'motley thousands' (97) of rapparees who besiege Glindarragh, on the pretext of seeking some allegedly stolen cattle. There is a pitched battle just before which, during the initial parlay, Garrett makes sure the name of King James is audibly insulted by the hot-tempered and outraged Willoughby, thus providing the charge of treason. Eventually, the castle is taken and Willoughby and his daughter are at the mercy of Garrett and his rapparees.

Grace Willoughby has already been rescued once from the clutches of a particularly ugly and grotesque rapparee, called Desmond Hogan, by an unknown and handsome dragoon, who is recognised by her old nurse as Torlogh Dhuv, or 'Dark Torlough', a scion of the ancient O'Brien family, who are the real owners of Glindarragh castle. The ancient Gaelic prophecy says that when the one with the shamrock mark on his brow is seen on Glindarragh Bridge, then the O'Briens will return to Glindarragh. It seems that the O'Briens were driven out at the dissolution of the monasteries and that the Willoughby family was subsequently given the castle by the 'old queen', Elizabeth.

Just at the moment of Garrett's triumph, Torlogh O'Brien appears with a troop of dragoons and takes over from him. O'Brien thus, for the first time, enters what is arguably his own property. He quarters his men at the castle and takes personal charge of Garrett's prisoners, escorting them himself to Dublin for the trial. It is plain that the honourable and kindly O'Brien has no sympathy for Garrett and every sympathy for Willoughby and his daughter, despite the fact that they are, technically, his enemies.[21]

James II enters Dublin, and we catch a glimpse of his Privy Council tetchily discussing Willoughby's case. In Dublin, thanks to the machinations of Garrett and his associates, who manipulate one of the key witnesses into betraying Willoughby, the trial goes against the old man. O'Brien, having declared himself to Grace Willoughby and been accepted, helps her to plead secretly with James himself for her father's life, but the King rejects her plea and her father is thrown into jail to await execution.

However, Garrett discovers that the Glindarragh estate has been set up in such a way that it will revert, not to the state, but to another party on

Sir Hugh's death. It is imperative therefore that he not be hanged, while they search for the deed and destroy it. So Sir Hugh obtains a temporary reprieve, which is reported with teasing irony.

Meanwhile O'Brien has been obliged to rejoin his unit. He fights with Sarsfield's cavalry all the way through from Boyne Water to the battle of Aughrim where he is wounded, and we find him lying in the vaults of St Mary's Abbey towards the end of the book, very weak, but protected from the incursions of Protestant Williamite soldiery by a ragged crew of rapparees.

Garrett, who has in the meantime characteristically turned coat and become a Williamite, and is an officer in the Protestant forces, has been overtaken by history and fails in his project. Glindarragh is eventually reclaimed by O'Brien with Grace Willoughby as his bride and the old man carries on in residence, as the current but temporary owner. Garrett is finally killed by Ned Ryan, one of his neighbouring rapparees, in a skirmish after a cattle raid. The villain is thrown into a ravine, and his corpse is found by children picking 'frahans' (whortleberries).

Rhetoric

I am deliberately simplifying the plot in the above summary to reveal its main lines. It is clear that this plot is again reconciliatory, and that the story is sympathetic, in the manner of earlier writers of Irish romance, Lady Morgan and Charles Maturin, to 'the O's and the Mac's', the ancient Catholic (but also pagan) nobility of Ireland who were the original owners of the land. Willoughby, the doughty old Whig peer (a rather rare character in Le Fanu: a good (i.e. a high-toned) Whig, and O'Brien, the Milesian who resembles a 'Moorish prince', come to recognise one another because they share a common trait: honour. They are both true Irishmen, whatever their religious persuasions, family histories, and ancestral claims to the same piece of property.

This sentimental convention is, in a sense, a class recognition. Garrett, the ambitious villain, is a hypocrite opportunist who is born 'low'. He is typical of the 'New Interest'. There is a range of minor characters who occupy the place of other stereotypes hovering between the fictional and the historical. Another 'low' character, Old Tisdal, the respectable tenant of Glindarragh's manor farm at Drumgunniol, and follower of Sir Hugh, who betrays him and testifies against him, is a highwayman turned Puritan, whose pious exterior masks his murderous past. This again, though not simple hypocrisy, is an important version of 'lowness' which Le Fanu will exploit in the villains, and sometimes, in a twist of expectations, the sympathetic characters, of his later romances.[22]

The new frame: the magic mirror

The Prologue of this text is a rhetorical feat, which goes some way towards providing Le Fanu with a solution to the conflict between the Gothic (i.e. the indirect and retributory) use of 'attestation' he has invented for the short story in *The Purcell Papers*, and the pressure of the historical romance towards panorama and overview, which implies a 'central' narrative voice, a more stable, or at least a more visible, relationship between implied author and reader:

> In the summer of the year 1686, at about ten o'clock at night, two scenes were passing, very different in all the accidents of place, plot, and personage; and which although enacted, the one in London, and the other near it, yet exercised an influence upon the events and persons of our Irish story, so important and so permanent, that we must needs lift the curtain from before the magic mirror, which every author, in virtue of his craft, is privileged to consult, and disclose for a minute the scenery and forms which flit across its mystic surface.[23]

At first sight, this device is simply mechanical: it is evidently a dramatic way of providing a 'back-story' for the novel's plot, whose main action begins in 1689. But it has certain oddities about it, which are in excess of this function. What is a *curtain* doing in front of the 'mirror'? The reader is metaphorically in the dark: a member of the audience at a fairground show, or perhaps a fantasmagoria.[24] And the author? A mixture of Gypsy Rose Lee, Hecate from *Macbeth*, and the Master of Ceremonies at a peepshow. Narration is a kind of prophecy about the past. We stare into the essence of the scene, and we watch while its 'forms' – characters shorn of names and all but the accidental properties of their clothing, bearing, and environment – act out a proleptic dumbshow of the novel's narrative.

But we are not just metaphorically in the dark. This process plainly teases the reader with their very distance from the images in front of them; our (modern) position of almost total ignorance and helplessness is mocked by the insistent intimacy of this partial realisation. How for example can we (even the early-nineteenth-century reader) identify whether these 'forms' are 'fictions' or representations of historical characters?

> In the chamber into which we are looking, there burns a large lamp, which sheds through its stained-glass sphere a soft, rose-coloured light on all the objects which surround it; and eight wax lights, flaring

and flickering in the evening breeze which floats lightly in at the open windows, tend an additional distinctiveness to the forms that occupy the room.

These are four in number: two lean over a table, which stands near the window, and seem to be closely examining a map, which nearly covers the board over which they stoop – the one sharp-featured, sallow, somewhat slovenly in his attire, his short cloak hanging from his shoulder, and his high-crowned hat (then an obsolete fashion) dangling in his hand, leans over the outspread plan, and with eager gestures and rapid enunciation, and yet with a strange mixture of deference, appears to harangue his listening companion. *He* is a strong, square-built man, somewhat perhaps, beyond the middle age, gravely and handsomely dressed – his huge perriwig swings forward and rests his chin upon his jewelled hand, and fixes upon the chart before him a countenance bold and massive, in which the strong lines of sense and sensuality are strikingly combined.[25]

We are placed in the position of one who must deduce from the signs the meaning of this scene. The 'chart' – as in a stage play – indicates planning, if not conspiracy. But the text tells us nothing directly. Our sensory targets are confined to the visual sign – the sound has effectively been turned off. The figures are seen from a distance, and with an uncertainty that represents our own ignorance in advance – the first form 'appears to harangue' the second, for example – of its actual appearance.

The first of these figures is a fiction: it is the villain of this novel, Miles Garrett, whose clothes and manners betray his lowly origins and his country fashions. The second figure is the brother of Richard Talbot, Earl of Tyrconnell, and is a historical figure. (The emphasis on 'He' may convey a clue to an Irish reader of the 1840s, but it is a rhetorical gamble, which looks more like teasing to me.) It might be supposed that the next chapter would begin by explaining all this. But no such revelation follows. How do I know this? Because after 144 pages, or twenty chapters, the author suddenly adds a series of 'casual' afterthoughts:

... this was the very individual whom Sir Hugh had that day pointed out to his daughter as the "lay priest", and brother to the Earl of Tyrconnell, while the procession was passing beneath the windows of the Carbrie; let us add too, that this is the identical person whom we described in the earliest chapter of this book as leaning over a certain map, in company with Miles Garrett, upon a soft summer's night in the year 1686, in a rich saloon in London.[26]

The fictional Garrett then, in the magic-mirror image, is setting up the first stage of his plan to gain Glindarragh castle – hence the map. The rest of the first magic-mirror scene is an equally unknowable mixture of fictional plot and historical fact:

> Pacing to and fro, and sometimes pausing half abstractedly at this table, looking for a moment at the outspread paper, and betraying the absence, and, perhaps, the agitation of his mind by his wandering gaze and the restless drumming of his knuckles on the table; then turning again to resume his rapid walk across the floor, and stealing occasionally a hurried and uneasy look towards a figure who sits alone upon a sofa in the obscurest part of the chamber, is seen a man of commanding stature and lofty mien, though somewhat tending to corpulence, richly dressed in a suit of dark velvet, sparkling with jewels, his neckcloth and ruffles fluttering with splendid point, having in his countenance a certain character of haughty command, according well with the high pretensions of his garb.

We are plunged again into the activity of deduction or guesswork. This must be 'Lying Dick Talbot', the Earl of Tyrconnel himself, a historical figure of great importance. The implication is that he is aware of the conspiracy which his brother is entering into with Miles Garrett, but is too distracted to find it of interest.

That is because of his apparently guilty interest in the fourth 'form':

> Another figure remains to be described, it is that toward which the regards of him we have just examined are so often turned: the form is that of a female, seated, as we have said, upon a sofa, and wrapped in a close travelling cloak, the hood of which falls over her face, so that, excepting she is tall, and possesses hands and feet of singular beauty and slimness, we can pronounce nothing whatever of her *personnel* – she is evidently weeping, her dress shows the vibration of every sob, and the convulsive clasping of her small hands, and the measured beating of her tiny foot upon the floor, betoken her inward anguish.[27]

This is Lady Willoughby, a fictional character, whose affair with Tyrconnell has become known to Garrett, who in his turn intends to use this knowledge as a means of convicting her husband, Sir Hugh Willoughby, of treason and thus gaining the object of his desire, the possession of Glindarragh castle in Limerick, the Willoughby seat.

Again, I infer this from having read the novel. I could not actually 'deduce' it from what is in front of me, so completely is it reduced to the bare 'forms' and 'figures' of the magic mirror's images. It intrigues me, of course; but the mirror reveals a drama I am explicitly forbidden at this stage to enter, and, indeed, for much of the novel to come. To read at this point is to enter the space of darkness. And yet the author – the showman-prophet – teases me mercilessly with my own efforts to infer meaning from the text in front of me, which he is in the act of creating:

> Lo! there must have been some sudden sound at the door! They all start and look toward it – the lean gentleman, in the shabby suit, clutches his map; his brawny companion advances a pace; the tall aristocrat arrests his walk, and stands fixed and breathless; while the lady shrinks further back, and draws her hood more closely over her face.
>
> Their objects, then, must be secret.
>
> It is, however, a false alarm, they resume their respective postures and occupations – and so leaving them, we wave the wand which conjured up the scene, and in a moment all is shivered, clouded, and gone.[28]

The frustration of that hackneyed old picturesque opening device of 'the hypothetical observer' becomes explicit here, as the narrator turns the parodic screw on the melodrama of the early Victorian reader's expectations, fed on a diet of Ainsworth, Reynolds, Dickens, Eugène Sue, and Sir Walter Scott.

What is interesting are the expressionistic lengths to which Le Fanu is prepared to go and what he is prepared to risk to gain his effect of readerly 'darkness'. The frame is an assimilation of reading – and specifically, the state of expectation – to the early cinema, and the darkness that descends between each scene. No sooner is the mirror 'wiped', than a second scene appears, just as obscure as the first. This time the reference-points are more obviously 'Gothic'; we seem to be in an undercroft or even burial vault of some kind:

> … it represents the dim vistas of a vaulted chamber, spanned with low, broad arches of stone, springing from the stone floor. Two blazing links, circled with a lurid halo from the heavy damps which hang there, in thin perpetual fog, shed a dusky, flickering glare upon the stained and dripping roof, and through the dim and manifold perspective of arches, until it spends itself in vapoury darkness. (3)

One thinks here of the numerous underground scenes (often Catholic – *Rookwood*, or *Guy Fawkes*, for example) in Harrison Ainsworth's novels, much read at this time; and of the Jacobite climax to Scott's *The Black Dwarf*, which takes place in an underground chapel. But here we are treading the line of the frame, not the text proper: there is little clue as to what is happening. In fact, the rhetoric works hard to deny us information, undermining the reader's position of privilege once again, so that the 'fitful glow' of the turpentine torches acts as a metaphor for our state of knowledge as much as it 'illuminates' the characters before us:

> A group of some seven or eight figures stands in the fitful glow of this ruddy illumination – gentlemen of wealth and worship, it would seem, by the richness of their garb: some are wrapt in their cloaks, some are booted, and all wear their broad-leafed, low-crowned hats. Strong lines and deep shadows mark many a furrowed and earnest face. This is no funereal meeting, as the place would seem to indicate – no trappings of mourning are visible, and the subject of their conversation, though deep and weighty, is too earnest and energizing for a theme of sorrow; neither is there, in the faces or gestures of the assembly, a single indication of excitement or enthusiasm. The countenances, the attitudes, the movements of the group, all betoken caution, deliberation, and intense anxiety. From time to time are seen, singly, or in couples, or in groups of three, other forms in the shadowy distance, as richly dressed, gliding like ghosts through the cloistered avenues, and holding with themselves, or one another anxious debate.[29]

All we are allowed to know from the text is that this is the summer of 1686. One year, that is, after the failure of the Monmouth rebellion. We are somewhere near London. I infer from the atmosphere that this is the beginning of the real rebellion against James II by leading Protestants who had grown tired of watching the transformation of England into a catholic state, a move which eventually led to the invitation to the Prince of Orange to invade their country and which was to lead to civil war in Ireland. There is a touch of irony about the odd use of 'wealth and worship' in the above (does 'worship' here refer to religion, or 'adulation based on', or even 'of', material prosperity? This is precisely the ambiguity of the demonic Vanderhausen, from 'Schalken the Painter') which suggests that the leading interests here might well be 'the New Interest' of the Whigs. This is no romantic, Jacobite conspiracy, for a lost kingdom; but a serious, worldly, and above all feasible affair.

The scene is suddenly animated:

> And now, a tall and singularly handsome man, in gorgeous military uniform, turning from an elder personage in a velvet cloak, to whom he has been deferentially listening, moves a pace or two toward the detached parties, who walk slowly up and down, as we have described, and raising his plumed hat, he beckons them forward; and so they come, and must with the rest; whereupon the elder gentleman, in the velvet cloak, draws forth a letter, and with a brief word or two of preface, as would seem, reads it for the rest, pausing from time to time to offer and receive remarks. This over, he says something further, whereupon he and all the rest raise their hats for a moment, and then he shows the letter to one of the company nearest himself, who takes it, looks to the end, and then to the beginning, and so passes it on to another, and so from hand to hand it goes, until again it first reaches him who first produced it; and then, with the same solemn and earnest looks and air, they, one by one, take leave, shake hands, and glide away, until the old gentleman in the cloak, and one other remain. Then he in the cloak holds the corner of the momentous letter to the flaring link, and now it floats to the ground in flame, and now all that remains of the mysterious paper, is a light black film, coursed all over by a thousand nimble sparkles.[30]

I am obliged to guess here. Among these shades of the obscure and dead, I take the leading conspirators to be the young Duke of Marlborough, second-in-commmand of James's army and a known plotter, and Anthony Ashley Cooper, the Earl of Shaftesbury, who had already been imprisoned in the tower for fomenting the Monmouth rebellion. This fateful letter is a draft of the invitation to William, Prince of Orange, son-in-law to King James, to invade the country and oust James from the throne. Either that, or it is James's reply. But Le Fanu would then have had to have moved it forward by two years because that did not occur until 1688, so I assume that this scene in the summer of 1686 perhaps represents the solemn undertaking to invite, rather than William's acceptance. Hence, everyone is given the opportunity to comment, finally, on the wording, and then health is wished to the enterprise and loyalty and respect are expressed towards the Protestant Prince, the arrangement is checked, sealed by handshakes, and this copy of the letter destroyed.

The nature of the image and what it represents is interesting. The Gothic vault is a fiction: the condensation of a set of underground political actions into a set of 'forms', not an attempt to portray realistically those actions. The reader's attempts to identify are kept at bay by the technique of (what we would call in modern jargon) defamiliarisation.

This is worthy of Pinewood Studies or Hollywood. Le Fanu shows he would have probably written for the movies if he had lived in the twentieth century. The Reader of the 1840s is invited to think of this as a version of the Fantasmagoria – a kind of magic-lanthern show of resurrected apparitions. Le Fanu has appropriated this literal phenomenon for its metaphorical value in alluding to the process of reading. The conceit sets the reader outside the text, and is an elaborately new form of framing and distancing, while ostensibly whipping up, the reader's responses. It establishes the dark space we enter when we read – the space of ignorance and 'superstition' and secrecy, which is there to be manipulated and preyed upon by the fictional text.[31] Le Fanu continues to insert, in other words, even in the leisurely overview of the romance genre, his estrangement of the reader from the text.

And, I think secondly, through the metaphor of 'forms' or 'figures', normally a temporary rhetorical device, he re-introduces a chiaroscuro effect into the frame of the fiction itself. This replaces, or shifts into a different form his earlier rhetoric of 'attestation'. It clearly assimilates the reading process to that of drama: and yields a space between the reader and the text, a kind of 'stage' on which the text performs itself, a non-mimetic plane, on which a complete mingling can take place between the discourses of history and fiction.

3
'Cyclopean History': *The House by the Churchyard*

The ghost narrates

This time Le Fanu chooses a ghost to narrate the tale – his own ancestor, Charles de Cresseron, the Huguenot refugee from Caen, in Louis XIV's France, who fought on King William's side and who was granted land in reward for his services, thus founding the Irish branch of the Le Fanu dynasty. His imagined descendant – the double of the author – is an old man in the 1860s, looking back to a scene in his youth. This ironical figure projects much of the 'merriness' and 'jollity' of the vanished eighteenth-century Protestant culture; but in a doubleness of register, the rhetoric of darkness threads its way through the narrative's surface – a chattily self-conscious use of Charles's spoken voice – in what amounts, even in the comic scenes, to a persistent use of mock-heroic conceits about death and horror.[1]

The opening of the novel is an elaborate set of frames. Charles is a living witness to the social history of Chapelizod, an 'outpost' village of Dublin. He takes us back, across the growing industrialism of the early nineteenth century, into the vanished past, the heart of a 'dream' of pastoral solidity:

The broad old street looked hospitable and merry, with steep roofs and many-coloured hall-doors. The jolly old inn, just beyond the turnpike at the sweep of the road, leading over the buttressed bridge by the mill, was the first to welcome the excursionist from Dublin, under the sign of the Phoenix. There, in the grand, wainscoted back-parlour, with 'the great and good king William', in his robe, garter, periwig, and sceptre, presiding in the panel over the chimney-piece, and confronting the large projecting window, through which the river, and the daffodils, and the summer foliage looked so bright and quiet, the

> Aldermen of Skinner's Alley – a club of the "true blue" ' dye, as old as the Jacobite Wars of the previous century – the corporation of Shoemakers, or of Tailors, or the Freemasons, or the musical clubs, loved to dine at the stately hour of five, and deliver their jokes, sentiments, songs and wisdom, on a pleasant summer's evening. Alas! the inn is as clean gone as the guests – a dream of the shadow of smoke.[2]

The last ambiguous remark casts its own shadow on this bright scene. The shadow is cast backward, but also proleptic: the implication is that its pastoral tranquillity never really existed, except as the (compensatory) nostalgic dream of a later Victorian era. But the 'shadow of smoke' predicts the substance which is the novel's Victorian present, a prelude to the Whiggish vision of Victorian commerce and industry. Despite the leisured heartiness of Charles's tone, the topography is full of an ominous vacuity. It is all haunted: the solid brick inn is as mortal as its guests, and the very act of imagination itself is presented as a 'dream', a troubling mixture of ghost story and memory.

Against this search for a vanished past, is set the narrative present of the speaker, which continuously and explicitly puts truth and fiction at odds with one another. This book is profoundly hybrid: Charles is a narrator in the tradition of Cervantes and Sterne's Tristram. Charles writes from 'memoranda' (I, 18), and the text is full of the device of digesting pre-existent records: for example, Chapter 5 begins:

> If I stuck at a fib as little as some historians, I might easily tell you who won the prizes at this shooting on Palmerstown Green. But the truth is, I don't know; my granduncle could have told me, for he had a marvellous memory, but he died, a pleasant old gentleman of fourscore and upwards, when I was a small urchin.[3]

Charles self-consciously employs early on in the text an aesthetics of interruption which distances the reader from the plot of the novel, despite the drive to truth of its 'mystery' structure. The digest of true records, beyond which the narrator has nothing to say, is a paradox about the notion of a 'true history', which depends on fiction. Cervantes is, as he says in the Preface to *Don Quixote*, not the author, but the 'step-father' of his novel, because he depends on the records of another, the historian Cidi Hamete Benengeli. He loosens the relationship between the author as an authority-figure, and the author as a narrator who merely *redacts* – i.e. condenses into narrative form – a set of historical records. 'History' is a notoriously ambiguous item of discourse in Cervantes: it connotes narrative and authenticity – fiction and truth. This 'Cervantick' paradox is then taken over by Sterne as 'the history of what passes in a man's own mind'.[4]

Of course, Scott is not unaware of this paradox about the novelist's relation to history, and we may think of Scott as Le Fanu's immediate model. But there are a number of references to Cervantes and Sterne in this book, which suggest to me that the comedy tradition has a special significance. Besides, the evidence suggests that Le Fanu may well have thought of Scott as, like Byron, a romantic heir to this comic and sceptical tradition. Or perhaps like Charles Maturin, his nearest Irish reference-point, who also alludes to this comic tradition and who appeals, in the 'two brothers' plot of his *Melmoth*, to the divided nature of Irish society after the land appropriations of the Cromwellite invasion.[5]

The narration is anyway in a tradition of paradox; Charles twice alludes to the early part of his narrative as a 'winter's tale' – beyond Cervantes and his subversive framing of fiction lies Shakespeare's hybrid last plays and his use of 'old tales' – superstitious old tales – which are framed in a self-conscious manner, but which turn out to be indistinguishable from the framing device itself; the 'superstitious' contains the rational or self-reflective.

The Prologue and first chapters of the novel form a microcosm of these narrative tensions. They are a set of vanishing frames, giving way to one another into earlier and earlier historical periods. Charles establishes himself in the first scene as a witness. He is fourteen, and is present at the comically Gothic grave-digging scene with his uncle, the then curate of Chapelizod (NB: probably about 1805 – if Charles is 70 in 1861, the novel's time of narration, then he was born in 1791 and is 14 in 1805 ...). The corpse of an old lady, Rebecca Darby, has been brought by stages back from Sligo to Chapelizod (from the West back to the East) and now the plot must be prepared:

There was a great flat stone over that small parcel of the rector's freehold, which the family held by a tenure, not of lives, but of deaths, renewable for ever. So that my uncle, who was a man of anxious temperament, had little trouble in satisfying himself of the meerings and identity of this narrow tenement, to which Lemuel Mattocks, the sexton, led him as straight and confidently as he could have done to the communion-table.

My uncle, therefore, fiated the sexton's presentiment, and the work commenced forthwith. I don't know whether all boys have the same liking for horrors which I am conscious of having possessed ... .[6]

A skull is accidentally thrown up by the sexton. The scene is clearly an echo of Hamlet and Yorick, and this leads the reader on to Sterne. The skull appears to have two sets of grotesque wounds in it, heavy blows and an apparent gunshot wound, and as they stand around discussing it, the curate speculating 'with a melancholy sort of horror' that the undoubtedly murdered owner had been both shot and struck down, they are corrected by a voice:

> 'Twasn't a gunshot, Sir; why the hole 'id take in a grape-shot,' said an old fellow, just from behind my uncle, in a pensioner's cocked hat, leggings, and long old-world red frock-coat, speaking with a harsh reedy voice, and a grim sort of reserved smile.
>
> I moved a little aside, with a sort of thrill, to give him freer access to my uncle, in the hope that he might, perhaps, throw a light upon the history of this remarkable memorial. The old fellow had a rat-like gray eye – the other was hid under a black patch – and there was a deep red scar across his forehead, slanting from the patch that covered the extinguished orb. His face was purplish, the tinge deepening towards the lumpish top of his nose, on the side of which stood a big wart, and he carried a great walking-cane over his shoulder, and bore, as it seemed to me, an intimidating, but caricatured resemblance to an old portrait of Oliver Cromwell in my Whig grandfather's parlour.[7]

Enter the monocular retrospective prophet from the past, who speaks with the authority of one who was present, one who knows the 'true history', and whom Charles regards as the (thrillingly horrifying) voice of the whole tradition. The portrait of Cromwell has damningly come alive to offer an underground history of the Whig succession.

But this is a caricature, a fiction. The effect is chequered: one of a crossing of fictional genres and discourses, in which the Gothic 'tale of terror' (I, 15) which the old soldier has just begun and for which the fourteen-year-old Charles, on his own admission, 'thirsts' (I, 15), is framed by the sceptical humour of Charles the old man, a narrator in the Cervantick tradition who playfully holds the notion of a 'true history' at bay. This is clearly a 'winter's tale' yet it is claimed as true, and the truth of the whole narrative here is founded upon the oral testimony of the old boy, which the reader is not allowed to hear, itself authenticated by the corroborating testimony of Charles and the unexpected arrival of a written source. Charles interrupts the old boy, just as he is settled in the parlour of the house by the churchyard with his punch, beginning his story – the plot of the novel we are reading – to give us this information:

> Many years after, as will sometimes happen, a flood of light was unexpectedly poured over the details of his narrative; on my coming into possession of the diary, curiously minute, and the voluminous correspondence of Rebecca, sister to general Chattesworth, with whose family I had the honour to be connected. And this journal, to me, with my queer cat-like affection for this old village, a perfect treasure – and the interminable *bundles* of letters, sorted and arranged so neatly, with little abstracts of their contents in red ink, in her own firm thin hand upon the covers, from all and to all manner of persons – for the industrious lady made fair copies of all the letters she wrote – formed for many years my occasional, and always pleasant winter night's reading.[8]

We are given no access to the content of these papers at this point, only their form. The process of transmission at once belongs to the drive to truth and the writing of fiction – it authenticates, and provides a rhetorical distraction from the story itself. We no more begin *here* than we did with the old soldier's tale.

The trick is to give the reader facts – indeed, to give away the plot in advance – but at a stage when he or she cannot possibly understand their significance. To keep the reader 'in the dark': a phrase which connotes a state of suspended rationalism, of 'superstition', of guessing. This is evident in the dramatic scene in Chapter 2, whose Gothic vocabulary of hellish darkness is mixed with an infuriatingly teasing manner which dangles the facts before the reader, and hides them at the same time. A secret burial, at midnight on a dark and rainy night:

> A great oak shell: the lid was outside the porch, Mr Tressels was unwilling to screw it down, having heard that the entrance to the vault was so narrow, and apprehending it might be necessary to take the coffin out. So it lay its length with a dull weight on the two forms. The lead coffin inside, with its dusty black velvet, was plainly much older. There was a plate on it with two bold capitals, and a full stop after each, thus:-
>
> R.D.
> obiit May 11th
> A.D. 1746.
> aetat 38.

And above this plain, oval plate was a little bit of ornament no bigger than a sixpence. John Tracy took it for a star, Bob Martin said he knew it to be a Freemason's order, and Mr Tressels, who almost overlooked it, thought it was nothing better than a fourpenny cherub. But Mr Irons, the clerk, knew that it was a coronet; and when he heard the other theories thrown out, being a man of very few words he let them have it their own way, and with his thin lips closed, with their changeless and unpleasant character of an imperfect smile, he coldly kept this little bit of knowledge to himself.

Earth to earth (rumble), dust to dust (tumble), ashes to ashes (rattle).

And now the coffin must go out again, and down to its final abode.

The flag that closed the entrance of the vault had been removed. But the descent of Avernus was not facile, the steps being steep and broken, and the roof so low. Young Mervyn had gone down the steps to see it duly placed: a murky, fiery light, came up, against which the descending figures looked black and cyclopean.[9]

We have now, in a single chapter break, gone back some forty or fifty years from the Prologue. The mystery is laid before reader and characters alike – only Mr Irons knows that the tiny mark is a coronet, the sign of an Earl, and he is firmly keeping his knowledge from everyone, including the reader. Young Mervyn has brought his father 'home' from England to the family vault. The Latin inscription on the nameless coffin should read: Robert Dunoran/Died May 11th/AD 1746/Aged 38. The disgraced Earl, who committed suicide in 1746, after having been convicted (wrongly) of the murder of Mr Beauclerc at Newmarket, is unable, officially, legally, to be buried in consecrated ground. The melancholy heir, Mr Mervyn, has written to the rector of Chapelizod, Dr Walsingham, who has agreed to turn a blind eye to the proceeding. But he has refused to perform the ceremony himself. Mervyn has brought his own (English? Irish, retired?) clergyman to perform the theogically unacceptable and perhaps illicit act, who is described earlier as hovering, in his surplice and white whig, like a 'white bird of night'. These facts explain some of the detachment and even comedy that lurks at unexpected moments in what is otherwise a wonderfully 'dark' scene.

The *OED* gives two senses for 'cyclopean': (1) an allusion to an ancient race of giants, traces of whom exist in prehistoric architectural sites; and (2) an allusion to the specific Homeric example of the troglodytic one-eyed race, the famous representative of whom is Polyphemos, outwitted by Odysseus in the Odyssey. There are hints of both senses in what we have just read: the 'flat stone' in the graveyard is a cyclopean

touch, which will reappear right across Le Fanu's later work. The old soldier in the graveyard is a monocular witness. A 'cyclopean history'
therefore is a kind of contradiction; it is a history of the survival of the
'cyclopean', the earlier, cruder, mythic, epic phase of the culture, which
was indeed revived with the Victorian cult of the Druids and would
have been quite recognisable to Le Fanu's Victorian English audience
in the 1860s.[10]

This furtive burial ceremony is parodied in a series of rumbles and rat-
tles. Its agency is removed – no one throws the earth. The lurid glow of
the vault is a Drury Lane glow as much as it is an observed event – its
fictionality is flaunted – we already know Charles can't *really* have
seen it, on his own admission. And this perhaps explains the pagan
allusion – to the sixth book of Virgil's *Aeneid*, the descent into Hades, in
which the poet prays for strength to describe the horrors of the underground world, which has an effect at once mock-heroic and Gothic, and
hence the notion of a pagan, pre-Christian underground world is used
in a rather complex fashion here, as a comparison with the benign corruption of the Christian one. Le Fanu devotes a whole chapter of *Uncle
Silas* and 'Carmilla' to 'the descent of Avernus', different in each case. It
is clearly one of Le Fanu's armoury of metaphors for the slippery slope
down which his two heroines slide. It is also a standard Gothic allusion,
used by Maturin in *Melmoth the Wanderer*. And Le Fanu, like Maturin
before him, has the project (and the gift) of combining comedy and horror, so that the tone of his writing dances, constantly, delicately,
between the two extremes.

The ghost of a hand (a twice-told tale)

This is the most famous, and obviously Gothic aspect of this book,
which often appears to editors to stick out like a sore thumb – the notorious Chapter 12 – 'Some Odd facts About the Tiled House – Being An
Authentic Narrative of the Ghost of a Hand'. This chapter has been
treated traditionally by editors as a self-contained short story, and
indeed fictional tradition made sure that this would happen because it
was made into a much more famous short story by W.F. Magee, 'The
Beast With Five Fingers', which in its turn contributed to the expres-
sionist movie, *The Hands of Orlac*, with Peter Lorre.

As we have seen, Le Fanu often likes to offer two versions of a narrative – one that belongs to the common people, and the other which
bristles with a more modern, sceptical, legalistic or scientific vigilance. If
we take this famous ghost story – one indeed of the most powerful and

original of the whole Gothic tradition – and put it back into its context, we get, I think, some interesting results.

Arthur Mervyn, alias Mordaunt, is impersonating his cousin, Lord Castlemallard's other nephew, who was 'ruined at Paris' – that is, *decently* ruined. He has brought home the body of his ruined and disgraced father, the Earl Viscount Robert of Dunoran, and buried it in the family vault and he now hovers at the Tiled House, the only thing left of his father's estate. A stranger in his own house. The young man is himself, effectively, a ghost (he is described as an 'apparition' (I, 36): despite his beauty and elegance, he cannot marry and renew his fortunes, which, at the age of 30 or 31, he desperately needs to do, because of the family dis- grace. He cannot even inherit the Tiled House itself, which belongs to him and which has gone to rack and ruin, because, although he is of age, he must clear the family name first, before he can pay the debts his father has left him. Credit would otherwise be impossible. According to his callous uncle, he has the aspect of a vampire:

> 'Yes, Sir, he's a very pretty young man, and very well dressed,' said his Lordship, with manifest dissatisfaction: 'but I don't like meeting him, you know. 'Tis not his fault; but one can't help thinking of – of things; and I'd be glad his friends would advise him not to dress in velvets, you know – particularly black velvets, you can understand. I could not help thinking, at the time, of a pall, somehow. I'm not – no – not pleasant near him. No – I – I can't – his face is so pale – you don't often see so pale a face – no – it looks like a reflection from one that's still paler – you understand – and in short, even in his perfumes there's a taint of – of – you know – a taint of blood, Sir.'[11]

The discourses of economics and Gothic horror are perfectly blended here. It irritates his uncle that Mordaunt has returned to the family house, and is beginning to restore it: one of his Irish agents, the Artillery doctor, Sturk, has been urging him to take advantage of the fact that the house is reputed to be haunted and no servants will live in it, to buy it. As a property, it adjoins his own estate. The historical discourse at the outset of the novel, in 1767, overlaps perfectly with the Gothic motif. Mordaunt is a product of aristocratic inbreeding, as his extreme degree of pallor suggests: his father married his beautiful cousin, and ruined her. He has her huge beautiful melancholy eyes, and already pale skin.

Le Fanu as usual tells the same story twice. Chapter 11 gives us the history of the haunting of the Tiled House in this context, from the point of view of 'old Sally', the maid of Lilias, the Rector's daughter, as a 'winter's tale'. After the ruin and disgrace of the Earl's indictment for

murder and suicide in 1748, his wife and young child, the brother or
sister of Mordaunt, stayed in the Tiled House and died there within a
short time. The manner of delivery is typically self-conscious. The novel
is set back in the Enlightenment period, which is an important counterpoint to the survival of its Protestant culture:

> 'There are people, Sally, now-a-days, who call themselves free-
> thinkers, and don't believe in anything – even in ghosts,' said Lilias.
>   'A then the place he's stoppin in now, Miss Lily, 'ill soon cure him
> of free-thinking, if the half they say about it's true,' answered Sally.
>   'But I don't say, mind, *he*'s a free-thinker, for I don't know anything
> of Mr Mervyn; but if he be not, he must be very brave, or very good,
> indeed. I know, Sally, I should be horribly afraid, indeed, to sleep in
> it myself,' answered Lilias, with a cosey [sic] little shudder, as the aer-
> ial image of the old house for a moment stood before her, with its
> peculiar malign, scared, and skulking aspect, as if it had drawn back
> in shame and guilt among the melancholy old elms and tall hemlock
> and nettles.
>   'And now, Sally, I'm safe in bed. Stir the fire, my old darling.' For
> although it was the first week in May, the night was frosty. 'And tell
> me all about the Tiled House again, and frighten me out of my wits.'
>   So good old Sally, whose faith in such matters was a religion, went off
> over the well-known ground in a gentle little amble – sometimes sub-
> siding into a walk as she approached some special horror, and pulling
> up altogether – that is to say, suspending her knitting, and looking with
> a mysterious nod at her young mistress in the four-poster, or lowering
> her voice to a sort of whisper when the crisis came. [12]

The concentration on transmission is quite inseparable here from the
content of the scene: narrative is the subject of narrative, the oral is
asimilated to the written. Lilias, like the narrator, Charles de Cresseron,
loves a 'horror'. The scene is one of perfect comfort. The enjoyment of
horror is tied to the survival of religion. Hence the joke that the evoca-
tion of horror for Sally is a special article of faith – apparently a parody
of orthodox religion. This is the frame, in which the ghost story is
received by the reader – one which foregrounds a variety of explanations
from the superstitious to the atheistical and Voltairean.
  So Sally runs through the witnesses, who all corroborate one another,
a kind of parody of Charles de Cresseron himself, the authenticator:

> Mick Daly, when he had the orchard, used to sleep in the loft over the
> kitchen; and he swore that within five or six weeks, while he lodged

there, he twice saw the same thing, and that was a lady, in a hood and a loose dress, her head drooping, and her finger on her lip, walking in silence among the crooked stems, with a little child by the hand, who ran smiling and skipping beside her. And the Widow Cresswell once met them at night-fall, on the path through the orchard to the back-door, and she did not know what it was until she saw the men look-ing at one another as she told it.[13]

Mordaunt has brought his father, the Earl, over the water 'home', but, as Sally goes on to tell Lily, her narrative intensifying into horror in the process, it is in fact for the second time. He is already there and has been so since the occasion on the night of his death, when the 'hand' first makes its appearance:

> 'The very night he met his death in England, old Oliver, the butler, was listening to Dalton – for Dalton was a scholar – reading the letter that came to him through the post that day, telling him to get things ready, for his troubles wor nearly over and he expected to be with them again in a few days, and *may-be almost as soon as the letter*; and sure enough, while he was reading, there comes a frightful rattle at the window, like someone all in a tremble, trying to shake it open, and the earl's voice, as they both conceited, cries from outside, "Let me in, let me in, let me in!" '[14] (my italics)

This is a reprise of the most famous instance, outside Tennyson's *In Memoriam*, of a disembodied hand in Victorian literature: the 'return' of the dead Catherine to Heathcliff. Le Fanu even repeats her despair-ing cry 'Let me in!'. The conjunction of the letter and the 'hand' (refer-ring to handwriting) is the first instance of the homonymic that Le Fanu uses immediately after this, in *Wylder's Hand*, the plot of which is based on the forgery of the handwriting of a dead man. The naturalistic level is still present: the Earl was gambling, as ever, that he would not be indicted, and so optimistically wrote his letter to his servants. However, the judgement went against him, and he killed himself instead, the letter immediately acquiring a metaphysical overtone, because (as with all letters) the hand that wrote it, freed from the ten-ancy of the body and yet eternally excluded from it too, arrives at the same time:

> ' "It's him," says the butler, " 'Tis so, bedad," says Dalton, and they both looked at the windy, and at one another – and then back

again – overjoyed, in a soart of a way, and frightened all at onst. Old
Oliver was bad with the rheumatiz in his knee, and went lame-like. So
away goes Dalton to the hall-door, and he calls "who's there?" and
no answer. "Maybe," says Dalton, to himself, " 'tis what he's rid
round to the back-door;" so to the back-door with him, and there he
shouts again – and no answer and not a sound outside – and he began
to feel quare, and to the hall-door back with him again. "Who's
there? do you hear? who's there?" he shouts, and receiving no answer
still. "I'll open the door at any rate," says he, "maybe it's what he's
made his escape," for they knew all about his troubles, and wants to
get in without noise, so praying all the time – for his mind misgave
him it might not be all right – he shifts the bars and unlocks the door;
but neither man, nor woman, nor child, nor horse, nor any living
shape was standing there, only something or another slipt into the
house close by his leg; it might be a dog, or something that way, he
could not tell, for he only seen it for a moment with the corner of his
eye, and it went in just like as if it belonged to the place.'[15]

The superstitious servant immediately realises that his master is dead.
The allegory is complete. It encompasses the relation between body and
soul, and the economic and cultural alienation of the journey back
'across the water', across the Styx, from England to Ireland. A journey
impossible to finish, for the Earl, and yet impossible not to keep on making. The House is from this point in the mid-eighteenth century
haunted by the Hand, until we encounter it at the beginning of the
novel's main action in 1767, occupied by Young Mervyn, alias
Mordaunt, who is, thus, one of the ghosts who just happens to be nom-
inally alive, his substance (economic and biological) wasted. The House
is thus a multiple symbol, of the individual and the estate, in this case
the ruined Dunoran dynasty, just as it is in the traditional Gothic from
Walpole onwards.

The much more famous Chapter 12 then defamiliarises this story,
telling it over again during the intervening ten years, after the death of
the Earl, and mimicking the ignorance, bewilderment, and fear of the
new (rising) bourgeois tenants. Lord Castlemallard, not knowing what
to do with the property he is obliged to look after, lets it to a
'Corporation fellow', a Dublin Alderman, who in turn sublets it to his
son-in-law, a Mr Prosser.

Again, the text creates an ironical overlap between the superstitious
and the rational by means of a typical disclaimer from Charles. This
time, we are in the medium of a written culture, the very emblem of

modern, rational scepticism:

> I'm sure she believed every word she related, for old Sally was vera-
> cious. But all this was worth just so much as such talk commonly is –
> marvels, fabulae, what our ancestors called winter's tales – which gath-
> ered details from every narrator, and dilated in the act of narration.[16]

There is however an 'objective' mystery. Charles has one of Miss Rebecca
Chattesworth's letters of 1753, but the publisher won't let him do anything except paraphrase it for us:

> I was for printing the entire letter which is really very singular as well
> as characteristic. But my publisher meets me with his *veto*; and I
> believe he is right. The worthy old lady's letter *is*, perhaps, too long;
> and I must rest content with a few hungry notes of its tenor.[17]

This is a glimpse of some *real* evidence, though Aunt Becky isn't a sceptic.
We have already had this made clear to us:

> Some people said she was a bit of a Voltarian, but unjustly; for though
> she now and then came out with a bouncing social paradox, she was
> good bitter Church-woman.

But Charles's own sense of the negotiable nature of the text he is writing
crosses over, quite openly, as part of the game of reading, with the
rhetorical production of horror here, which uses the sense of rationality
built into the material medium of fiction-writing in the 1860s as a
sophisticated public process, bristling with editors and an impatient and
critical general public, only to subvert it, repeating exactly the patterns
of the oral – one narrator builds upon another, and one incident is there,
not to be authenticated, but *capped*, by the next. The legalistic format of
Chapter 12, the drive for 'authenticity' (i.e. the language of documentation) is thus part of a rich dialogue, internal to the novel, between truth
and fiction. The intensity of the claims of one side is transferred to the
other: so documentation makes space for the marvellous, the horrific,
and the grotesque, which outpaces the perceptions of the 'superstitious'
servants in Chapter 11:

> There was a candle burning on a small table at the foot of the bed,
> beside the one he held in one hand, a heavy ledger, connected with
> his father-in-law's business being under his arm. He drew the curtain

at the side of the bed, and saw Mrs Prosser lying, as for a few seconds he mortally feared, dead, her face being motionless, white, and covered in a cold dew; and on the pillow, close beside her head, and just within the curtains, was, as he first thought, a toad – but really the same white, fattish hand, the wrist resting on the pillow, and the fingers extended towards her temple.[18]

The heavy ledger indicates the seriousness of Mr Prosser, who takes his work to bed with him. But the new merchant class meets its comeuppance in this instance, and it is poor Mrs Prosser, the daughter of a Dublin Alderman, who is unable to breathe, paralysed in mortal horror by the loathsome hand of the old Earl. This is a deathbed scene from Le Fanu's early work, the burning candle indicating the consciousness of the subject, adapted into a haunting.[19]

Years later, Charles, who is too young to have known the Prossers personally, eventually does manage to draw closer to his source, and meet his principal witness, the cousin of the young Prosser child, James, who has been haunted in the nursery of the Tiled House:

In the year 1819, at a college breakfast, I met a Mr Prosser – a thin, grave, but rather chatty old gentleman, with very white hair, drawn back into a pigtail – and he told us all, with a concise particularity, a story of his cousin, James Prosser, who, when an infant, had slept for some time in what his mother said was a haunted nursery in an old house near Chapelizod, and who, whenever he was ill, over-fatigued, or in anywise feverish, suffered all through his life as he had done from a time he could scarce remember, from a vision of a certain gentleman, fat and pale, every curl of whose wig, every button and fold of whose laced clothes, and every feature and line of whose sensual, benignant, and unwholesome face, was as minutely engraven upon his memory as the dress and lineaments of his own grandfather's portrait, which hung before him every day at breakfast, dinner and supper.[20]

Lo and behold, the features, finally, of Mordaunt's father, 'R.D.', Viscount Lord Robert of Dunoran, the owner of the hand, who condenses in the mixture of qualities in his face the contradictions of his class. How strange and repugnant the term 'benignant' is, when placed so precisely between 'sensual' and 'unwholesome' – it seems a perfect example of a Freudian slip for 'malignant' – and yet this is the contradiction, that the Earl's fat and toadlike hand is the very image of the *waste* of its owner, perpetually open, never grasping and holding anything material, but letting it slip through its fingers. The bourgeois ledger that is thrown at it – at which it 'withdraws' – is a open joke about the peculiarly simple, polarised relation between these two classes.[21]

Gothic and mixed style: two examples

Here I am concerned with different levels of hybridity in this text, particularly the relation between 'horror', which is the master trope of the book, and comedy, romance, and a theatrical kind of grotesque. Reading needs to be alive to the subtlety of these chiaroscuro effects, because the text is often reversing conventions – be they literary, at the level of style or genre, or behavioural. And because Le Fanu's career as a writer of romance suffered as a result of these impurities of genre.

Let me give two examples, first, of the delicacy, and then, of the power of this mixed style first. Both of them show how the master trope of Gothic horror appears in the writing, like unexpected colours in shot silk.

First, the handling of romantic love. The rhetorical principle here is Shakespearian. It is an interesting paradox that the two main pairs of lovers, Mervyn/Mordaunt, and Gertrude Chattesworth, and Captain Devereux and Lilias Washington are given attention in the reverse order of their importance. The text is crowded with doubles, and clearly some principle of natural selection has to operate. Gertrude and Mordaunt have some importance in the 'mystery' plot, in that Gertrude is being proposed to by the two 'vampires' of the book – Mordaunt and Dangerfield, and she eventually chooses the survivor, the noble heir, Mordaunt. But their characters are not highly developed. On the other hand, Lilias and Devereux are placed in the foreground, though neither of them is of any importance in the unravelling of the mystery. Yet theirs is the love that is spectacularly not to be. Instead, Lily rejects Devereux, even though it is made clear to the reader that she loves him. It is then revealed that she is dying of consumption, though she cannot have known this when she made her decision. By the standards of realism, it is an apparently perverse and uneconomic distribution. By the standards of Victorian melodrama, it is a missed opportunity – we could have had a lovely romantic death. Instead, Charles comments on it, as a truth he couldn't divert from, a part of the fiction he couldn't manage:

> I had plans for mending this part of the record, and marrying her to handsome Captain Devereux, and making him worthy of her; but somehow I could not. From very early times I had known the sad story. I had heard her beauty talked about in my childhood; the rich,

clear tints, the delicate outlines, those tender and pleasant dimples, like the wimpling of a well; an image so pure, and merry and melancholy withal, had grown before me, and in twilight shadows visited the now lonely haunts of her brief hours; even the old church, in my evening rambles along the upland of the Park, had in my eyes so saddened a grace in the knowledge that those slender bones lay beneath its shadows, and all about her was so linked in my mind with truth, and melancholy, and altogether so sacred, that I could not trifle with the story, and felt, even when I imagined it, a pang, and a reproach, as if I had mocked the sadness of little Lily's fate ... .[22]

The convention of negotiating the plot with the reader in the course of the narrative is essentially comic – it comes from Cervantes into the eighteenth-century novel. One thinks of Fielding's narrator in *Tom Jones*, who reveals that he has allowed Tom to sleep with his mother. But the language here is quite inappropriate – it is wistful and devoted, insisting on both truth and melancholy, insisting on death as a truth that cannot be balked by the romantic or melodramatic conventions of fiction. This is a good example of the way the mixed style works to create the bittersweet tone, which keeps wrongfooting the reader. Charles even goes on to justify this decision, ethically, in another switch of tone, which reveals him to be a devoted reader of his own narrative, who still feels some doubts about it:

And after all, what difference should it make? Is not the generation among whom her girlish lot was cast long passed away? A few years more or less of life. What of them now? ... Had she married Captain Devereux, what would her lot have been? She was not one of those potent and stoical spirits, who can survive the wreck of their best affections, and retort injury with scorn. In forming that simple spirit, Nature had forgotten arrogance and wrath. She would never have fought against the cruelty of changed affections if that or the treasons of an unprincipled husband had come. His love would have been her light and life, and when that was turned away, like a northern flower that has lost its sun, she would have only hung her pretty head, and died, in her long winter. So viewing now the ways of wisdom from a distance, I think I can see they were the best, and how that fair, young mortal, who seemed a sacrifice, was really a conqueror.[23]

Charles commits the sin of a reader here, who dreams up endings for the narrative that lie beyond its scope. He pleads with us to find ways of accommodating the unconsoling truth of his fiction. The final comment is interesting: it heralds a long line of fascinating studies of the 'perversity' of the female psyche in Le Fanu's work, which hark back to Richardson. Lilias[24] refuses to be seduced by the seducer, the Rochester figure, Devereux, and thrown aside. The scene of their parting is a masterpiece of 'perversity'. Devereux has been courting Lily for some time, and he has, despite himself, fallen in love with her. But both are proud. There is a misunderstanding between them, and she thinks (in simple friendship, not knowing her feelings) that he was going to leave without speaking to her, and feels betrayed. He *has*, in fact, resolved to leave her alone for a month, because he too has felt betrayed by a certain coldness and distance he thinks he has detected in her manner, and his pride tells the philanderer that he cannot be a slave to a woman like this. But the rake is in love. He can't help trying to seduce her, and when the unexpected news of his posting comes, he seeks her out near the river, at the very site where he sang her a charming lyric and touched her heart. The dialogue between them is tense and full of realistic impulse and switches of mood. At the same time, it is shot through with jokes about death that mix the sentimental and the Gothic:

> 'My dreams take wing, but my follies will not leave me. And you have been ill, Miss Lilias?'
> 'Oh, nothing: only a little cold.'
> 'And I am going – I only knew last night – really going away.' He paused; but the young lady did not feel called upon to say anything, and only allowed him to go on. In fact, she was piqued, and did not choose to show the least concern about his movements. 'And I've a great mind now that I'm leaving this little world,' and he glanced, it seemed to her, regretfully towards the village, 'to put you down, Miss Lily, if you will allow it, in my codicil for a legacy—'
> She laughed a pleasant little laugh. How ill-natured! but, oh, wasn't it musical?[25]

The cold will turn to consumption, but no one knows this except Charles, the narrator. Played against Devereux's almost unconsciously pleading, emotional backmail – the soldier anticipates his death on the battlefield – Lily's spirited and piqued rejection of him is mixed – heartbreakingly – with the real charge of her death. Comically, in a parody of Rochester, he gets it all wrong, and tries to leave her his monkey. She hovers between satire and gravity, choosing the latter, and confirming her rejection of what to him is both a ploy and a real emotion. Then she realises, from something he says, that he *has* been to her house that morning to say goodbye, as a friend, and her emotions, disguised by the banality of her question, 'You are then really going?', become inexplicably complex – Charles comments 'so that no one would have guessed how strangely she felt at that moment'. They shake hands, and say goodbye, hovering on the edge of a declaration of love:

> She was frightened lest he should possibly say more than she knew how to answer.
> 'And somehow it seems to me, I have a great deal to say.'
> 'And I've a great deal to read, you see;' and she just stirred old Miss Wardle's letter, that lay open in her hand, with a smile just the least in the world of comic distress.
> 'A great deal,' he said.
> 'And farewell again,' said Lilias.
> 'Farewell! dear Miss Lily.'
> And then, he just looked his old strange look upon her; and he went: and she dropped her eyes upon the letter.[26]

The spareness of this writing is admirable – the surface is almost banal. But it is also charged with restrained emotion, focused in the glimpse we get of Lilias's smile as 'just the least in the world of comic distress'.

The bittersweet moment of 'perversity', the intense concentration and dramatisation of this moment, comes now, at the point of victory. Charles gives us all viewpoints: his, hers, and his own, as he brings us all the confusion and bafflement of Lilias's 'victory':

> He had got into the far meadow, where the path makes a little turn round the clump of poplars, and hides itself. Just there he looked over his shoulder, a last look it might be, the handsome strange creature that had made so many of her hours pass so pleasantly; he that was so saucy with every one else, and so gentle with her; of whom, she believed, she might make anything, a hero or a demi-god! She knew a look would call him back – back, maybe, to her feet; but she could not give that little sign. There she stood, affecting to read the letter, one word of which she did not see. 'She does not care; but – there's no one like her. No – she does not care.' He thought; and she let him think it: but her heart swelled to her throat, and she felt as if she could have screamed, 'Come back – my only love – my darling – without you I must die!' But she did not raise her head. She only read on, steadily, old Miss Wardle's letter – over and over – the same half dozen lines.

> And when, after five minutes more, she lifted up her eyes, the hoary poplars were ruffling their thick leaves in the breeze – and he gone; and the plaintive music came mellowed from the village, and the village and the world, seemed all on a sudden empty for her.[27]

Lily the conqueror is Lily the defeated. The cliché of romantic love ('Without you I must die!') is not enough. With or without him, she must die. They both must die. The moment of rejection, which exists within the conventions of 'romance', is Lily's sudden consciousness of her own mortality, conveyed in the touch of sublime in the sudden emptiness of the landscape; and this is the real subject of the passage. Lily is Christ, and the river-bank scene her Gethsemane.

The hyrid nature of the writing, the shift of tone from social comedy to horror and back, is extended by the nature of the dialogue between Gertrude and Lily. They both persistently use the language of Gothic horror about love. Gertrude is in love with Mervyn, a ghost, and Lily senses this quality in him too:

> ... Mervyn acquiesced serenely in the existing state of things, and seemed disposed to be 'sweet upon' pretty Lilias Walsingham, if that young lady had allowed it; but her father had dropped hints about his history and belongings which surrounded him in her eyes with a sort of chill and supernatural halo. There was something funeste and mysterious even in his beauty; and her spirits faltered and sank in his presence. Something of the same unpleasant influence, too, or was it fancy, she thought his approach seemed now to exercise upon Gertrude also, and that she, too, was unaccountably chilled and darkened by his handsome, but ill-omened presence.[28]

At this point neither Lilias nor the reader knows that Gertrude and Mordaunt are only pretending not to be in love. Lily's father has merely told her about Mervyn's family disgrace, which is mainly a social and economic question of his reputation and currency in the marriage market. But the passage is edging (from 'unpleasant' to 'darkened') towards the Gothic all the time: 'funeste', Lily's Gothic signal, is going to be one of Maud's key words about Silas.

And Gertrude, quite independently, when trying to confess her secret to Lily, without actually telling her what's going on, is made to use exactly the same 'turn' into the language of darkness and death:

> 'I hate the light, Lily,' repeated Gertrude, not looking at her companion, but directly out through the bow-window upon the dark outline

of the lawn and river bank, and the high grounds on the other side. 'I hate the light – yes, I hate the light, because my thoughts are darkness – yes, my thoughts are darkness. No human being knows me; and I feel like a person who is *haunted*. Tell me what you saw when you came into the parlour just now.'[29]

Mervyn, her lover, whose shadow Lily has glimpsed at the window, has been reduced to the 'form of a man', a ghost, through the economic and social limbo in which he hovers. The language of 'darkness' intensifies, as Gerty tries to get back on terms with her old friend, after a long period of secrecy, until there's almost a contradiction between the language she is using, and what she is trying to say about the absoluteness of the state of being in love. She is 'possessed', and has died to the world:

> 'Gertrude, dear, I ought not to have come in so suddenly.'
> 'Yes, 'twas but right – 'twas but kind in you, Lily – right and kind – to treat me like the open-hearted and intimate friend that, Heaven knows, I was to you Lily, all my life. I think – at least, I think – till lately – but you were always franker than I – and truer. You've walked in the light, Lily, and that's the way to peace. I turned aside, and walked in mystery; and it seems to me I am treading now the valley of the shadow of death. Walking and talking, I am, nevertheless, in the silence and darkness of the grave.'[30]

The irony of this speech is that it is Lily who is dying, in reality, though neither of them knows it and both think of themselves as 'haunted' by love – Gertrude by Mervyn and Lily by Devereux. This is the first appearance of the language of darkness in Le Fanu as a code for the description of romantic love; and the irony of women's friendship, the intense closeness and love between women, is that it is subject to the absolute passivity demanded by the convention. 'Darkness' is Irish for secrecy. This puts the two women in a mirror-image relationship to each other, where their lives are both haunted, as Gertrude calls it – plagued by a world of secrets, of 'darknesses'. 'I'm no agent now', says Gertrude, as she (actively) swears Lily to secrecy, 'but simply passive in the matter' (II, 21). This looks forward to 'Carmilla' and to the extraordinary later romance, *Haunted Lives*, which sets out to explore this Gothic metaphor of 'haunting' for the predatory, undermining 'darkness' (the self and other-betrayal, division into secrecy) of romantic and sexual love.

My second example of the hybrid style in action is the male resurrection plot, and the almost Jacobean set of mixed signals we get from the scene in which Dr Sturk, the witness to Dangerfield's past crimes, is trepanned by the brutal surgeon, Black Dillon. Structurally, this scene might have come from a stage comedy, but the master-stroke is the way it is seen from the totally restricted point of view of the tremulously agitated Mrs Sturk, and the servants, who are outside the door. This gives a special underlay of pathos in the comedy, which makes the effect of the writing very paradoxical, emotionally. We laugh and wince at the same time, as the village barber arrives, accompanied by Mrs Sturk who hovers, trying to get even a glimpse at the sick-room door:

> 'Come in here, then. Come in, will you?' cried the doctor, hauling him in with his great red hand.
>
> 'There now – there now – there – there,' he said gruffly, extending his palm to keep off poor Mrs Sturk.
>
> So he shut the door, and poor Mrs Sturk heard him draw the bolt, and felt that her Barney had passed out of her hands, and that she could do nothing for him now but clasp her hands and gasp up her prayers for his deliverance; and so great indeed was her anguish and panic, that she had not room for the feminine reflection how great a brute Doctor Dillon was.[31]

The sawbones is a comic eighteenth-century type. But here Le Fanu has invested the scene with all kinds of unexpected tones. The horror of the 'great red hand' which is to perform the terrible operation on her Barney, meddling even in his very brains, and which bars the way to Mrs Sturk, and then – to cap it all – draws the bolt on her, is a secular version (one of several in the novel) of the hand that haunts the Tiled House. Charles intervenes to give the 'feminine reflection' which his character can't give, drawing our attention to his role as a writer of fiction in a kind of George Eliot parody, and adding an interesting detachment to the scene. Like Wilkie Collins, Le Fanu is always interested in women and servants.

Now we are firmly excluded, and we can only hear and imagine from outside the room, through the filter of Mrs Sturk's anguish, the momentous scene that is taking place in the bedroom:

> So she heard them walking this way and that, but could not distinguish what they said, only she heard them talking; and once or twice a word reached her, but not very intelligible, such as –
>
> 'Twas Surgeon Beauchamp's – see that.'
>
> 'Mighty curious.'

Then a lot of mumbling and
'Cruciform, of course.'

This was said by Doctor Dillon, near the door, where he had come
to take an addditional candle from the table that stood there; as he
receded it lost itself in mumble again, and then she heard quite
plainly –
'Keep your hand there.'

And a few second after.
'Hold it there and don't let it drip.'

And then a little more mumbled dialogue, and she thought she heard –
'Begin now.'

And there was a dead silence of many seconds; and Mrs Sturk felt as
if she must scream, and her heart beat at a gallop, and her dry, white
lips silently called upon her Maker for help, and she felt quite wild,
and very faint; and heard them speak brief and low together, and
then another long silence; and then a loud voice, in a sort of shriek,
cry out that name – holy and awful – which we do not mix in tales
like this. It was Sturk's voice; and he cried in the same horrid shriek,
'Murder – mercy – Mr Archer!' [32]

The restriction of viewpoint is essential to the effect of this writing
which suddenly here has a grotesque theatricality about it. The vague-
nesses and then sudden clarities, dependent on where ('on stage') the
protagonists happen to be, for example, are perfectly rendered through
the eavesdropper's straining faculties. What does 'don't let it drip' refer
to, for example? The candle? The idea that the red-hot wax could drip
on to the man's skull, or even into his brains, hardly bears thinking of,
and yet surely this is what the reader must wildly entertain, even if
Mrs Sturk can't manage to. The silences, the mutterings, all are drawn
out. And then, we may smile even as the dead man sits up and blas-
phemes, and Charles primly intervenes to draw a veil over his language,
again showing us the fiction at work. And yet this is a solemnly awful
moment, on all kinds of levels. The shriek is 'horrid': meaning, it makes
the knotted and combined locks stand up. It is a literal resurrection of
the dead, a motif, which, as we have seen elsewhere is of vital symbolic
importance to Le Fanu. The dead man speaks, even though he has been
in a coma for weeks. And he is immediately plunged back into the terrible moment of his murder, as his killer raises himself on his toes to
deliver with all his strength the final blow to his head. For the reader, of
course, we now know who killed him, though Archer has not been fully
identified at this stage as Dangerfield. The author now offers an open

challenge to the reader at this moment to guess the identity of his villain, Dangerfield.

One of the Victorian reviewers picked out Dillon as a remarkable character, and indeed he is. We start out here with a comic stereotype – a drunken Hogarthian brute with his gold-topped cane, reduced to the flagrant metonym of his hand. But he is treated in an unusual way: a criminal debtor, neglected by his profession, he is bribed by the villain, Dangerfield, to perform the operation. He takes pride in besting the ignorant fools who surround him, and succeeds – only too well.

On one level the scene is Gothic: it is a material version of the motif of revenancy, and, at the level of plot, it is the moment at which Dangerfield, who seeks to manipulate chance, is defeated by the perverse pride of Black Dillon, himself equally a believer in chance. Here is the conversation between them which clinches the deal. Both men feel 'discomfort' over the unexpressed subject of their conversation, which is, effectively, murder:

'You want to have him speak? Well, suppose there's a hundred chances to one the trepan kills him on the spot – what then?' demanded the surgeon, uncomfortably.

Dangerfield pondered also uncomfortably for a minute, but answered nothing; on the contrary, he demanded –

'And what then, Sir?'

'But here, in this case,' said Black Dillon, 'there's no chance at all, do you see, there's no chance, good, bad, or indifferent; none at all.'

'But *I* believe there *is*,' replied Dangerfield decisively.

'You believe, but *I* know.'

'See, sir,' said Dangerfield, darkening, and speaking with a strange snarl; 'I know what I'm about. I've a desire, sir, that he should speak if 'twere only two minutes of conscious articulate life, and then death – 'tis not a pin's point to me how soon. Left to himself he must die; therefore, to shrink from the operation on which depends the discovery both of his actual murderer and of his money, sir, otherwise lost to his family, is – is a damned affectation! *I* think it – so do *you*, sir; and I offer five hundred guineas as your fee, and Mrs Sturk's letter to bear you harmless.' [33]

Dangerfield has his man. The surface reportage of this looks realistic. As hypocrites (i.e. actors), they are both skirting around the issue without saying what it is. There is no difference between them; both see the world as a matter of chances, except that Dangerfield operates on a principle of will, and it is he who is the much greater, the *real* hypocrite, in the scene. We see the chess game, in a typically overlapping manner, partly from his point of view. So, the word 'decisively' gives us a clue to what he is up to. Dillon has given him what he wants – his final confirmation about the patient's chances. He wants to kill the patient, not revive him. If there is no chance, then this is *his* chance and he must take it. When Dillon challenges him, he makes his play, and the Gothic note creeps in at the word 'darkening', just at the point when he is gearing up to lie absolutely to Dillon, presenting himself as a rational (and therefore plausibly unsentimental) philanthropist. But the reader already knows at this point that he has 'persuaded' poor innocent Mrs Sturk with a lot of bullying legal flummery to write the note that will get Dillon out of the Marshalsea, in order to do the job. So we are watching the signals of evil at work, not just crime. The structure of the scene is the temptation by the devil. Dillon is 'Black', but Dangerfield (as his name suggests) is so much blacker that he becomes darkness visible.

Charles, the narrator, is enigmatic about the allegorical level of the chess game Dangerfield is playing throughout the novel, and yet the signs are there for the reader. For example, after a scene in which we see him distributing charity, and hear the approval of the Chapelizod worthies, Charles produces a joking analogy:

> And thus it is, as the foul fiend, when he vanishes, leaves a smell of brimstone after him, a good man leaves a fragrance; and the company in the parlour enjoyed the aroma of Mr Dangerfield's virtues, as he buttoned his white surtout over his vest, and dropped his vails into the palms of the carbuncled butler and fuddled footman in the hall.[34]

This is a perfect example of how the mixed style of the novel works – the insinuating pastiche of a comic intervention, bounced off the superstitious version of the devil – in this case Shakespeare's Poor Tom and his 'foul fiend' – which forms a teasing hint to the reader to reverse the ideas of good and evil in the act of reading the scene we have just read; and yet, does not supply us with the information with which to make that reversal.

Plot and narrative method

The central opposition of the plot is between chance and design, between doubt and faith, and the mixed style of the novel presents this as a paradox about appearance and reality. All we all have is the chess game. It is clear from the pathos of Mrs Sturk, as she buttonholes the embarassed village doctor, that her mere blind faith is not enough:

> 'And he's so much better already, you see, and I know so well how he gets through an illness, 'tis wonderful, and he certainly is mightily improved since we got him to bed. Why, I can *see* him breathe now, and you know it *must* be a good sign; and then there's the a merciful God over us – and all the poor little children – what would become of us?' And then she wiped her eyes quickly. 'The promise, you know, of length of days – it often comforted me before – to those that honour father and mother; and I believe there never was so good a son. Oh! my noble Barney, never; 'tis my want of reliance and trust in the Almighty's goodness.'
>
> And so, holding Toole by the cuff of his coat, and looking piteously into his face as they stood together in the door-way, the poor little women argued thus with inexorable death.[35]

This is fierce satire (because so full of compassion) and it challenges the Victorian reader. Anthropomorphism (i.e. 'superstition') of this type is no good at all. We know, beyond her, (1) that Sturk was a desperate blackmailer, and (2) that he has been murdered in cold blood, and is about to die. Charles's intervention comes hard on the heels of her 'comforting' idea of goodness. He pulls back, and over her head, offers the reader an allegorical image, which adumbrates the central theme of the novel, the relation between chance and necessity or pattern:

> Fools, and blind! when amidst our agonies of supplication the blow descends, our faith in prayer is staggered, as if it reached not the ear of the Allwise, and moved not His sublime compassion. Are we quite sure that we comprehend the awful and far-sighted game that is being played for us and others so well that we can sit by and safely dictate its moves?
>
> How will Messrs Morphy or Staunton, on whose calculations, I will suppose you have staked £100, brook your insane solicitations to spare this pawn or withdraw that knight from prise, on the board which is but the toy type of that dread field where all the powers of eternal intellect, the wisdom from above and the wisdom from beneath – the stupendous intelligence that made, and the stupendous sagacity that

would undo us, are pitted against one another in a death-combat, which admits of no reconciliation and no compromise.[36]

God made the world, but the Devil, his chess opponent – in this case, Paul Dangerfield, the fake-convert to 'goodness' – rules it. Both move in mysterious ways, via the medium of chance. The 'far-sighted game' is built on a series of calculations which reveal themselves to our restricted and fallible viewpoint, poor mortals, as only chance, inexorable but without pattern. Either way, it's death in this combat. Sometimes, as in the case of Dangerfield, a gambler succeeds in controlling the chances for a time. But God is a more powerful computer – he is more like the betting-shop that calculates the odds in advance, than the Devil is, who is the tremendous punter, pulling his victories off against those odds. For us, Death is the inevitable outcome, and the only problem is what kind of death. We, like the Sturks, are no more able to bilk the inexorability of death than a captured pawn can protest against the rules of chess.

This rather bleak version of the universe explains a number of things about this strange and fascinating book. It explains the detailed attention given to Dangerfield's confession towards the end of the book. He can see no reason why he should have failed – he is satisfied that he made the right calculations. He could not have afforded to let Sturk die in a coma, in case he woke up of his own accord and denounced him. He had to act. All the evidence pointed to the fact that Sturk would die without speaking after the trepan; that Ezekiel Irons would not find the courage to talk. These are both chances which he could not, reasonably, have predicted. 'So, Sir,' says Dangerfield to Mervyn in his condemned cell, 'you see I've nothing to blame myself for – though all has broken down.' (III, 296)

There are two major omissions in all this. (1) The lack of all moral sense except his own interest, and (2) his neglect of the fact that the past never goes away. Because he is a gentleman, like the Devil, when the game is up and life is over for him, Dangerfield declares that he will help Mordaunt clear his father's name, so at least the heir can inherit, and begin to build the family reputation again, with his beautiful young wife, Gertrude. The second omission, however, is more revealing and less stereotypical. The rule in Le Fanu is that the past never goes away. Just as Mordaunt is the victim of his 'blood' and is therefore described, as we have seen, as a vampire, so Dangerfield, too, is haunted by blood and by his murderous deeds of the past. And this is where the cross-over occurs between the plot and the rhetorical level. We are even allowed to glimpse a rare private moment of weariness in this indefatigably 'long-headed' creature. Charles is on hand to let us know that naturalistic conventions of presentation, in this instance, will *not* be obeyed:

> All this was not, as we sometimes read, 'mentally ejaculated', but quite literally muttered, as I believe everyone at times mutters to himself. 'Charles Archer living – Charles Archer dead – or, as I sometimes think, neither one nor t'other quite – half man, half corpse – a vampire – there is no rest for thee: no sabbath in the days of thy work. Blood – blood – blood – 'tis tiresome. Why should I be a slave to these d——d secrets. I don't think 'tis my judgement, so much as the devil that holds me here.[37]

He asks himself if instinct or calculation is 'oftener right'. Potentially, he is aware of the futility of the game he is playing. Why stay here at all? Unfortunately, the way he puts it to himself ('oftener') reveals the corruption of a gambler's question. Dangerfield is potentially noble – his name, Paul, indicates a conversion in reverse – his 'respectable' later-life disguise is more like Saul before Damascus than Paul after. The gamester – with his Roman villa by the aside of Lake Como ready for him – has crawled into the life of a gentleman by being the agent of another. He could cut and run, but it is indeed the devil that is driving him, and this is the Gothic irony of this passage. Charles appears to choose the greater realism of muttering aloud; but another way of seeing it is that of the Shakespearian soliloquy. Dangerfield is associated in the text with Hamlet, the arch-soliloquiser, and Richard III just before the battle of York facing his 'file of ghosts'.

Chance exists on both sides of the equation. God's grace looks exactly like chance. He is defeated by testimony from the past about the past. The vampire struggles rationally to free himself from a past to which he is linked by blood – he lives out a kind of death-in-life, this time, not through inheritance and suicide, but murder. Here, perhaps, we can see the rhetorical principle of the book at work, and how its fictional self-consciousness, which tends to work in the opposite direction – links to its thematic drive to foreground 'plot'. It is the act of witnessing, which the law treats like material evidence, and which religion treats as the foundation of our knowledge of Christ's miracles, an ambiguity which dominates the fictional method of the book. This is why the problem of testimony is allowed, anarchically, to democratise the act of witnessing; even Mrs Sturk has her point of view and it may indeed coincide with the truth.

It is the storyteller who forms the relation, as Charles, in an unusually complex intervention at the beginning of III, XIV, makes clear:

> The buzz of a village, like the hum of a city, represents a very wonderful variety of human accent and feeling. It is marvellous how a few families thrown together will suffice to furnish forth this *dubia coena* of sweets and bitters.
>
> The roar of many waters – the ululatus of many-voicd humanity – marvellously monotonous, considering the infinite variety of its ingedients, booms on through the dark. The story-teller alone can take up the score of the mighty medley, and read at a glance what every fife and fiddlestick is doing. That pompous thrum-thrum is the talk of the great white Marseilles paunch, pietate gravis; the whine comes from Lazarus, at the area rails; and the bass is old Dives, roaring at his butler; the piccolo is contributed by the audacious schoolboy, whistling over his Latin Grammar; that wild, long note is Mrs Fondle's farewell of her dead boy; the ugly barytone, rising from the tap-room, is what Wandering Willie calls a sculduddery song – shut your ears, and pass on; and that clear soprano, in nursery, rings out a shower of innocent idiotisms over the half-stripped baby, and suspends the brawl upon its lips.
>
> So, on this night, as usual, there rose up toward the stars a throbbing murmur from our village – a wild chaos of sound, which we must strive to analyse, extracting from their hurly-burly each separate tune it may concern us to hear.[38]

This is an explicit defence of the storyteller's role – and therefore of fiction. The comparison between the village and city is totally anti-pastoral, though it may owe something to George Eliot. There is also a passing allusion to Scott's 'Wandering Willie', often extracted from his fiction as a Gothic tale. There is none of the feeling of a Wordsworthian privileging of landscape, or the assimilation of mankind to the pre-industrial past in it. This is not how the eighteenth-century pastiche works at all. Instead, the city and the village are versions of each other – the vision of total contingency, of each voice, however insignificant, claiming its place in the cacophony, despite the fact that no one can hear it. No one, that is, except the storyteller, who conducts this chaos and therefore who has the antenna to pick up each 'voice', if necessary, but certainly 'each separate tune it may concern us to hear'. This mysterious qualification is significant – it suggests the intervention of something as a prior motive for selection. But is it (novelistic) 'plot', or (fabular) 'story'? Truth or fiction? With a scheme of universal contingency like this, what are the principles of exclusion?

The paradox of this passage is perfectly poised: there is a drive *against* contingency too. What is also distinctive about the passage is its biblical resonance. The roaring waters, the darkness (and presumably silence, though, oddly, this is *not* invoked) of universal death against which the voices form their strangely monotonous roar to all except the storyteller. And some of the examples of purely contingent voices are also highly significant. One of the blueprints for the plots of Le Fanu's late romances is the biblical parable of Dives and Lazarus, the rich man and the poor man, and the reversal of their relation in the end, so that Dives is tormented by the sight he is granted of Lazarus enjoying the company of God and the angels in Paradise, which forms an important part of his own particular hell. For Lazarus is not forgotten by the all-seeing God. Silas invokes this fable to describe his relation to Dr Bryerly, in *Uncle Silas*. This is one of Christ's fables from the gospels, which enters these romances at the level of plot, but which has an allegorical, rather than a realistic significance.

Charles also uses this parable to describe the relation between Dangerfield and Sturk, so it functions in his passage as an allusion to the plot of this novel itself. The whole variety of the novel invoked here is likely to collapse at any moment into 'darkness'. The 'dubia coena' (the 'doubtful dinner' – a joke about rotten shellfish) is not Plato's *Symposium*, but the last supper, with doubting Thomas and Judas – its bitterness – challenging and chequering strangely the sweetness of the occasion. The dynamism of the rhetoric works in this way downwards towards darkness, not upwards towards light, nor even outwards towards contingency.

So laughter itself is the death's-head, not the eighteenth-century 'jollity', and it is paradoxically Charles's role as 'conductor' that gives him the licence to produce this special dark colour that dominates the novel's spectrum of hybridity.[39]

Part II
Gothic Hybrids

4
Dreadful Witness: Narrative Perversity and *Wylder's Hand*

The ghost (of a ghost) narrates

In *Wylder's Hand*, the techniques of self-conscious narration are adapted to a different mood and tone. The fictional space which the reader inhabits is quite significantly narrower. Some of this shift in tone is attributable to the fact that Le Fanu signed a contract – or gentleman's agreement – after *The House by the Churchyard*, not to set his fiction in Ireland, and to make it 'of modern times'.[1] The leisurely eighteenth-century pastiche of Quixote and Sterne which Charles de Cresseron uses as a comic mask of hybridity – the 'Churchyard laugh' – has the effect in the earlier novel of foregrounding an explicitly paradoxical relation between fiction and truth. In that novel, Charles lets us know when he is making things up, and when his records do not stretch to a picture which he needs for his narration.

But when Le Fanu uses Charles again in *Wylder's Hand* he plays a different game. This novel is concerned to maintain a sustained mood of horror; its comedy is in a very minor key. This is a sleeker more 'modern' version of that paradoxical relation between truth and fiction; the question of fiction is not so much explicitly raised, as implicitly conveyed, in the structure of the narration. Charles narrates the story from the end, in both novels; but in *Wylder's Hand*, the position and angle of narration is much odder and flaunts its own contradictions in front of the reader.

Charles de Cresseron is a family historian, who has been working on the family papers for ten years when the novel's action opens. Charles's account of what happens in the 1850s to the Brandon and Wylder families of Gylingden (i.e. Buxton) in Derbyshire – of which he himself is a remote scion – is a strange mixture of the eye-witness and the omniscient narrator. Charles himself is a kind of ghostly version of his former, Irish self, fading without explanation from one position to another. Witnessing, of course, is a vital part of the cultural thematics of Le Fanu's Gothic; but for the moment, I want to concentrate on the formal problem of the angle of narration.

The result is that Charles's position, as a narrator, is frequently impossible. He writes like an eavesdropper on very intimate conversations, and yet he draws the reader's attention to the fact that he was not present. This is a constant and maddening problem about authority which the reader of this complex and hybrid novel has to negotiate. It is a game in the text which forms a curious floating space of epistemological doubt, in which, as readers, we are confined. Charles is a kind of machine for stimulating readerly inference, which has the constant effect of keeping the narrative at arm's length.

Let me give a concrete example of this effect. Charles begins Chapter XXXV by commenting on his own position, in such a way that we know he cannot have been present at the conversation, between the two villains, Captain Stanley Lake and the lawyer, Josiah Larkin, in the breakfast room of Larkin's house, 'The Lodge' in Gylingden, a conversation which he has just reported to us in intimate detail:

> By this time your humble servant, the chronicler of these Gylingden annals, had taken his leave of magnificent old Brandon, and of its strangely interesting young mistress, and was carrying away with him, as he flew along the London rails, the broken imagery of that grand and shivered dream. He was destined, however, before very long, to revisit these scenes; and in the meantime heard, in rude outline, the tenor of what was happening – the minute incidents and colouring of which were afterwards faithfully communicated.[2]

'By this time' refers specifically to (1) the end of the previous chapter, i.e. a textual *place*; and (2) the moment in narrative time at which the two characters have the conversation we have just (apparently) witnessed. It is clear from this intervention, that Charles is constantly aware of his own absence from the narrative, but not from the text; and of the paradox for the reader which this creates. His point of view is both omniscient and restricted to that of an eye-witness. The text is layered, because it is made to include both these levels – the restricted point of view of the direct witness, and the general point of view of the editor. Indeed, it plays one off against the other. Charles narrates from the end, from a point at which all the 'mystery' is known, his discourse being set, not exclusively at the time of narrating, but sometimes occupying a curiously *displaced*, editorial position. But he seems also unable to reveal to the reader what he does not know at first hand, for Charles is also a protagonist, the protagonist of his own narration, entering it and leaving it, in time and space: in the passage above, for example, he speaks of himself in the third person, using a convention of Victorian letter-writing, as if narrating himself as a character.

The flaunted inconsistency of this makes it a privileged, but not actually a Godlike, position. Charles feels he must justify himself in the teeth of this paradox. Even if he wasn't there at the time, gossip, and then finally records – documents, and testimonies – whether written or spoken, we presume they are recorded in the strictest accuracy – provide him with an authority beyond the limitations of his own role as an eye-witness. So the aesthetic effect of interruption – of the removal of the eye-witness – is not interruption at all, in reality:

> I can, therefore, without break or blur, continue my description; and to say truth, at this distance of time, I have some difficulty – so well acquainted was I with the actors and the scenery – determining, without consulting my diary, what portions of the narrative I relate from hearsay, and what as a spectator.[3]

Charles's frankness about his confusion here – and Le Fanu's corresponding disingenuousness – is disarming. The 'real' is not the surface reportage, but the inner drama that is going on all the time; and it is at this level that the rhetoric of this self-conscious narration is linked to horror and the Gothic – for, what is *really* going on, says Charles, is a kind of nightmare of the abyss which is both inside himself and outside in the world:

> But that I am so far from understanding myself, I should often be amazed at the sayings and doings of other people. As it is, I discover in myself an abyss, I gaze down and listen, and discover neither light nor harmony, but thunderings and lightenings, and voices and laughter, and a medley that dismays me. There rage the elements which God only can control. Forgive us our trespasses; lead us not into temptation; deliver us from the Evil One! How helpless and appalled we shut our eyes over that awful chasm.[4]

This extraordinary and unexpected modulation marks the delicate layering of the text – the way that it moves between the rational, and indeed the sceptical – the legal aspect of witnessing – and the 'superstitious', the religious aspect of witnessing which we are all subject to, in the old Greek sense of 'martyras' – that we witness by our existence and our consciousness, the existence of evil. Those in hell or heaven are all witnesses in this old sense. The text produces the overlap and challenges the reader with the apparent continuity of the rational and the 'superstitious'. Hence, the curious effect of deficiency of point of view which is acknowledged, even in the very excess and overproduction of narration that Charles goes in for. The narrative has a strange, hollow centre – a teasingly removed object of knowledge – that the reader is not allowed direct contact with.

Resurrections

Early on in his narrative, Charles treats the reader to a meditation about memory, which shows how much the thematics of the novel are translated into these connundra about narration and point of view. At their first meeting, the apparently cold and aloof Dorcas Brandon suddenly asks Charles about her mother, who died in her infancy, and Charles gives her 'the sad and pretty picture that remained, and always will, in the vacant air, when I think of her, on the mysterious retina of memory'.[5] Afterwards, he reflects on the nature of such 'pictures':

How filmy they are! the moonlight shines through them, as through the phantom Dane in Retzch's outlines – colour without substance.

How they come, wearing for ever the sweetest and pleasantest look of their earthly days. Their sweetest and merriest tones hover musically in the distance; how far away, how near to silence, yet how clear! And so it is with our remembrance of the immortal part. It is the loveliest traits that remain with us perennially; all that was noblest and most beautiful is there, in a changeless and celestial shadow; and this is the resurrection of the memory, the foretaste and image which the 'Faithful Creator' accords us of the resurrection and glory to come – the body redeemed, the spirit made perfect.[6]

The tenderness of this picture is belied by the threat in the Shakespeare analogy, which is one of the great source texts for the Gothic tradition. Our memories are like the ghost of Hamlet's father – we 'see' them. The reference to painting is also ominous, despite Charles's lyricism. Painting is a magic art For Le Fanu, whose novels often refer to the

Gothic convention of the portrait which comes alive, painting is a form of haunting. Charles appeals to Retzch, as he did in *Churchyard*, when talking about the Wandering Jew. The term 'filmy' is the favourite metaphor of Maud in *Silas*, too which suggests the connexion between outer phenomena and inner vision: 'colour without substance'.[7]

Narration is a form of memory, for Charles, stimulated by the memories of others. The piety and orthodoxy and, indeed, optimism, of this quotidian symbol of resurrection to come is parodied in the novel's plot, which centres on a profane resurrection, that of Mark Wylder, whose ring bears the family motto: 'Resurgam', and the inscription in Persian, which turns out, on several levels, to be a nightmare parody of Christ's utterance in the gospels: 'I will come up again' (Matthew 26:32).

Le Fanu's text is obsessed by the Pauline metaphor, which finishes the passage above: 'the body redeemed, the spirit made perfect'. It seems to create, ironically, in a playful, murderous fashion, the conditions of a resurrection that is mockingly material, and set them against the orthodox consolation of St Paul. When Rachel Lake is deep in despair, in the middle of the story, after having become an accessory to Mark Wylder's murder, which the reader only dimly understands, she consults the vicar, William Wylder. Wylder, paraphrasing Paul's Corinthians, tries to offer Rachel the orthodox consolatory paradox of despair as a means to hope:

'Come!' said he, 'Miss Lake, bethink you; was there not a time – and no very distant one – when futurity caused you no anxiety, and when the subject which has grown so interesting, was altogether distasteful to you. The seed of the Word is received at length into good ground: but a grain of wheat will bring forth no fruit unless it die first. The seed dies to outward sense, and despair follows: but the principle of life is working in it, and it will surely grow and bring forth fruit – thirty, sixty, an hundred-fold – be not dismayed. The body dies, and the Lord of Life compares it to the death of the seed in the earth; and then comes the palingenesis – the rising in glory. In like manner He compares the reception of the principle of eternal life into the soul to the dropping of a seed into the earth; it follows the general law of mortality. It too does – such a death as the children of heaven die here – only to germinate afresh with celestial power and beauty.' Miss Lake's way lay by a footpath across the corner of the park to Redman's Dell. So they crossed the stile, and still conversing,

(a)

(b)

Figure 1 '...it seemed to her...that his face was growing like that of Leonora's phantom trooper...'. From 'Retzsch's Outlines to Burger's Ballads' (London, 1840), BL Shelfmark 506.aa.16., Plates 5 & 6, Illustrations to Burger's 'Lenore'.

(a)

(b)

Figure 2 'the phantom Dane' from 'Retzsch's Outlines to Shakespeare' (London, 1828), BL Shelfmark, 840.m.3. Illustrations to 'Hamlet', Act 1, Sc. 3, and Act 1, Sc. 4.

followed the footpath under the hedgerow of the pretty field, and crossing another stile, entered the park.[8]

'Futurity' here is code for life after death in general, and resurrection in particular. The Vicar quotes the Greek Testament: 'Palingenesis' means, literally, 'the process of being born again'. This is the orthodox doctrine of Christian consolation, which includes the resurrection of the body as a spiritual phenomenon.[9]

I have included the switch into what looks like plain narrative here, in the last paragraph, because this is the point at which it becomes apparent that the plot of the novel, which centres on that unhallowed patch of ground, Redman's Dell, frequently associated with Vallom-broso, or the Valley of the Shadow of Death, and the profane resurrec-tion which is to take place in it, swings in here as a demonic counterpoint to The Rev. Wylder's speech, placed in apparent innocence and neutrality by Charles, but offering a parody of the orthodox doc-trine of spiritual resurrection. Here the discourse of the Gothic enters: Redman's Dell is also associated (by Lord Chelford, 168) with 'Der Freischütz', the short story by Appel, which was made into an opera by Weber and which features again as a subtext in *Uncle Silas*. Even Larkin, the villainous lawyer, who 'was not given to fancy, nor troubled with superstition' (192) is reminded, when confronted by a mysterious figure, a kind of 'grey monkey', which cries out to him, ambiguously, 'Mark!', of a buried set of German associations that are like a form of subtextual telepathy:

This cry of 'Mark!' was beginning to connect itself uncomfortably in his mind with his speculations about his wealthy client, which in that solitude and darkness began to seem not so entirely pure and disinter-ested as he was in the habit of regarding them, and a sort of wood-demon, such as a queer little schoolfellow used long ago to read a tale about in an old German story-book, was now dogging his darksome steps, and hanging upon his flank with a vindictive design.[10]

Charles the narrator conspires here with Larkin's memory to resurrect the 'wood demon' from 'Der Freischütz', actually Mad Uncle Julius Brandon, who prophecies that Mark Wylder will arise again.

This corpse, like Hamlet's 'something … rotten in the state of Denmark' is an object of knowledge, of memory, partly resurrected, but hidden from the reader by the narrative itself. But the hidden dictates what is real;

when, in Chapter XXI, called 'In Redman's Dell', Rachel Lake is walked home by Lord Chelford, who indicates to her that he is very attracted to her, the narrative makes the contrast between illusion and reality explicit:

> There was not much in this little speech, but it was spoken in a low, sweet voice; and Rachel looked down on the ferns before her feet, as they walked on side by side, not with a smile, but with a blush, and that beautiful look of gratification so becoming and indescribable. Happy that moment – that enchanted moment of oblivion and illusion. But the fitful evening breeze came up through Redman's Dell, with a gentle sweep over the autumnal foliage. Sudden as a sigh, and cold; in her ear it sounded like a whisper or a shudder, and she lifted up her eyes and saw the darkening dell before her; and with a pang, the dreadful sense of reality returned.[11]

The reader has been invited to infer, but not allowed to know, by this point, exactly what this 'dreadful sense of reality' is, though it is clearly connected with death, and the death of Mark Wylder. Chapter 17 of the novel is very obscure, but we infer when we read it that when Wylder and Stanley confronted one another in Redman's Dell, and Stanley tried to blackmail Wylder into giving up Dorcas Brandon, by invoking a disgrace Wylder has incurred at a club, Wylder replied by a counter-blackmail, seeking to enlist Stanley's help in trying to marry Rachel, with whom he was still in love, despite the fact that she had already rejected him some years previously. After Stanley has killed Wylder in the Dell, he panics and comes to Rachel's cottage at Redman's Farm. She then is obliged to play Lady Macbeth, and screw his courage to the sticking place by accompanying him back to the corpse, urging him on, and standing by while he buries it in a shallow grave.

Several scenes in this sequence of the plot are missing, omitted by Charles, who has himself been confronted by the Gothic figure of 'Uncle Lorne' Brandon in his bed-chamber, and the seeming confirmation of the 'ghost' of the portrait in the daylight. For example, at the end of Chapter XIV, about the coming confrontation between Stanley Lake and Mark Wylder, he remarks teasingly:

> If one could only see it, the manoeuvring and ultimate collision of two such generals as he and Lake would be worth observing.[12]

But he doesn't observe it, and the reader is left in the dark. Equally, the burial of Wylder's body is tantalisingly missing from the text. We see

Stanley arrive, overhear him persuade Rachel to go back with him, and we see Rachel leave with him. We then see them return, not knowing what it is they have done. It is immediately after this scene (on which Charles drops the curtain) that Stanley conceives the idea of 'resurrecting' Wylder, pretending he is still alive by forging a number of letters from him, and having them posted in London, initially by Rachel, who will then have provided him with an alibi. We see him do this without any explanation from Charles. Effectively, Rachel is forced to sacrifice her good name, in order to accomplish this stratagem: heavily veiled, she lets herself be seen at Dollington station in the company of a 'gentleman' (actually Stanley, but, to all intents and purposes, Wylder) and buys two tickets for London: one for herself and one for her companion. She then stays in London for three days, pretending, and coopting beloved old Tamar, her servant, into pretending, that she is ill, but having successfully allowed the diversionary inference to arise in the mind of anyone who discovers the facts (i.e. Larkin), that she is actually having an affair with Wylder, even while he is engaged to her cousin and closest friend, Dorcas.

This double pack of lies is, we infer, a source of total agony to Rachel. We don't learn all of this for sure until the end of the novel, though we do see Stanley arrive at her house that night, and Charles, making sure that we know he couldn't possibly have been there, 'eavesdrops' on the conversation which they then have, full of revelation for Rachel, but not necessarily for the reader. This is the night from which the eclipse of Rachel's life dates, and that eclipse proceeds from gaps in the text through which the object of knowledge is doubly removed, and yet, at the same time, asserted in both fabula and discourse. Stanley appears in the middle of the night and calls for wine before he can explain:

> 'There is the key. There's some wine in the press, I think.'
> He tried to open it, but his hand shook. He saw his sister look at him, and he flung the keys on the table rather savagely, with, I dare say, a curse between his teeth.[13]

Does he curse here, or not? Is the pious Charles just being coy here, with his 'I dare say'; is he out of ear-shot, or is he showing the reader he doesn't know? These doubts draw our attention to the fact that he can't have been an eye-witness to this scene, but, at best, has heard it recounted, probably more than once, by both the participants. The texture of the scene, despite the detail of the reportage, is actually that of a reconstruction, a fictional hypothesis, hence its free undertone of artifice and pastiche. Charles's act of imagination is a kind of cooperative dream within a set of facts he cannot fully, at this stage, reveal to us. We are condemned to watch and guess, knowing the scene is fictional, but lured by its dreadful truth into giving it credibility, as it unfolds and Rachel suddenly begins to understand:

> Rachel took the key with a faint gleam of scorn on her face and brought out the wine in silence.
>
> He took a tall-stemmed Venetian glass that stood upon the cabinet, an antique decoration, and filled it with sherry – a strange revival of old service! How long was it since lips had touched its brim before, and whose? Lovers', maybe, and how How [sic] long since that cold crystal had glowed with the ripples of wine? This, at all events, was its last service. It is an old legend of the Venetian glass – its shivering at touch of poison; and there are those of whom it is said, 'the poison of asps is under their lips'.
>
> 'What's that?' ejaculated Rachel, with a sudden shriek – that whispered shriek, so expressive and ghastly, that you, perhaps, have once heard in your life – and her very lips grew white.
>
> 'Hollo!' cried Lake. He was standing with his back to the window, and sprang forward, as pale as she, and grasped her, with a white leer that she never forgot, over his shoulder, and the Venice glass was shivered on the ground.
>
> 'Who's there?' he whispered.
>
> And Rachel, in a whisper, ejaculated the awful name that must not be taken in vain.
>
> She sat down. She was looking at him with a wild, stern stare, straight in the face, and he still holding her arm, and close to her.
>
> 'I see it all now,' she whispered.[14]

We don't know what Rachel 'sees', and neither, at this point, does her brother. The textual experience here is Salome-like: the object of knowledge is partly veiled from both reader and character, so we watch Rachel's gradual *éclaircissment* dawn, without full knowledge, ourselves, of exactly what has happened. But we know that it is worse than Rachel thinks, and we can guess ahead of her, that it is a fatal case. The superstitious rhetoric about the shattered Venetian glass is entirely Charles's interpolation; there is room for the breaking of the glass to be a purely natural event, caused by their panic. Charles again holds his own narrative at arm's length, as he actively engages the reader ('you') about the accuracy of describing Rachel's cry as a 'whispered shriek', which must seem oxymoronic, unless the reader has heard such a rare but terrible sound. The more than faint echo of *Macbeth*, in the rhythmn of their abrupt questions, brings the artifice of the Gothic subtext fully to the fore. They are frozen, deliberately, like actors who have escaped from a performance of Shakespeare's tragedy, around an object of knowledge too dreadful to name. The method strikingly anticipates that of Henry James:

> 'Who – what – what is it?' said he.
>
> 'I could not have fancied *that*,' she whispered with a gasp.
>
> Stanley looked around him with pale and sharpened features.
>
> 'What the devil is it! If that scoundrel had come to kill us you could not cry out louder,' he whispered, with an oath. 'Do you want to wake your people up?'
>
> 'Oh! Stanley,' she repeated in a changed and horror-stricken way. 'What a fool I've been. I see it at last; I see it all now,' and she waved her white hands together very slowly, as mesmerisers move theirs.
>
> There was a silence of some seconds, and his yellow ferine gaze met hers strangely.
>
> 'You always were a sharp girl, Radie, and I think you do see it,' he said at last, very quietly.
>
> 'The witness – the witness – the dreadful witness!' she repeated[15]

What Rachel seems to see here is that this whole affair is now a question of murder, and that she herself is implicated, to the point of ruin, with Stanley. She is herself 'the dreadful witness' – 'dreadful' meaning precisely 'full of dread', and she knows that, from this moment on, she will be forced into a position of guilt in order to save her wretched, cowardly brother. She will be obliged to look upon the corpse of Mark Wylder with her own eyes. She will need to force the panicking Stanley to bury it, and perhaps even help him, in order to save them both. This is the point at which the Gothic nightmare meets the mundane facts of the case: 'witness' either means 'accessory' in the legal sense, or 'witness' in a religious sense (i.e. 'participant in') to a reality that lies beyond the material realm of the senses. For the stress here on 'dreadful witness', which belongs to the text and not the character, also refers to to what Rachel will see: the object of knowledge itself, the corpse of Wylder, which will eventually rise from the earth, its hand finally showing itself, to denounce them all.

Much of the novel is concerned with the 'eclipse' of darkness which Rachel suffers at this moment and afterwards. Her despair echoes that of Susan Bennett in the 1850s. We know that Le Fanu had at that time been through a period before his wife Susanna died, in which she questioned her faith and he tried his best to defend it, desperately swatting up his theological knowledge to be prepared for the niceties of her despair. This passage, for example, also seems very close to what had happened to Le Fanu himself:

> The young lady was so intelligent that William Wylder was obliged to exert himself in controversy with her eloquent despair; and this combat with the doubts and terrors of a mind of much more than ordinary vigour and resource, though altogether feminine, compelled him to bestir himself, and so, for the time, found him entire occupation.[16]

Charles also talks about another of Susan Le Fanu's apparent symptoms, Rachel's 'hypochondria':

> I think that Stanley was right, and that living in that solitary and darksome dell had helped to make her hypochondriac.[17]

and also her horror and 'hysteria' after Stanley's visits:

> When Stanley took leave after one of these visits – stolen visits, somehow, they always seemed to her – the solitary mistress of Redman's Farm invariably experienced the nervous reaction which follows the artificial calm of suppressed excitement. Something of panic and horror, relieved sometimes by a gush of tears – sometimes more slowly and painfully subsiding without that hysterical escape.[18]

The passage into despair is absolute, like a conversion, a change of personality. It coincides with a modern-looking study of depression.

Rachel begins like Lilias Walsingham in *Churchyard*. Her beauty and independence, her courage and good-humour, are undoubted. 'The young belle' is happy with her limited means and she toys innocently with 'good horror', like Lilias Walsingham, as she asks Tamar to tell her grisly stories:

> 'So, my dear old fairy, here's your Cinderella home again from the ball, and I've seen nothing so pretty as this since I left Redman's Farm. How white your table is, how nice your chairs; I wish you'd change with me and let me be cook week about; and really the fire is quite pleasant tonight. Come, and make a cup of tea, and tell us a story, and frighten me and Margery before we go to our beds.[19]

The Victorian childhood delight in horror, however, which endorses the pastiche of the horror tradition in the novel's rhetoric, and its connection with the fairytale, ironically plays into a real descent into hell after she has become the slave of Stanley, her corrupt and evil brother. Later on, the Gothic fairytale of Lady Ringdove has become a 'true allegory':

> 'I beg your pardon, dear Tamar, but you must first tell me that story you used to tell me long ago of Lady Ringdove, that lived in Epping Forest, to whom the ghost came and told something she was never to reveal, and who slowly died of the secret, growing all the time more and more like the spectre; and besought the priest when she was dying, that he would have her laid in the abbey vault, with her mouth open, and her eyes and ears sealed, in token that her term of slavery was over, that her lips might now be open, and that her eyes were to see no more the dreadful sight, nor her ears to hear the frightful words that used to scare them in her lifetime; and then, you remember, whenever afterwards they opened the door of the vault, the wind entering made such moanings in her hollow mouth, and declared things so horrible that they built up the door of the vault and entered it no more ...'
>
> 'Yes, it is true – a true allegory, I mean Tamar. Death will close the eyes and ears against the sights and sounds of earth; but even the tomb secures no secrecy. The dead themselves declare their dreadful secrets, open-mouthed, to the winds. Oh, Tamar! turn over the pages, and try to find some part which says where safety may be found at any price; for sometimes I think I am almost bereft of – reason.[20]

The dead are the ultimate witnesses, and Rachel herself, since her cooption into the secret of Wylder's murder, and the subsequent fake resurrection of Wylder through forged letters, has died to the world. She is described, from the outset, as an 'anchorite' at Redman's Farm. But she is of a limited independence. As soon as Stanley appears, this independence, which is humorously referred to at the outset, is progressively doomed to total isolation and despair. This Gothic folktale of Lady Ringdove corresponds to 'slavery', in Rachel's case, to a secret which she can reveal to no one, not even to her beloved cousin Dorcas, who is by this time married to Stanley.

Lord Chelford, who is in love with her, perceives there is a change in Rachel. He thinks of it as Undine before and after her entry into mortality:

> As Rachel came forward in her faded gardening costume, an old silk
> shawl about her shoulders, and hoodwise over her head, somehow
> very becoming, there was a blush – he could not help seeing it – on
> her young face, and for a moment her fine eyes dropped, and she
> looked up, smiling a more thoughful and a sadder smile than in old
> days. The picture of that smile so gay and fearless, and yet so femi-
> nine, rose up beside the sadder smile that greeted him now, and he
> thought of Ondine without and Ondine with a soul.[21]

The analogy with the story of Undine becomes an increasingly important one in Le Fanu's romances for thinking about the lives of his
women. It is a complete subtext in *The Tenants of Malory*, which
describes the wanton destruction of a proud and independent girl by
marriage to Cleve Verney; and the motif also appears in *Haunted Lives*,
which acts as a late scherzo on these themes.

Chelford's perceptive view of Rachel here prefaces the perversely
presented love scene between them, to which, as usual Charles is *not* a
witness, and the lights and shades of which he can thus render with all
the paradoxical confidence of one who knows what must have happened, and therefore is willing to invent what did. Slave to her secret,
her reputation potentially compromised, Rachel is forced – like Lilias
Walsingham in *The House by the Churchyard* – to reject Lord Chelford
with perfect decorum, even though she is in love with him:

> 'Oh! Rachel, darling, you must not say that – I love you so – so
> *desperately*, you don't know.'
> 'I can say nothing else, Lord Chelford. My mind is quite made up –
> I am inexpressibly grateful – you will never know how grateful – but
> except as a friend – and won't you still be my friend? – I never can
> regard you.'
> Rachel was so very pale that her very lips were white as she spoke
> this in a melancholy but very firm way.
> 'Oh, Rachel, it is a great blow – maybe if you thought it over! –
> I'll wait any time.'
> 'No, Lord Chelford, I'm quite unworthy of your preference; and
> time cannot change me – and I am speaking, not from impulse, but
> from conviction. This is our secret – yours and mine – and we'll

forget it; and I could not bear to lose your friendship – you'll be my friend still – won't you? Good-bye.'

'God bless you Rachel!' And he hurredly kissed the hand she had placed in his, and without a word more, or looking back, he walked swiftly down the wooded road towards Gylingden.

So, then, it had come and gone – gone for ever.

'Margery, bring the basket in; I think a shower is coming.'

And she picked up the trowel and other implements, and placed them in the porch, and glanced up towards the clouds, as if she saw them, and had nothing to think of but her gardening and the weather, and as if her heart was not breaking.[22]

Such occasions only come but once in life. The artificial language of Victorian romance is juxtaposed with the Gothic horror of her real situation here. Rachel is a ghost of her former self, haunted by her complicity in Wylder's murder. Lawyer Larkin, the grotesque, rat-like sleuth, falling for the false trail she (in some degree, unconsciously) and Stanley have laid, gets as far as believing that she is Wylder's secret lover. When he tries, later, to insinuate this to Chelford, the Viscount rejects all such suggestions out of hand, despite the fact that we know he has no evidence, and in spite of the probability that Rachel's mysterious attitude in this scene might well have suggested something of this nature to him. His blind faith in her essential nobility only increases the tragedy of her 'slavery' to Stanley's secret.

There is irony throughout the text in Rachel's relationship to her beautiful dark-haired cousin, Dorcas Brandon. Dorcas is perverse and passionate, and the two beautiful women, the dark and the fair, are open and frank and loving with each other. However, having been 'sacrificed' by Stanley, Rachel begins to avoid Dorcas, even after Dorcas, having been open enough to confess all to her, has married him in a passionate fit of perverse love. They are like Lilias and Gertrude, whose frank and open relationship in *House by the Churchyard* is equally marred by a 'secret', which Gertrude cannot speak of and which has to do with a man. But there is a physically close, mirror-image feeling, between Dorcas and Rachel:

And she threw her arms round her cousin's neck, and brave Rachel at last burst into tears.

Dorcas, in her strange way, was moved.

'I like you still, Rachel; I'm sure I'll always like you. You resemble me, Rachel; you are fearless and inflexible and generous. That spirit belongs to the blood of our strange race; all our women were so. Yes, Rachel, I do love you ...

The young queen looked on her kindly, but sadly, through her large, strange eyes, clouded with a presage of futurity, and she kissed her again, and said –

'Rachel, dear, I have a plan for you and me: we shall be old maids, you and I, and live together like the ladies of Llangollen ...' (110)[23]

The ladies of Llangollen in their delightful half-timbered house and garden, Plas Newydd, were famous by the mid-Victorian period. It is, however, even at this stage in the novel, a fantasy which has the wishful, unreachable status, for the reader, of Lear's cry to Cordelia in the fourth act of Shakespeare's play:

> We two alone shall sing like birds i' the cage ...
>
> (V. iii. 9)

It is already too late for Rachel, who has fallen into the depressive hell of her secret. She has become Undine 'with a soul'. Later, however, she is able to pluck up courage and tell Dorcas, who in her turn is transformed into Lady Macbeth (the title of Chapter 66). From that point on, Dorcas, haunted by Stanley's evil (i.e. blackmailed into covering up for him) turns 'witch-like'; and the intensity of the love between the two women, at once joined together and isolated by their involvement with the unspeakable crime of Stanley, increases:

'You and I against the world, Radie!' said Dorcas, with a wild smile and a dark admiration in her look, and kissing Rachel again. 'I used to think myself brave; it belongs to women of our blood; but this is no common strain upon courage, Radie. I've grown to fear Stanley, somewhat like a ghost; I fear it is even worse than he says', and she looked with a horrible enquiry into Rachel's eyes.

'So do *I*, Dorcas,' said Rachel in a firm, low whisper, returning her look as darkly.

'What's done cannot be undone,' said Rachel, unconsciously quoting from a terrible soliloquy of Shakespeare.[24]

Dorcas has 'fallen' now, too, and she and Rachel occupy the same impossible space: they have the same blood, and they both love each other, and they are both 'haunted' – despite all, they love, and are blackmailed by, one as a wife and the other as a sister – the same hideously cowardly, corrupt and cruel man. They are both unconsciously acting out the tragedy of Lady Macbeth, forced into full conscious involvement with murder, in order to survive. We are not far here from Carmilla. The language of Gothic horror and the uncanny is being used to describe the reality of their perverse and isolated mirror-image situation. The eavesdropping Charles's final picture of them in the last lines of the novel is of two Undines, two spirits risen from the waters, Sirenic, perversely celebrating the loss of their Byron, who cannot be resurrected:

> Some summers ago, I was, for a few days, in the wondrous City of Venice. Everyone knows something of the enchantment of the Italian moon, the expanse of dark and flashing blue, and the phantasmal city, rising like a beautiful spirit from the waters. Gliding near the Lido – where so many rings of Doges lie lost beneath the waves – I heard the pleasant sound of female voices upon the water – and then, with a sudden glory, rose a sad, wild hymn, like the musical wail of the forsaken sea:–
>
> The spouseless Adriatic mourns her lord.
>
> The song ceased. The gondola which bore the musicians floated by – a slender hand over the gunwale trailed its fingers in the water. Unseen I saw. Rachel and Dorcas, beautiful in the sad moonlight, passed so near we could have spoken – passed me like spirits – never more, it may be, to cross my sight in life.[25]

The rings of the Doges are supposed to return to Venice, an echo of the ring inscribed 'Resurgam' on Mark Wylder's hand. The trailing hand belongs to one or other of them; it doesn't matter which, because they have become one 'spirit'; ringless, lingering, in its conjunction of spirit and matter, it echoes, and mocks, the gross, bodily, retributive hand of Wylder:

> Something like a stunted, blackened branch was sticking out of the peat, ending in a set of short thickish twigs. This is what it seemed. The dogs were barking at it. It was, really, a human hand and arm, disclosed by the slipping of the bank, undermined by the brook, which was swollen by the recent rains.
>   The dogs were sniffing and yelping about it.
>   'It's a hand!' cried Wealdon, with an oath.
>   'A hand?' I echoed.
>   We were both peering at it, having drawn near, stooping and hesitating as men do in a curious horror.

It was, indeed, a human hand and arm, disclosed from about the elbow, enveloped in a discoloured coat-sleeve, which fell back from the limb, and the fingers, like it black, were extended in the air.[26]

Stanley has reckoned without this act of witnessing – he is the victim of a pun: he has sought to 'resurrect' Wylder by writing in his 'hand'. But Wylder's prophesied bodily resurrection (his 'hand', in the other literal sense) emerges from the soil to defeat him, and destroy him.

The Cyclopean

Charles as a device is constantly teasing and tantalising the reader. He sets the narrative against the text. The layered text is constantly finding coincidences between the 'modern' and the 'ancient'; between psycho-somatic conditions and the ancient tales of the Gothic and the folk. 'Superstition' is constantly made to echo the grotesque nature of reality: William Wylder's money troubles are referred to as a 'gigantic Brocken spectre', and when Rachel faints away on their return to her house after the burial of Wylder, Charles describes Stanley as he bathes her temples of her forehead in self-consciously Gothic terms:

It was the dark and pallid scrutiny of a familiar of the Holy Office, bringing a victim back to consciousness. (79)[27]

This is pure Radcliffe, but it is also purely self-conscious, its 'Gothic' effect hovering in the discourse – and yet it overlaps perfectly with the horror of what is happening. Charles even overlays the 'historical' regis-ter with a term from folktale here: 'familiar', which implies witchcraft. Stanley is the exquisite torturer of his sister.

The external reflex of this overlap between the past and the present, between 'superstition' and police-court melodrama, is in the develop-ment of a subtext of the 'cyclopean' which began in *The House by the Churchyard*. Charles, as intimate and family historian, first uses the expression in describing the old house, which has swapped hands between the Brandons and the Wylders in one bloody feud after another. The house is self-consciously 'Gothic':

To my mind, there is something indescribably satisfactory in the intense solidity of those old stairs and floors – no spring in the planks, not a creak; you walk as over strata of stone. What clumsy grandeur! What Cyclopean carpenters! What a prodigality of oak![28]

This the beginning of a Gothic revenge of the past on the present. The old landowning estates of Ireland are full of 'grand old timber' which is oak, hundreds of years old, like stone. The worst crime an landowner can commit is 'waste': the selling and burning-off of this timber. Thus references to the 'Cyclopean', to a rugged patriarchal order of a prehistoric type, which built in vast blocks of crude stone, are opposed to the modern.

Mark Wylder himself belongs by lineage and by temperament to this world. Having been rejected again by Rachel Lake at the supper party in Chapter IV, tries to interfere with the arrangements for driving her home; and at the point when he realises, this will not work, he is described by Charles in 'Cyclopean' terms:

> ... as the gay good-night and leave-taking took place by the door-steps, Mark drew back, like a guilty thing in silence, and showed no sign but the red top of his cigar, glowing like the eye of a Cyclops in the dark.[29]

The glance at *Hamlet* and the ghost of Hamlet's father here, who in Shakespeare's phrase, 'started like a guilty thing', confirms the notion of a Cyclopean haunting – Mark himself is a kind of prophetic, haunting presence.

The motif occurs again after his death, when Rachel is at Dollington station at the end of Chapter XVIII and gives Stanley his alibi by pretending to be travelling with Wylder:

> The sleepy clerk that night in the Dollington station stamped two first class tickets for London, one of which was for a gentleman, and the other for a cloaked lady, with a very thick veil, who stood outside on the platform; and almost immediately after the scream of the engine was heard piercing the deep cutting, the Cyclopean red lamps glared nearer and nearer, and the palpitating monster, so stupendous and so docile, came smoothly to a stand-still before the trelliswork and hollyhocks of that pretty station.[30]

Charles is at his most typically indirect here, and the result is to force all information into coded form. The modern and the ancient coincide in the Cyclopean monster, which also links us to the specific plot of Wylder's death and the lineage of the Brandons.

The term signifies 'rough-hewn, ancient, troglodytic, and monstrous', but also, in a sense, 'noble'. There is one sarcastically inverted allusion to these values, when Charles describes Lawyer Larkin's office in XXXII, when

William Wylder, trapped by the wily hypocrite into asking him to take on his case, is treated to a typical piece of Larkinesque self-advertisment:

> 'My dear Sir, I only wish I could; but my hands are so awfully full,' and he lifted them up and shook them, and shook his tall, bald head at the same time, and smiled a weary smile. 'Just look there,' and he waved his fingers in the direction of the Cyclopean wall of tin boxes, tier above tier, each bearing, in yellow italics, the name of some country gentleman, and two baronets among the number; 'everyone of them laden with deeds and papers. You can't have a notion – no one has – what it is.' (151)[31]

The 'Cyclopean wall of tin boxes' is a parody of the rough-hewn irregular architecture of the aristocracy which Larkin is busy replacing by a set of legal frauds, as he seeks to climb into the position of a gentleman. Charles is very sarcastic throughout the novel about this, taking advantage of his editor's role to add 'sic' after the term 'gentleman', when Larkin describes himself thus.

Larkin is the opposite of the 'Cyclopean'. He is the point at which Charles reveals the connection in Le Fanu's mind between the growth of Dissent, and the anti-Semitic stereotype of the Jewish moneylender. The hideous 'rat-like' Larkin begins as a lapsed Methodist hypocrite, 'conforming to Methodism, but returned to the Church' (20). Charles is taken aback by his vehemence, as he finds himself representing him as a deaths-head:

> Perhaps his *personnel* prejudiced me – though I could not quite say why. He was a tall lank man – rather long of limb, long of head, and gaunt of face. He wanted teeth at both sides, and there was rather a skull-like cavity when he smiled – which was pretty often. His eyes were small and reddish, as if accustomed to cry; and when everything went smoothly were dull and dove-like, but when things crossed or excited him, which ocurred when his own pocket or plans were concerned, they grew singularly unpleasant, and greatly resembled those of some not aimiable animal – was it a rat, or a serpent. It was a peculiar concentrated vigilance and rapine that I have seen there. (19–20)[32]

Here Charles is unequivocally the witness to this almost imperceptible, symbolic change of aspect. But the whole description is a form of mythic code: Larkin, like Uriah Heep, is 'long-headed', which is code for 'calculating' – here metonymised in Larkin's deathly skull. As he gets more prosperous, and approaches his Dickensian comeuppance, Larkin is metamorphosed by Charles into an honorary Jew:

'He shall be like a tree planted by the water-side, that will bring forth his fruit in due season. His leaf shall not wither. So thought this good man complacently. He liked these fine consolations of the Jewish dispensation – actual milk and honey, and a land of promise on which he could set his foot'.[33]

This is the beginning of a whole series of unfortunate subplots in Le Fanu's romances which develop this theme of an association between Dissenters and Jews, as cheating, materialistic parasites battening on the Cyclopean patrimony of a lost aristocracy. This is Whig culture: for Charles de Cresseron, a Gothic nightmare of 'vigilance and rapine', which no one is allowed to escape. We are not surprised when, towards the end of the book, Stanley declares himself ready to stand for parliament 'on the old Whig principles'. Wylder, Larkin, and Stanley are all the same, Charles tells us.

The evidentiary mode

This strange mixture of omniscience and restricted viewpoint in the novel's method of narration is to become a standard vehicle of the mixed form of Le Fanu's later romances. Charles is a kind of 'familiar', a ghost at the reader's elbow, who every now and then reminds us of his presence as a character in the story. The epistemology of narration itself is continually under scrutiny in this enigmatic space, which is an overlap between the legal and the religious senses of witnessing.

Indirection, and the alienation of the reader's position as judge, are necessary to the end, and beyond the end, of the plot. Charles, when discussing the secret horrors of the Vicar William Wylder, at one point has an outburst about 'frankness'. His point – a very Protestant one – is that 'secrecy' is necessary to the consciousness of a Christian, and that such 'reserve', far from being incompatible with Christian morality, is essential to it:

The best man, the simplest man that ever lived, has his reserves. The conscious frailty of mortality owes that sad reverence to itself, and to the esteem of others. You can't be too frank and humble when you have wronged your neighbour; but keep your offences against God to yourself, and let your battle with your own heart be waged under the eye of Him alone. The frankness of the sentimental Jean Jacques Rousseau, and of my coarse friend, Mark Wylder, is but a damnable form of vicious egotism. A miserable sinner have I been, my friend, but details profit neither thee nor me. The inner man had best be known only to himself and his Maker. I like that good and simple Welsh parson, of Beaumaris, near two hundred years ago, who with a sad sort of humour, placed for motto under his portrait, done in stained glass, *nunc primum transparui*. [I have now for the first time become transparent.] (My translation.)[34]

It is not surprising that Charles is anti-Rousseau: the 'openness' of Dissenters revolts him, and seems merely a form of hypocrisy. Rousseau betrays his Calvinism by opening his heart. This can only really be imagined at the last trump – as the Welsh parson's joke testifies.

This commitment to 'reserve' has a strong link to the attraction of the 'mystery' format for Le Fanu. His method of withholding information from the reader, telling the story more than once, and so on, which is very like that of Ann Radcliffe, is part of a Protestant tradition of doubt and caution before the mystery of the human heart. The reader needs to experience this indirection at first hand, hence the self-conscious construction of a space of doubt in which we are obliged to exist. Even the dénouement of this novel's tortuous and elusive plot raises doubts which the text does not solve, but leaves to the reader's own judgement. For example, when the dying Stanley finally makes a statement, the reader expects to have Rachel's hand in the proceedings explained. But Lake is lying:

> He said that on the night of Mark Wylder's last visit to Brandon, he had accompanied him from the Hall; that Mark had seen someone in the neighbourhood of Gylingden, a person pretending to be his wife, or some near relative of hers, as well as he, Captain Lake, could understand, and was resolved to go to London privately, and have the matter arranged there.[35]

This improbable vagueness is presumably Stanley's way of protecting himself. He still thinks at this point he will survive. We understand this; but it doesn't help us with the question of Rachel's position. In fact, it drives us mad if we are simply looking for cut and dried 'facts', seeking narrative closure through the convention of stable information. A few pages later, Stanley Lake realises he is really dying, and the reader finally is given some indication of Rachel's role in the affair. Charles, as usual, intervenes heavily on Lake's confession:

> Lake admitted that Rachel had posted the letters in London believing them to be genuine, for he pretended they were Wylder's. It is easy to look grave over poor Rachel's slight, and partly unconscious share in the business of the tragedy. But what girl of energy and strong affections would have had the melancholy courage to surrender her brother to public justice under the circumstances? Lord Chelford, who knew all, says she 'acted nobly'.[36]

Charles's phrase 'partly unconscious share' conceals as much as it reveals. How much did Rachel understand of what she was doing? This seems to be for the reader to feel and understand. But her horror and despair is not compatible with too much 'unconscious-ness'. She knows she is an accessory to murder, and she knows she has been involved in a cover-up generated by Stanley. She doesn't want to know about the letters plot. She tries to stop her ears. But she knows that Stanley is 'resurrecting' Wylder, because when Stanley comes to her a second time, in Chapter XXV, they have the following conversation:

> 'I said *he* should go abroad, and so he shall,' said Lake, in a very low tone, with a grim oath.
> 'Why do you talk that way? You terrify me,' said Rachel, with one hand raised toward his face with a gesture of horror and entreaty, and the other closed on his wrist.
> 'I say he *shall*, Radie.'
> 'Has he lost his wits? I can't comprehend you – you frighten me, Stanley. You're talking wildly on purpose, I believe, to terrify me. You know the state I'm in – sleepless – half wild – all alone here. You're talking like a maniac. It's cruel – it's cowardly.'
> 'I mean to *do* it – you'll see.'
> Suddenly she hurried by him, and in a moment was in the little kitchen, with its fire and candle burning cheerily. Stanley Lake was at her shoulder as she entered, and both were white with agitation.[37]

The tragedy here is that Rachel cannot 'unknow' what she already knows. She tries to draw the line: 'I'll hear no secret', she says. Charles de Cresseron is doing his usual thing of representing the two of them as actors on stage, in a drama which we must judge for ourselves. And it is for the reader to calculate whether Rachel *can* rid Stanley's words of meaning like this. Whether her innocence extends to the successful evacuation of the signified in his temptation into meaning. Charles specifies he is 'at her shoulder', which suggests the devil's temptation of Christ. But it seems impossible for Rachel to draw the line she wants to – it would offend against consciousness itself. Her stage 'horror' here – a diversionary tactic, clearly – covers a contradiction which the reader, as a privileged member of the jury, needs to make a judgement about.

The final word is Charles's, who invokes the Gospels in his quest for a liberal view:

> 'Now, Joseph, being a just man, was minded to put her away privily.' The law being what? That she was to be publicly stigmatised and punished. His *justice* being what? Simply that he would have her to be neither – but screened and parted 'with privily'. Let the Pharisees who would have *summum jus* against their neighbours, remember that God regards the tender and compassionate, who forbears, on occasion, to put the law in motion, as the *just* man.[38]

The case is Matthew 1:18–19, in which Joseph of Nazareth learns that his wife is pregnant, and sees fit to keep her from public judgement. It turns out that she is pregnant by the Holy Ghost, and so there is a providential aspect to this little test. Joseph behaved rightly by invoking, not the letter, but the spirit of the law. But to invoke the spirit of the law is admit mystery, secrecy and indirection into human affairs. It is this which the novel sets against the 'transparency' of the Pharisees, the hypocritical 'openness' of Lawyer Larkin, who is ready to make the case against Rachel as a loose woman for his own corrupt reasons, which Charles is quite ready to explain to the reader as the typical indirection of the Pharisee.

5

Magic Lanthern: *Uncle Silas*, Narrative Indirection and the Layered Text

Peephole narration

After a number of experiments with third-person writing, Le Fanu dispenses with his ghostwriter, Charles de Cresseron, and lets Maud, his principal protagonist and witness, speak for herself. This gives the text a different kind of focus and seductive power. But those earlier experiments in holding narrative at arm's length, follow through into this text, too, in the tension between the spoken and the textualised voice, and the multiple perspectives which are opened up, by that tension, in the very act of narration. This apparently transparent text is, above all, a self-conscious representation. *Uncle Silas's* Gothic, its rhetoric of 'superstition', darkness and horror, is an intimate presence in its narrative indirectness, traversing the hybridity of its effects.

It is part of this text's peculiarly indirect relationship with the reader. That relationship fragments the means of narrative by framing devices, and the assimilation of narrative to testimony, which has the powerful double effect of invoking an orthodox doctrine and leaving room for superstition, its power deriving simultaneously from religious and legal contexts – the presumption of first-person witnessing as truthful. All this has the powerful double effect of bringing testimony forward against authority. Maud, the *ingénue*, is a rebel because she is a dreamer; and she lets loose a set of thoughts in the reader which reach far beyond the conventionalities of her present utterance, or even her own future self.[1]

Uncle Silas is a layered text. There are levels beyond the speaker, Maud, perpetually present. The device of the first-person *ingénue* narrator does its work very effectively, catching the reader in the folds of the text like a butterfly in a net. But Maud is ventriloquised, a composite, only part *ingénue*: she is, like Pip in *Great Expectations*, looking back upon her former childhood self. To be precise, as a thirty-one-year-old, she looks back to herself at seventeen years and nine months.

The first paragraph is an anti-Gothic 'feint'. It describes a room, rugged, old fashioned, empty of all but the signs of human presence. The writing mimics an easy transparency, a spoken voice, in which it seems almost inevitable that the 'you' of the implied reader should be comfortably acknowledged at the end of the paragraph:

It was winter – that is, about the second week in November – and great gusts were rattling at the windows, and wailing and thundering among our tall trees and ivied chimneys – a very dark night, and a very cheerful fire blazing, a pleasant mixture of good round coal and spluttering dry wood, in a genuine old fireplace, in a sombre old room. Black wainscoting glimmered up to the ceiling, in small ebony panels; a cheerful clump of wax candles on the tea-table; many old portraits, some grim and pale, others pretty, and some very graceful and charming, hanging from the walls. Few pictures, except portraits long and short, were there. On the whole, I think you would have taken the room for our parlour. It was not like our modern notion of a drawing-room. It was a long room too, and every way capacious, but irregularly shaped.[2]

Le Fanu first wrote 'hollooing' in the magazine text for the wind's action here, which he cut out. It smacks a little too much of ghostly hunters, perhaps. Either that, or it is too redolent of the spoken voice's delicate transaction with the written word. The point is to ban equivocation about 'darkness'. The darkness which presses in, and is also already inside, in the 'sombre' room and the 'black wainscoting', is firmly kept at bay by the cheerfulness of the candles and the fire. 'Our parlour' and 'our modern notion of a drawing room' are plainly different forms of 'our': the first belongs to the family or owners of the room, and the second to 'you and me', the outer frame – contemporary late Victorians whose drawing-rooms are regular in shape and character. But the room is empty, except for portraits and we cannot 'see' the speaker who mediates the present and the past, the unfamiliar and the familiar.

The pleasure of finding out who is speaking is already before us. And the text then self-consciously 'pictures' the speaker in the room:

A girl, of little more than seventeen, looking, I believe, younger still; slight and rather tall, with a great deal of golden hair, dark grey-eyed,

and with a countenance rather sensitive and melancholy, was sitting
at the tea-table, in a reverie. I was that girl.[3]

So 'I' is doubled, already represented, subject and object. The paradox
comes when the speaker says 'I believe' and we wonder immediately
about this qualification, and the break with the former self it implies.
She now cannot re-enter, because there are limits to what she can know.
How can you know you looked younger than seventeen? Total honesty
would refer, not just to the mirror, but to the opinions of others. So,
coming from the older Maud, 'I believe' is an honest and a modest qualification, a modest admission of second-hand knowledge. The speaker
tries to picture her former self, and reveals the limits of her perspective.
There is a sense in which the art of 'picturing', for Maud (not yet
named), is an important part of the act of memory. But the device is not
just naturalistic: the rhetoric of portraiture is a textual manoevre that
lies beyond her point of view. She is to fall in love with one of these portraits: the portrait of Uncle Silas. In the meantime, the picture of herself
speaks: 'I was that girl'; and the gap between present and past is
revealed, even as it is crossed.

But at the same time 'I believe' is also the opposite of a qualification:
it is an act of faith. It signifies the imaginative leap the speaker makes to
cross the gap, to go from outside to inside, and back again. Reading the
book is a constant shuttling between a restricted and a less restricted set
of viewpoints. Logically, this should yield revelation and the constant
feeling of things being exploded or explained: but instead, it buries
meaning; it creates ambiguity and 'atmosphere', the 'prismatic film' that
lies over objects and people which is such a delicate and distinctive part
of the novel's impact.

Take, for example, the extraordinary scene in the first chapter when
Dr Bryerly, whom Mrs Rusk describes as 'a great conjuror among the
Swedenborg sect', arrives at Knowl. Maud calls him 'Mr Bryerly', which
is a significant error, stemming from Rusk's prejudicial description,
('conjuror' imples fraud, and the devil – the conjuring of spirits) and
which automatically deceives the reader.

The next day the young Maud dutifully knocks before entering her
father's study, and the scene her ignorant and superstitious eyes are
presented with is conveyed to the reader in all its mystery and
embarassment:

I suppose they were too intent on other matters to hear, but receiving
no answer, I entered the room. My father was sitting in his chair, with

his coat and waistcoat off, Mr Bryerly kneeling on a stool beside him, rather facing him, his black scratch wig leaning close to my father's grizzled hair. There was a large tome of their divinity lore, I suppose, open on the table close by. The lank black figure of Mr Bryerly stood up, and he concealed something quickly in the breast of his coat.[4]

This is very bizarre and nothing is done to clarify the mystery for Maud, or the reader either, of what they are up to. They are as embarrassed as if they have been caught together in a sexual act. And what is the thing which Bryerly puts into his waistcoat pocket?

This scene is never specifically explained. Instead, the misunderstanding is built on, as we look at them through Maud's ignorant, but scandalised eyes. For her, it is not sexuality that dictates their bizarre intimacy, but religion:

> I remember so well the kind of shock and disgust I felt in the certainty that I had surprised them at some, perhaps, debasing incantation, a suspicion of this Mr Bryerly, of the ill fitting black coat, and white choker, and a sort of fear came over me, and I fancied he was asserting some kind of mastery over my father, which very much alarmed me.[5]

This is a double defamiliarisation: Maud is superstitious, but orthodox; her attitudes are the product of exclusion. She perceives 'dangers' which are dictated by the suspicion of heresy: 'some debasing incantation' and 'confession', both of which are heretical to an Anglican Protestant of Maud's stripe. Her father, although he has left the Church for 'some odd sect', has taken care that she be brought up in the orthodox faith; but in her benign neglect, she is also subject to the fears and prejudices of Mrs Rusk, whose name suggests a hale and hearty rural Protestantism, anti-Catholic and anti-Dissenter. The old housekeeper's phrase for the Swedenborgian who takes Maud for a walk in Chapter II is: 'that limb of darkness', which is consciously a part of the text's Gothic rhetoric of Heaven and Hell and darkness.

Through this fear, beyond her point of view, we connect the child's sense of the Other with specific doctrinal and behavioural transgressions in Victorian culture. The story is taking place sometime in the late 1840s, anticipating 1848, the year of revolutions, and the Papal Aggression of 1850. This was a particularly suspicious time. Cardinal Newman went over to Rome in 1845. But the story is also being told post-1850, uncovering another layer of threat, when mid-Victorian Anglican England was riddled with Methodism and Puseyism,

Tractarianism and fears of fifth-columnism, and Le Fanu's Ireland was beginning to be convulsed by Fenianism. Conspiracy is in the air.[6]

But Maud is totally unreliable here. She is wrong, and the text allows, and then shows, her to be wrong. Wrong to call him *Mr* Bryerly, just because of his clothes, and to assume that, if he is a Doctor and one of *them*, then he must be a Doctor of Divinity, i.e. Black Arts. Bryerly is, as he makes quite clear later on, a Doctor of Medicine and proud of it; and here he is taking Maud's father's pulse. The thing he slips into his pocket is a watch. And the men deceive her, not because they are guilty; but because they seek to protect her from the knowledge that her father is fatally ill.

All this we have to infer; it is not explained at all. Brought up largely by the servants, Maud's mind is 'very uninstructed as to the limits of the marvellous' (I, 13); and it is in this mind that the reader must remain, even though that very statement implies the later Maud who has received instruction and indeed who knows the truth. Such is the degree of conviction which the convention of first-person witnessing carries from outside its fictional context. This is the strange thing about the book's rhetoric: it recreates successfully – re-inhabits – the ignorance of its *ingénue* narrator. And, through the invitation of transparency, by the silent contract of her anguish, we are forced to live in the world of the adolescent girl's superstitions, even though at another level, they are constantly exploded.

These early chapters are a brilliant study of how the girl is deprived of knowledge by her father, and creates her own power out of the very weakness of her position, the very paucity of her knowledge. The scene above is doubly defamiliarised, because Maud, although she is in fact seventeen and nine months, instead of having his illness even mentioned, let alone explained to her, is told that her Father is 'going upon a journey' and that a 'friend' will call for him. An explanation which she takes literally, and associates with Bryerly himself, thus confirming the 'limb of darkness' idea. But then, she finds out that he knows nothing about it and we find her extremely puzzled.[7]

Pre-texts: fairytale and Gothic romance

The textual layers I've been discussing are not entirely distinct: as we should expect from a seventeen-year-old upper-middle-class girl of the 1840s, Maud is herself a reader of fairytales and romances (Gothic or otherwise) and she assimilates her story (the completed story we are about to read) in Chapter 3 to the reproof of female curiosity, which is the traditional moral of Bluebeard:

> Why is it that this form of ambition – curiosity – which entered into the temptation of our first parents, is so specially hard to resist? Knowledge is power – and power of one sort or another is the secret lust of human souls; and here is, beside the sense of exploration, the undefinable interest of a story, and above all, something forbidden, to stimulate the contumacious appetite.[8]

The 'something forbidden' is one of the prime conditions, as Vladimir Propp found out about Russian folktales in the 1920s, of narrative. Prohibition provides the forward drive, as Maud implies. Much more than this, the passage suggests that all stories are ultimately the story of the Fall of Man, in which we ourselves (Maud's readers) are, by our human definition, included. We cannot resist her story, because our relation to narrative itself is one of appetite: we are fallen and driven by curiosity, the vehicle of power, the 'secret lust of human souls'. All stories are our story, especially if we happen to be women: the 'first parent' is not Adam here, but Eve. Maud herself cannot resist her own story. Contumacy is the sign of original sin: it is a form of stubbornness and waywardness, the presence of what is referred to, by the later Maud reflecting on her former self, as 'the old man' (the unregenerate Adam) in her, in all of us. Silas is the ultimate form, the objective correlative, of that 'old man'.

Hence the following dialogue about the key is another joke about Bluebeard and the fairytale prohibition; and it indicates that the plot of the novel in which we find ourselves is a re-write of the folktale:

> And pausing, he looked in my face as he might upon a picture.
>
> 'They *are* – yes – I had better do it another way – another; yes – and she'll not suspect – she'll not suppose.'
>
> He looked steadfastly upon the key, and from it to me, suddenly lifting it up, and said abruptly, 'See, child,' and after a second or two – '*Remember* this key.'
>
> It was oddly shaped and unlike others.[9]

There are several levels of representation concealed in this pastiche. Maud is already represented, an unreal presence for her father; he 'looked in my face as he would upon a picture'. In some sense she isn't there, as an original, but only as a representation towards which he has an aesthetic response, which is a (chilling) metaphor for his detachment.

Figure 3   'Remember – this key.' From Gustave Doré, 'Les Contes de Perrault' (Paris, 1862), BL Shelfmark 1871 f. 11.

Unlike her original in Perrault, Maud wouldn't dream of crudely opening the cabinet at this stage: Madame does it for her by opening the desk, just as, in the end, she dies in Maud's place too. The Bluebeard figure has also been 'decomposed' (as McCormack has shown) into the two brothers, Austin and Silas, both of whom conspire to keep Maud in the dark and issue prohibitions. The dialogue above is part of a running set of allusions in the text to 'Bluebeard.' For example, in Chapter XVI the transition is very uneasy when, just after having delivered the orthodox consolation from St Paul about Maud's fear of death, her cousin, Lady Knollys, switches into fantastic mode, casting Silas as Bluebeard, in order to dispel Maud's fears:

> 'So this great wind, you say, is blowing toward us from the wood there. If so, Maud, it is blowing from Bartram-Haugh, too, over the trees and chimneys of that old place, and the mysterious old man, who is quite right in thinking I don't like him; and I can fancy him an old enchanter in his castle, waving his familiar spirits on the wind to fetch and carry tidings of our occupations here.'[10]

This is meant as a distraction for Maud, but its total effect is to remind us that the plot of the novel we are reading *is* built on 'Bluebeard' and Silas makes a very good analogy: it reminds us uneasily of the danger he poses.

And once she has reached Bartram-Haugh, Maud reminds us again of the folktale:

> I had not half seen this old house of Bartram Haugh yet. At first, indeed, I had but an imperfect idea of its extent. There was a range of rooms along the one side of the great gallery, with closed window-shutters, and the doors generally locked. Old L'Amour grew cross when we went into them, although we could see nothing; and Milly was afraid to open the windows – not that any Bluebeard revelations were apprehended, but simply because she knew that Uncle Silas's order was that things should be left undisturbed ...[11]

Precisely, that is what Bluebeard does: issue prohibitions about where the women can go in his castle. The plot of the novel reveals itself in such uneasy and self-contradictory disclaimers, to be a repetition of a romance at a higher level of detail, not a realistic refutation of 'fairy-tale' or 'romance'. Even the social jokes are invaded by the allusion: at a point of comedy and maximum relief, away from Silas, in Cousin Monica's comfortable anti-Gothic house of Elverston, when Maud, attracted to Lord Ilbury, is trying to snoop on him in *Burke's 'Peerage'*, she suddenly reminds us where she really is:

> One day, all being quiet, I did venture, and actually, with a beating heart, got so far as to find out the letters 'Il', when I heard a step

outside the door, which opened a little bit, and I heard Lady Knollys, luckily arrested at the entrance, talk some sentences outside, her hand still upon the door handle, as Mrs Bluebeard might the door of the chamber of horrors at the sound of her husband's step, and skipped to a remote part of the room, where Cousin Knollys found me, in a mysterious state of agitation.[12]

The transgression here is trivial, but the way it is approached is quite dissonant; Maud's metaphorical joke shows what is on her mind, and brings back to the reader banished thoughts of Silas and Bartram Haugh, the dark world, polluting momentarily the light and safety of 'reality'.

The antithesis in the rhetoric of the novel between reality and illusion, the *fiction* of romance and fairytale, is constantly in a state of collapse into the mundane. The 'Gothic' rhetoric (a composite of references to ghosts, resurrected corpses, superstitions, Radcliffean romance and fairytale) is built on disclaimers of the Gothic, which imply a form of realism, but discredit it at a higher level. Fairytales don't happen in the real world of the nineteenth century, says the reader's prejudice, masquerading as scepticism; but the fiction of romance turns out to be the best way of describing an otherwise indescribably frightening and horrible reality.

The most obvious example of this trick comes in the description of Madame's execution which is grotesque realism, or realism upside down:

Madame was breathing in the deep respiration of heavy sleep. Suddenly, but softly, he laid, as it seemed to me, his left hand over her face, and nearly at the same instant there came a scrunching blow; an unnatural shriek, beginning small and swelling for two or three seconds into a yell such as are imagined in haunted houses ...[13]

Maud, the narrator, assimilates the true to the imagined, and her comment gathers up this horrifying climax into the ghost-story nightmare where it evidently belongs. But in this context nightmares are true fictions; pictures which possess the soul of the viewer, representations which, like the Bluebeard plot, 'prefigure', not copy, reality, even in its most banal, police-court form.

The plot of the novel is a variant of the Bluebeard plot which is presented as if simply embedded in it as a set of allusions. This is a direct allusion to the Gothic Romance which, from Radcliffe on, is itself originally built on the Bluebeard plot. Ann Radcliffe's *Mysteries of Udolpho*, for example, featuring the abduction and incarceration of the heiress in a dilapidated castle, is clearly a variant. Maturin's *Melmoth* features allusions to and even epigraphs from the tale. When describing Emily's capacity to explore what she is clearly terrified of, the passages of the castle, Radcliffe herself eloquently describes the curiosity motif from Bluebeard, mapping it on to the Burkean sublime:

> But a terror of this nature, as it occupies and expands the mind, and elevates it to high expectation, is purely sublime, and leads us, by a kind of fascination, to seek even the object, from which we appear to shrink.[14]

and Le Fanu's Anglo-Irish forerunner, Charles Maturin takes this up in *Melmoth*, when Young John Melmoth, urged by his Guardians to return to college and complete his education 'as soon as proper', stays behind instead, to explore his uncle's decaying house:

> ... but John urged the expediency of paying the respect due to his uncle's memory, by remaining a decent time in the house after his decease. This was not his real motive. Curiosity, or something that perhaps deserves a better name, the wild and awful pursuit of an indefinite object, had taken strong hold of his mind.[15]

This dynamic perfectly describes Maud's exploration of Bartram Haugh. She casts herself quite explicitly as a Radcliffe heroine and replays the sado-masochistic psychology of 'pleasing terror':

> It was plain that not nearly a tithe of this great house was inhabited; long corridors and galleries stretched away in dust and silence, and were crossed by others, whose dark arches inspired me in the distance with an awful sort of sadness. It was plainly one of those great structures in which you might easily lose yourself, and with a pleasing terror it reminded me of that delightful old abbey in Mrs Radcliffe's romance, among whose silent staircases, dim passages, and long suites of lordly but forsaken chambers, begirt without by the sombre forest, the family of La Mote secured a gloomy asylum.[16]

Later, she reinforces this allusion, comparing herself, while she explores Bartram-Haugh's back passages and deserted wings, to Adelaide in Radcliffe's *Romance of the Forest* (350). Even at the end, when she is tense with despair, she makes a joke about this. Locked into her room by Madame, she casts herself jokingly as a 'Gothic' heroine and therefore does *not* see herself a Gothic heroine, trapped in a Bluebeard plot:

> I rushed into the next room, forgetting, if indeed I had observed it, that there was no door from it upon the gallery. I turned round in an angry and dismayed perplexity, and, like prisoners in romances, examined the windows.[17]

This is an allusion to the psychology of a romance readership, as much as it is to the actions of a character. The reader is the prisoner of improbability, or, at its strongest, impossibility. This has long been part of the Gothic tradition itself, as Maturin reveals by his allusion to it in Melmoth to describe his heroine, trapped in 'half-feudal' Spain into an imminent marriage she cannot go through with:

> 'All that day she thought how it was possible to liberate herself from her situation, while the feeling that liberation was impossible clung to the bottom of her heart; and this sensation of the energies of the soul in all their strength, being in vain opposed to imbecillity (sic) and mediocrity, when aided by circumstances, is one productive alike of melancholy and irritation. We feel, like prisoners in romance, bound by threads to which the power of magic has given the force of adamant.[18]

The romance tradition is self-conscious about the relation between the reader and the text, long before Le Fanu. He is alluding here to a long line of explicit meditation about the entrapment of the psyche by the impossible or the absurd through the sublime power of curiosity. Curiosity, that is, for *narrative*.

Dreadful witness

Part of the inheritance which derives from Le Fanu's study of the Gothic Romance is the habit of epistemological doubt and the corresponding narrative fragmentation which is the symptom of a testing struggle between doubt and faith in the Anglican Protestant tradition. Maud's orthodoxy and her fear that her faith is failing are both important to the experience of horror in the narrative of *Uncle Silas*:

> Oh, Death, king of terrors! The body quakes, and the spirit faints before thee. It is vain, with hands clasped over our eyes, to scream our

reclamation; the horrible image will not be excluded. We have just the word spoken eighteen hundred years ago, and our trembling faith. And through the broken vault the gleam of the Star of Bethlehem.[19]

Though this is retrospective, the isolation of the young girl's superstitious consciousness is the medium through which we apprehend the events of the story. For Radcliffe, and Maturin, before Le Fanu, the Gothic Romance is already a meditation on the relation between scepticism and belief, inherited from the eighteenth-century debates on miracles, for example, following in the wake of Hume's sceptical intervention on this subject in the mid-eighteenth century.[20] Though the texts are usually in the third person, Ann Radcliffe's narratives insist on the isolation of the perceiving subject, the young girl, and the reader is often forced into a position in which judgement is impossible because of a lack of information; even Emily's emotions – which she attempts to subject to rational critique, are at a distance from her self. Phenomena are misperceived, slowed down into enigmas, and held at arm's length. It is hard for Emily to remain rational in the face of so much mystery. Assent, in the Anglican tradition, is 'rational' and becomes what Maturin refers to as 'a labour', and that labour assumes the isolation of the human subject, judging, perceiving, sifting the evidence alone. The Gothic Romance rewrites the Book of Job. The overwhelming feeling for the reader is of the necessity, and yet the precariousness, of rational belief – Maud's 'limits of the marvellous' are hard to find and yet they must be found. We must travel on our own through 'the marvellous' to find its limits.

Maud's subjective narration – split and layered as it is – foregrounds the act of witnessing and much of its stylisation comes from this fragmentation of narrative means. And witnessing, as I have just been implying, is simultaneously a theme and a method in the book. The older Maud frames her own original testimony; but that testimony is vital to the impact of the story, because we, too, are alone with the frailty of our guarantees for the truth of what we can accept, our 'trembling faith'.

This procedure, of insistence on the eye-witness testimony, and therefore on scrupulously marking the place where it does not occur, imports two different demands for truth on the part of the fictional narrator: one, objectivity; and the second, faith, truth to herself in despite of the mystery of what she apparently perceives.

In the chapter 'Angry Words', the heated dialogue she overhears between Monica and her father about the hideous Madame de la Rougierre replays this very dilemma. Maud's father, in his scorn for both blind Protestant orthodoxy, and 'superstition', has become so isolated from everyone that he cannot believe his child's feelings of evil about her and see the danger of at least a common criminal in Madame. 'Are you *blind*?', cries Monica:

> '*You* are, Monica; your own unnatural prejudice – *unnatural* prejudice, blinds you. What is it all? – *nothing*. Were I to act as you say, I should be a *coward* and a traitor. I see, I *do* see, all that's real. I'm no Quixote, to draw my sword on illusions.'
> 'There should be no halting here. How *can* you – do you ever *think*? I wonder you can breathe. I feel as if the evil one were in the house.'
> A stern momentary frown was my father's only answer, as he looked fixedly at her.
> 'People need not nail up horseshoes, and mark their door stones with charms to keep the evil spirits out', ran on Lady Knollys, who looked as pale and angry in her way, 'but you open your door in the dark and invoke unknown danger. How can you look at that child that's – she's *not* playing,' said Lady Knollys, abruptly stopping.[21]

The 'limits of the marvellous' are notoriously hard to fix, especially when, from Austin's point of view, they have been falsely policed and Reason has been retarded by irrational fear. His opinion of women is that they are 'prejudiced', and violently judgemental. But from Monica's point of view – orthodox as she is – Austin is not using his common sense and common humanity. But she *expresses* herself in a fashion which adds to the 'Gothic' register: 'I feel as if the evil one were in the house.'

It turns out that she is right and he does not see what is in front of him. Monica knows Madame already, and knows her to be a petty crook, although she doesn't really explain this to Maud at this point, so the reader can only infer from what Maud reports, and wait. Gradually, we learn that she is a sham horror: her name is Mlle Blassemare, not the Gothic 'Madame de la Rougierre' (the pretentious name already parodied by the servants as 'Rogers' and 'Rougepot'), and that she's a thief, sent by Silas to Knowl to find out what is in Austin's will. But this is the reader's, not the terrified child's, point of view. This gap, between what is perceived and what is known, which is perpetual in the text, a gap between the restricted viewpoint and the general or retrospective overview, is promoted by the device of 'keyhole' narration, or first-person testimony: 'through the smallest aperture, for a moment, I had had a peep into Pandemonium'[22] says Maud, as she listens to the old housekeeper's description of Madame as a 'witch' and an 'old French hypocrite'.

In fact, in the incident of the 'pic-nic', Maud has indeed seen a conspiracy to abduct her at work for a moment, without having a vocabulary to express it, except the traditional language of Heaven and Hell. And this is the case with Monica too: she has only this language to express her fears for Maud, and so, paradoxically, though she is the consolatory voice of common sense and safety for Maud, she is also a prime source of the 'Gothic' register in the language of the text.

Nowhere is this confinement of perspective more evident than in the incident in which Maud falls asleep in a recess of her father's study, and wakes up to find Madame going through his desk:

> For about half an hour, I think, this went on; but at the time it seemed to me all but interminable. On a sudden she raised her head and listened for a moment, replaced the papers deftly, closed the desk without noise, except for the tiny click of the lock, extinguished the candle, and rustled stealthily out of the room, leaving in the darkness the malign and hag-like face on which the candle had just shone still floating filmy in the dark.[23]

The last image is typical of the chiaroscuro conventions of darkness and restricted lighting which occur in De la Tour and the Dutch painters Le Fanu was so interested in. The recording of the after-image has the visionary intensity of the marvellous: yet it is strict fact, strict eye-witness testimony. It is interesting to note that Le Fanu revised the wording of this passage: in the the magazine text, he wrote 'pictured on my retina' (*DUM*, 139) and altered it in the first edition to 'floating filmy in the dark'. The first expression, with its scientific clarity, while asserting the subjectivity of the perception, sacrifices the generality hidden in the restricted code of the viewer Maud, the 'film' that lies over all she sees. But the subjectivity is endemic in the dramatic situation anyway: the emendation challenges the reader with the paradox that the insubstantial is the true, the aethetic is the real, the Gothic melodrama of a Victorian production of *Macbeth* (which is what the effect of snapping out the lights strongly invokes) is the reality of a felony.

The transitions in the text from the eyewitness testimony to the 'circumstantial evidence' of retrospective narration are not concealed, as one might perhaps expect, but strongly marked for the reader. After Austin's death, for example, Maud emphasises the point:

> Henceforward all is circumstantial evidence – all conjectural – except the *litera scripta*, and to this evidence every note-book, and every

> scrap of paper and private letter, must contribute – ransacked, bare in
> the light of day – what it can.[24]

'*Litera scripta*' refers to writing, not speaking. Maud is reluctant to add
documentary evidence to what she herself sees and hears at first-hand:
she regards the very reading of her father's papers as a desecration, violation of his privacy. The text, on the other hand, teases us with its legalistic indirection at this point, raising the whole question of the legal
authority for the narrative's very knowledge of the facts and setting it
against the necessity of overview to make sense of the story.

This alienation effect is a pattern. For example, in Chapter VII, the
horrific *danse macabre* incident at Church Scarsdale – one of the great set-
pieces of the novel – is narrated from the child's terrified and outraged
point of view. The chapter finishes on a climax. But when we turn the
page and begin the next chapter, we are faced with a total anti-climax;
the childhood 'Gothic' is removed along with the eye-witness account,
and what happened next is *re*-told from 'circumstantial evidence':

> Three years later I learned – in a way she probably little expected, and
> then did not much care about – what really occurred there. I learned
> even phrases and looks – for the story was related to me by one who
> had heard it told – and therefore I venture to narrate what at the
> moment I neither saw nor suspected.[25]

We are left to guess at the identity of Maud's informant. (Probably
Milly... .) This 'realistic' anti-climax, however, generates (as it does in
Radcliffe and the traditional Gothic Romance) more subtle forms of horror, because it gives us a broader glimpse of the conspiracy at work
which Maud's 'superstition' has pre-figured. The discrediting of the
Grand Guignol confirms the Gothic hidden in the everyday, and
ultimately drives forward the 'Bluebeard' plot.

There are other examples of the marked transition from this epistemological self-consciousness in the text about the legal integrity of testimony
and the best evidence, the marking of transitions from the intensity of
first-person eye-witnessing to the second-hand use of sources.

But the legalistic technique of the narrative overlaps with the thematics of theological 'witnessing', the test of Maud's faith; this is why it is
so urgently and intensely presented, I think. Maud is incapable of
disbelieving; that is her strength as a narrator: she has no idea of the
'limits of the marvellous' and her 'superstition' – her fearful credulity –
is her most important claim to truth, not the retrospective scepticism, or

caution, or conscience, of herself at thirty, knowing all the facts in hind-sight. Her narrative, couched in the language of the metaphysical, sets truth against the lazy canons of 'probability'.

Witnessing is also the frail device of the New Testament for establishing the truth of Christ's miracles; and the Gothic Romance has from its outset borrowed the authority of the restricted viewpoint to establish the truth of its violation of *aesthetic* probability, the anti-miracle of 'the marvellous' which overlaps with the means of the miraculous. The greatest miracle is the Resurrection, as Bryerly the Swedenborgian reminds Maud, corrobo-rated by a 'cloud of witnesses', the chief of whom is St Paul:

> 'Remember, that when you fancy yourself alone and wrapt in dark-ness, you stand, in fact, in the centre of a theatre, as wide as the starry floor of heaven, with an audience, whom no man can number, beholding you under a flood of light. Therefore, though your body be in solitude and your mortal sense in darkness, remember to walk as being in the light, surrounded with a cloud of witnesses.'[26]

The tricky question of fiction is disguised here by the metaphor of the theatre, which is a way of making language cross from the letter to the spirit, from the *'litera scripta'* (the dead letter of the text) to the spiritual meaning of perception. The theme of isolation, the pernicious nature of the central premise of the Reformation, is denied here. The child is star-ing at her father's coffin without daring to look into it. Maud is not *really* alone, says Bryerly, and Death is just like walking out on a stage, dressed in your new body:

> 'Thus walk; and when the hour comes, and you pass forth unprisoned from the tabernacle of the flesh, although it still has its relations and its rights' – and saying this, as he held the solitary candle aloft in the doorway, he nodded towards the coffin, whose large black form was faintly traceable against the shadows beyond – 'You will rejoice; and being clothed upon with your house from on high, you will not be found naked. On the other hand, he that loveth corruption shall have enough thereof. Think upon these things. Good-night.'[27]

The consolatory rhetoric feeds the Gothic effect. Maud is figured here as dead. The Day of Judgement is like the actress's first performance, and the 'witnesses' are her audience. From certain points of view, this metaphor is heretical because too materialistic; the doctrine of the 'new body' is the subject of endless eighteenth-century pamphlets by

Protestants who attempt to answer St Augustine's proposition about the seed sown in corruption which results in the new body. And the orthodox Cousin Monica has already warned Maud about our modern materialism, in her own attempts to paraphrase St Paul's Corinthians.[28]

But the novel's trick is to take this clumsy attempt at consolation literally. The degree of the figurative in this declaration is precisely the grounds of its doctrinal uncertainty for the Victorian reader. Maud lives inside this cosmic drama as a phantom, already dead, and, in the novel's climax, as she looks down into the quadrangle at her own grave without understanding it, the 'starry floor of heaven' has become a nightmare of the real:

> I went up stairs with Madame like a somnambulist. I rather quickened my step as I drew near my room. I went in and stood, a phantom, at the window, looking into the dark quadrangle. A thin glimmering crescent hung in the frosty sky, and all the heaven was strewn with stars. Over the steep roof at the other side spread on the dark azure of the night this glorious blazonry of the unfathomable Creator. To me a dreadful scroll – inexorable eyes. the cloud of cruel witnesses looking in down in freezing brightness on my prayers and agonies.[29]

The witnesses are the guarantee of her remoteness and isolation, not her mingling with the community of saints: this is why they are so 'cruel'. Bryerly's account had omitted one important thing: some souls when they acquire their new body and walk forth will find themselves in Hell, cut off for ever from the community of saints and the face of God. There is a sense in which the text can not 'come back' from this moment of despair.

Death, and representation

Le Fanu is obsessed with metaphors drawn from painting. As critics have convincingly shown, chiaroscuro dominates the twilight world in which his characters live. In *Uncle Silas*, the analogy is explicitly between the portrait and the coffin. In the Gothic tradition, there is the ancient motif that representation reverses itself vampirically, steals the life of the original and endangers that of the perceiver. From Horace Walpole to Oscar Wilde and Bram Stoker's 'The Judge's House', via Maturin's *Melmoth*, and Poe's 'the Oval Portrait', the represented image comes to life and steps out of its frame, substituting itself for its original and drawing in the beholder into a world of unreality.

Chiaroscuro is the mode of Maud's perception of almost everything. She sees through a post-Radcliffean veil of 'superstition' and 'ghostiness', a register which is deeply romantic and 'Gothic', but largely mistaken as indeed it was for Ann Radcliffe's Emily. Early on, Maud has some very strange feelings about one of the portraits at Knowl. Monica says she 'falls in love' with it. She is fascinated by the image of a young man:

> It was a full-length, and represented a singularly handsome young man, dark, slender, elegant, in a costume then quite obsolete, though I believe it was seen at the beginning of this century – white leather pantaloons and top-boots, a buff waistcoat, and a chocolate coloured coat, and the hair long and brushed back.
>
> There was a remarkable elegance and a delicacy in the features, but also a character of resolution and ability that quite took the portrait out of the category of mere fops or fine men. When people looked at it for the first time, I have so often heard the exclamation – 'What a wonderfully handsome man!' and then, 'What a clever face!' An Italian greyhound stood by him, and some slender columns and a rich drapery in the background. But though the accessories were of the luxurious sort, and the beauty, as I have said, refined, there was a masculine force in that slender and oval face, and a fire in the large, shadowy eyes, which were very peculiar, and quite redeemed it from the suspicion of effeminacy.[30]

This is a Byronic stereotype. The reader might well think of Gainsborough's portrait of William Beckford as a young man, with the mention of 'the suspicion of effeminacy' – which is hardly kept out of that picture, yet which hovers ambiguously. The cleverness, however, and the 'fire in the large, shadowy eyes' suggest another notorious figure of the turn of the century: Le Fanu's great-uncle, Richard Brinsley Sheridan.[31]

Whatever is the most appropriate, at this moment Maud is drawn to the cause of this young man, and drawn into the picture, bewitched into pastness and deadness. A picture belongs to time and yet is out of it. This one is forty years old and yet Maud is excited by the thought that the original is still alive. She has entered a twilight world of representations at this point. Later, her father looks at her 'as he might upon a picture' (14), which indicates ironically how dead and non-existent as a human she is for him at that moment. In return, Maud perceives 'spectrally': in all that concerned her father's religion (i.e. his Swedenborgianism) 'there was to me something of the unearthly and spectral'. Everything

Maud sees and understands is covered in a 'film', a 'prismatic mist' (30) and the 'magic-lantern figures' (24) by which she is surrounded hover mid-way between images and demonically real people. A beautiful late description by Maud of the nature of her anxieties as a kind of meniscus of the soul applies this repeated metaphor of the 'film', not just to her perception of the outer world, but also to her own internal 'films of care':

> You will say, then, that my spirits and my serenity were quite restored. Not quite. How marvellously lie our anxieties, in filmy layers, one over the other! Take away that which has lain on the upper surface for so long – the care of cares – the only one, as it seemed to you, between your soul and the radiance of Heaven – and straight you find a new stratum there. As physical science tells us no fluid is without its skin, so does it seem with this fine medium of the soul, and these successive films of care that form upon its surface on mere contact with the upper air and light.[32]

Here we see how the 'film' is explicitly internal and external in the book's rhetoric. The text itself is layered in exactly this way; but, from the reader's point of view, these delicate, transparent layers do not always correspond to the ones which Maud can see in herself.

In the scene when she and Lady Knollys are looking at the oval portrait of Silas as a boy of nine, Monica's stare is a kind of traffic between life and death: '"A very singular face", she said, softly, as a person might who was looking into a coffin' (64). In the magazine text, Le Fanu wrote 'had been looking' but, in the first edition, he transferred it into the present perfect, pointing up the paradox about representation itself.

Maud transforms this full-length portrait of a young man 'either unspeakably vicious or unspeakably wronged' into a new picture of Christ, superimposing one painting on to another and entering into the picture as one of the crowd:

> We sat silent for a while, and I, gazing into vacancy, sent him in a chariot of triumph, chapletted, ringed, and robed through the city of imagination, crying after him, 'Innocent! innocent! martyr and crowned!' All the virtues and honesties, reason and conscience, in myriad shapes – tier above tier of human faces – from the crowded pavement, crowded windows, crowded roofs, joined in the jubilant acclamation, and trumpeters trumpeted, and drums rolled, and great organs and choirs through open cathedral gates, rolled anthems of praise and thanksgiving, and bells rang out, and cannons sounded, and the air trembled with the roaring harmony; and with a proud,

sad, clouded face, that rejoiced not with the rejoicers, and behind him the slave, thin as a ghost, white-faced, and sneering something into his ear: While I and all the city went on crying: 'Innocent! innocent! martyr and crowned!'[33]

This extraordinary passage condenses two fantasies into one: the erotic obsession with the portrait of her uncle and the Christian faith that runs strongly in all her personality. The original portrait ('the full length') is re-painted, or perhaps collaged, inside another painting, depicting the fantasy of vindication as an old-master epic painting, a Van Dyke of Christ's persecution, perhaps, in which Maud reduces herself to one of the crowd, her cries lost in theirs, an animated paint-fleck among others. Silas is, for Maud, the Christ-figure, but who is 'the slave, thin as a ghost, white-faced and sneering something in his ear'? The Devil? A Roman tormentor? Judas, the betrayer?

Unfortunately for Maud, her fantasy-painting is the wrong way round: she is Christ, the representative of her Father, and this 'slave' is really Silas himself, the pale sneering ghost who pursues a 'dubious, marsh-fire existence'. Her heroic ordeal to vindicate his reputation is founded upon a confusion. She has to enter the world of the dead past in order to understand his iniquity.

In another complex allusion, which involves a painting of Belisarius which hung over the Le Fanu family mantelpiece, Maud recalls a print by Scotin of a Van Dyke called 'Date Obolum Belisario' ('Give a Penny to Belisarius), which depicts the great Roman, blinded and begging by the side of the road.[34] She elides this with one of her childhood books, a coloured print of a young girl in Swiss costume flying in terror from a pack of wolves and 'flinging a piece of meat behind her which she had taken from a little market-basket hanging upon her arm'. Maud doodles idly: '£20,000. Date Obolum Belisario!' Silas here (in his real shape) is the leading wolf, 'the hoary brute that led the van' and Maud is flinging out bits of her fortune to him, piecemeal in instalments, in order to stop him from killing her. Then she hears a voice at the hearthstone: 'Fly the fangs of Belisarius!' (355). The mixed painterly and writerly allusions, in which the Van Dyke is undercut by the fairy-tale illustration, represents the fairytale as that which she dare not acknowledge to herself: the fact that Silas is not only a martyred hero, but the Big Bad Wolf, too.

When Maud first meets Silas at the age of seventy-four, he has gone back in time and become a Rembrandt:

The dark wainscoting behind him, and the vastness of the room, in the remoter part of which the light which fell strongly upon his

face and figure expended itself with hardly any effect, exhibited
him with the forcible and strange relief of a finely painted Dutch
portrait.[35]

Later, this becomes her Rembrandt-fantasy: 'Up rose my uncle, that
strangely venerable pale portrait, in his loose Rembrandt black velvet'
(238). This links him with her father, who is also said to have possessed
'the rugged features of a pale old Rembrandt'.[36] The Rembrandt-figure
is the vehicle of the Uncanny, an image of the Un-dead, whose very
darkness is like a dead dream, in which there is just a flash of 'phosphoric radiance covering something colder and more awful than the
grave' (353).

There is perhaps one more area of association between visual representation and the notion of death which should be mentioned. It concerns Madame de la Rougierre, or Mlle Blassemare, which is her real
name. The isolated, motherless Maud, has more of a horror of this wonderfully grotesque creature than she does of Silas himself, at least until
the end of the novel. Madame's is a theatrical performance: this is made
explicit at Church Scarsdale, when, seeking to terrify Maud, she performs a *danse macabre*, as Mme La Morgue – Missis Deadhouse! – in the
Churchyard, resulting in one of the great set-pieces of the Gothic as rich
and powerful in its way as Magwitch's 'resurrection' in the opening
scene of *Great Expectations* or the 'King Laugh' chapter of Stoker's *Dracula*.
Terrifyingly, she invites the child into the graveyard, across the small
brook which stands in for the Styx:

> 'Come, now!' cried Madam, raising her face, as if to sniff the air; 'we
> are close to them. You will like them soon as I. You shall see five of
> them. Ah, ça ira, ça ira, ça ira! Come cross quickly! I am Madame la
> Morgue – Mrs Deadhouse! I will present you my friends, Monsieur
> Cadavre and Monsieur Squelette. Come, come leetle mortal, let us
> play. Ouaah!' And she uttered a horrid yell from her enormous
> mouth, and pushing her wig and bonnet back, so as to show her
> great, bald head. She was laughing and really looked quite mad.[37]

The stereotypes here are interesting. Mme is French, and 'ça ira' is the
refrain from 'La Carmagnole', a revolutionary song. At the same time,
the French stereotype in the 1840s, looked at with hindsight from the
1860s, would anticipate that of 1848 (Maud likens her twice to a 'grim
genadier' which may suggest the adventures of Louis Napoleon, which
Le Fanu was worried about in the early 1850s). 'French' also traditionally

means 'sexually promiscuous'. 'Madame' is the name of a brothel-keeper (as she implies in 'Mrs Deadhouse' – a combination of the whorehouse and the grave). She is bald, probably because she is syphilitic. And she is imitating the woodcuts of the medieval *danse macabre*.

This grotesque piece of music-hall casts Madame as the pig-headed lady of the Breton ballad. When we add to this, her size, which Maud registers the first time she sees her, she is given a powerful appearance:

> Madame was on an unusually large scale, a circumstance which made some of her traits more startling, and altogether rendered her, in her strange way, more awful in the eyes of a nervous *child*, I may say, such as I was. She used to look at me for a long time sometimes, with the peculiar smile I have just mentioned, and her great finger upon her lip, like the Eleusinian priestess on the vase.[38]

Maud refers here to the Portland Vase and the figure of the Priestess of the cult of Demeter. The Duke of Portland deposited the vase in the British Museum in 1810. The famous image was engraved by Blake after Flaxman had enthused Josiah Wedgewood about the image, and Duke loaned it to him to model for his jasper ware. Blake made his engravings for Erasmus Darwin's poem, *The Botanic Garden* and it is Darwin who popularised the idea that the figure on the vase represented the Eleusinian Mysteries. The mystery cult of Demeter is a fertility cult, signified by the search by Demeter for her lost daughter who has been abducted by the King of Hades: Maud is the lost daughter who has entered the Kingdom of the Shades by the side of this 'awful' Eleusinian priestess who, 'her great finger on her lip', enjoins silence.[39]

Theatre: plot and theatrical form

The plot of this novel is a strange sado-masochistic exercise: Austin Ruthyn creates an 'ordeal' for his daughter, besides having its modern meaning, the term is deliberately archaic – a feudal word for a 'test' (masculine, and usually of arms, though it has left its mark on the legal sense of 'trial' too). Maud is to act as the 'bait' in a (posthumous) attempt by Austin to purge Silas's tarnished reputation, which has brought dishonour upon the family name. Austin will make a provision in his will, whereby the seventeen-year-old heiress will become his brother's ward until she comes of age. The financial temptation to the desperate Silas will be overwhelming: if no harm occurs to Maud, then

Figure 4   'Like the Eleusinian Priestess on the vase', from 'The Portland Vase' by D.E.L Haynes.

the slanders against Silas and the family name will be purged. The sacrifice of a daughter is a sublime motif from Byron's 'Hebrew Melodies'. In this conversation between the aged Jepthah and his daughter in the garden, young Maud is indoctrinated into the masculine values of honour, which will blind her eyes and make it impossible to see the other side of her uncle – a liar, a hypocrite and a coldly calculating materialist who will kill for money; Maud will only see him as he ought and pretends to be, a gentle wronged Christian *and* an innocent martyr:

> 'But I think little Maud would like to contribute to the restitution of her family name. It may cost you something – are you willing to buy it at a sacrifice? Is there – I don't speak of fortune, that is not involved – but is there any other honourable sacrifice you would shrink from to dispel the disgrace under which our most ancient and honourable name must otherwise continue to languish?'
>
> 'Oh, none – none indeed, sir – I am delighted!'
>
> Again I saw the Rembrandt smile.
>
> 'Well, Maud, I am sure there is *no* risk; but you are to suppose there is. Are you still willing to accept it?'

Again I assented.

'You are worthy of your blood, Maud Ruthyn.' (103)[40]

The most uneasy point of this dialogue is the strange remark of Austin about risk, which doesn't make sense: if there is no risk, then there is, surely, no ordeal. This is the moment of initiation into the value of masculine 'honour'. It is, for her, a sacred trust. It also corresponds to her fantasy. From this moment on, Maud's mistakes, the way she holds out blindly against Monica's dislike and distrust of Silas, are institutionalised and the reader is forced to live inside her blindness. Maud is the willing pawn of a neglectful, self-obsessed, older generation's desperate attempt to hang on to its reputation and power, just as her cousins Milly and Dudley are too. Her stubborn pride and family loyalty last to the end and almost cause her death.

Strangely, however, even Monica, when tested, also strenuously denies to Maud's face that she believes Silas guilty of the murder of Mr Charke, though it is clear from all she says that this is cannot really be quite true:

> 'But *you* did not suspect him, Cousin Knollys?' I said, trembling very much.
>
> 'No,' she answered very sharply. 'I told you so before. Of course I did not.'
>
> There was another silence.
>
> 'I wish, Cousin Monica,' I said, drawing close to her, 'you had not said *that* about Uncle Silas being like a wizard, and sending his spirits on the wind to listen. but I'm very glad you never suspected him.' I insinuated my cold hand into hers, and looked into her face with I know not what expression. She looked into mine with a hard, haughty stare, I thought.
>
> 'Of *course* I never suspected him; and *never* ask me *that* question again, Maud Ruthyn.'
>
> Was it family pride, or what was it, that gleamed so fiercely from her eyes as she said this? I was frightened – I was wounded – I burst into tears. (148)[41]

This is a genuinely ambiguous scene, because we are locked into Maud's perspective. Monica is desperate here not to go too far and confess that she thinks him a common criminal because that would prejudice and put undue pressure on the child. At the same time, the family pride seems absolutely real, and echoes Austin's fit of proud passion in the garden

with Maud which brings on his final apoplexy. Maud, who recognises
(as Austin has explained to her) that Monica is the source of a lot of *ghosty*
rhetoric about Silas, also cannot understand her cousin's sudden, passionate reticence after all the innuendos, and perhaps Monica herself at
this moment doesn't understand it either. Beneath all her cousin's chat-
ter, there runs a deep stream of mysterious feeling which compromises
Monica because, it seems, for all her daylight common sense and feminine intuition, she unexpectedly shares the masculine blind-spot of
'honour' with Maud herself.

Le Fanu tells us in the Preface that he took this plot from one of his
own short stories, 'Passage in the Secret History of an Irish Countess'
which was published in 'The Purcell Papers' sequence in the *DUM* in the
1830s. Margaret, Father Purcell's correspondent, is much more estranged
from her father than Maud is from hers:

> My father was what is called an oddity, and his treatment of me,
> though uniformly kind, flowed less from affection than from a sense
> of obligation and duty. Indeed, I seldom even spoke to him except at
> meal-times, and then his manner was silent and abrupt; his leisure
> hours, which were many, were passed either in his study or in solitary
> walks; in short, he seemed to take no further interest in my happiness
> or improvement than a conscientious regard to the discharge of his
> own duty would seem to claim. (4)[42]

This is presented as a standard form of eighteenth-century aristocratic
neglect. Consistent with this, Margaret's father doesn't seek to *persuade*
her, as Maud's does, to make her 'sacrifice', he simply leaves her to work
it out from the terms of his will:

> The object of this last provision I at once understood: my father
> desired, by making it the direct, apparent interest of Sir Arthur that I
> should die without issue, while at the same time he placed me wholly
> within his power, to prove to the world how great and unshaken was
> his confidence in his brother's innocence and honour, and also to
> afford him an opportunity of showing that this mark of confidence
> was not unworthily bestowed.
>
> It was a strange, perhaps an idle scheme; but as I had been always
> brought up in the habit of considering my uncle as a deeply injured
> man, and had been taught, almost as a part of my religion, to regard
> him as the very soul of honour, I felt no further uneasiness respecting
> the arrangement than that likely to result to a timid girl, of secluded

habits, from the immediate prospect of taking up her abode for the first time among total strangers. (25)

Margaret is indoctrinated, but not blackmailed like Maud is; just the clear victim of neglect and autocratic patriarchal power. Her final stroke of irony here ('I felt no further uneasiness ...', and so on) is a glimmer of pathos that conceals outrage. An outrage that becomes explicit after Edward, the ruffianly prototype of Dudley, has made his first insulting advance:

> I now keenly felt the unreasonableness of my father's conduct in placing me to reside with a family of all whose members, with one exception, he was grossly ignorant, and I bitterly felt the helplessness of my situation. I determined, however, in case of my cousin's persevering in his addresses, to lay all the particulars before my uncle, although he had never in kindness or intimacy gone a step beyond our first interview, and to throw myself upon his hospitality and his sense of honour for protection against a repetition of such scenes. (47–8)[43]

Here are the seeds of Maud's stubborn blindness and the the way she keeps on, in the face of all evidence to the contrary, appealing to her uncle as her kinsman. The appeal to 'honour' here, however, is a more reasonable and general assumption.

Maud's situation is more subtly and ironically presented: she wouldn't dream of questioning her father's judgement – indeed, she has assented to her own 'ordeal' and she is in love with the martyred image, the representation, of Uncle Silas before she meets him. She has the strongest possible interest in proving his innocence.

Margaret, on the other hand, is simply deceived by a hypocrite's theatrical performance:

> His manner was, or appeared to me, most fascinating; there was a mingled kindness and courtesy in it which seemed to speak benevolence itself. It was a manner which I felt cold art could never have taught; it owed most of its charm to its appearing to emanate directly from the heart; it must be a genuine index of the owner's mind. So I thought. (37)[44]

Here we are quite close to the traditional picture of the hypocrite from the theatrical comedies of the seventeenth and eighteenth centuries. Sheridan's characters are an attack on Shaftesburian 'benevolence'

which leads into the late-eighteenth-century 'man of sentiment' stereotype. Margaret, the *ingénue*, whose story is set back into the eighteenth
century, is deceived by the art of appearing spontaneously emotional. And
when she rejects Edward's advances, she suddenly sees the theatrical
performance for what it is:

> 'I tell you, madam, that having, without one word spoken in dis-
> couragement, permitted my son's most marked attentions for a
> twelvemonth or more, you have no right to dismiss him with no fur-
> ther explanation than demurely telling him that you had always
> looked coldly upon him; and neither your wealth nor your *ladyship*'
> (there was an emphasis of scorn on the word, which would have
> become Sir Giles Overreach himself) 'can warrant you in treating
> with contempt the affectionate regard of an honest heart.'[45]

We see graphically here one source for the marvellous set of equivocations that is Silas – the stage figure of the hypocrite, stretching back
to Shakespeare's Malvolio and Ben Jonson, and coming up through
seventeenth-century comedy, to Sheridan.[46]

These are elements of an (essentially comic) structure which Le Fanu
translates into the key of Gothic horror. At least one commentator has
noticed this. Walter C. Edens long ago suggested that Le Fanu is probably drawing for the strange figures of Austin and Silas on the plot of
what was a popular comedy of the Victorian period: Sheridan's *A School
for Scandal*. The story is of the two brothers, Charles and Joseph Surface,
one of whom, Charles, is profligate and addicted to gambling, but open-
hearted; and the other, Joseph, virtuous, financially stable, and full of
good sentiment. In the play, they are due to inherit from their Uncle
Oliver who has returned from the West Indies. There is an extraordinary
scene in which Charles, desperate for money, auctions off the family
portraits to Sir Oliver disguised as Mr Premium, a friend of a Jewish
moneylender (unfortunately, another frequent character in Le Fanu's
later novels; in *Silas*, he is killed off as Charke). But Charles, though
cheerfully ready to knock down most of his ancestors, refuses point-
blank to auction off Uncle Oliver's portrait and thus, despite appearances, much to Sir Oliver's satisfaction, retains his family honour. Joseph,
on the other hand, turns out to be a mean, coldly-scheming hypocrite
under an almost impenetrably thick varnish of sentiment. The plot is
clearly an allegory which has some resonance for *Uncle Silas*. And Le Fanu
gothicises this 'two brothers' plot in several novels after *Uncle Silas*.

Joseph Surface is a key figure in Le Fanu's anti-Whig polemics, which
is often about hypocritical materalism, in the form of the rascally

ex-dissenting lawyer Joseph Larkin who makes many appearances in the later romances from *Wylder's Hand* onwards. Charles, on the other hand, is Charles de Cresseron and later Charles Mannering. Consider the following privileged view of Charles and Harry, the Fairfield brothers, from *The Wyvern Mystery*:

> If there were eyes to see in the dark, they would have seen two countenances – one sincere, the other adjusted to that sort of sham sympathy and regret which Hogarth, with all his delicacy and power, portrays in the paternal alderman who figures in the last picture of 'Marriage a la Mode'.
>
> There was much anxiety in Charles' face, and a certain brooding same and constraint which would have accounted for his silence. In that jolly dog Harry was discoverable, as I have said, quite another light and form of countenance. There was a face that seemed to have discharged a smile, that still would not quite go. The eyelids drooped, the eyebrows raised, a simulated condolence, such as we all have seen.
>
> In our moral reviews of ourselves we practice optical delusions even upon our on self-scrutiny, and paint and mask our motives, and fill our ears with excuses and downright lies. So inveterate is the habit of deceiving, and even in the dark we form our features by hypocrisy, and scarcely know all this.(67)[47]

Le Fanu uses Hogarth here, but it makes no difference to the structure. He might have used Fielding or his favourite Sheridan, equally, from eighteenth-century satire. The argument, however, turns the traditional, satiric opposition between the two brothers – candour versus insincerity – into the doubled or divided self by which 'we practice optical delusions even upon our own self-scrutiny' – we are thus unconscious hypocrites, divided selves, all in a permanent moral darkness. This is a key to the later novels. Le Fanu has found a new language for his scepticism about the nature of the self. The old satirical dramatic structure provides him with a new version of the Gothic double, a way of discussing the split self.

The external social reflex of religion is encompassed by a similar act of transference from the old theatrical tradition. In Le Fanu's last novel, *Willing To Die*, Richard Marston, playing the part of Charles, approaches and idenitifies his opposite number the Catholic priest, Mr Carmel, who backs away:

> 'Why, what are you afraid of?' said Marston. 'You haven't, I hope, got a little French milliner behind your screen, like Joseph Surface, who,

I think, would have made a very pretty Jesuit. Why should you object to light?' (II, 312)[48]

Here we see the mapping between the old eighteenth-century structure and the Gothic anti-Catholic plot of this novel. We can see Le Fanu here creating his own new Gothic rhetoric out of a traditional set of moral oppositions between hypocrisy and candour.

6
Doubleplot I: *The Tenants of Malory*

Beatrice's phantom

This novel is intimately, but anonymously narrated. The framing is intratextual, not paratextual: it comes from its structure and teasing tone, and the seemingly casual introduction of a number of highly artificial motifs, including the codes of landscape and setting.[1] The novel is organised on Shakespearian lines: two separate but interlacing plots, both turning around the idea of 'possession'. The 'romance' plot, which opens the book, is the story of the winning of Margaret Fanshawe by Cleve Verney. Cleve is the local aristocracy's, the feudal Verneys', young bright hope. He is handsome, and knows how to manipulate his status. But he is also dependent on his unpleasant uncle, Kiffyn, who is the next in line for the baronetcy of the Verney family, an inheritance which is, however, at the opening of the novel, still under dispute. Financially, Cleve's prospects are not directly good – only good by association with his uncle.

Tenants have arrived at 'Malory', the site of a ruined sixth-century Augustinian priory just along the coast from Beaumaris, the old Friary and 'Steward's House' which, owned by the Verney family estate, have been made into modern accommodation and let to some unknown people. One of them is a beautiful young woman, whom Cleve glimpses in Church from his specially raised, family pew:

Leaning over the side of his pew, Mr. Cleve Verney prayed with a remarkable persistence in the direction of this seat. After the Litany he thought her a great deal more beautiful than he had before it, and by the time the Communion service closed he was sure he had never seen any one at all so lovely. He could not have fancied, in flesh and blood, so wonderful an embodiment of Guido's portrait of Beatrice

Cenci. The exquisite brow, and large hazel eye, so clear and soft, so
bold and shy. The face voluptuous, yet pure; *funeste*, but innocent.
The rich chestnut hair, the pearly whiteness, and scarlet lips, and
the strange, wild, melancholy look – and a shadow of fate. Three-
quarters, or full face, or momentary profile – in shade, now – in light –
the same wonderful likeness still. The phantom of Beatrice was
before him.[2]

Painting is often sinister in Le Fanu, and this is no exception: *funeste* is a
favourite signal in *Uncle Silas*. This particular painting is traditionally at
the uncanny end of the romantic spectrum. Beatrice is the subject of
tragedy; at the centre of a perverse family drama, in which incest eventually drives her to death. The painting – part of the romantic agony – is
invoked in Maturin's *Melmoth*. It was thought to be by Guido Reni, but
in fact is not. It forms the staple prototype of the Pre-Raphaelite woman
and the horrific current of Romanticism stemming from the Justine of
the 'Divine Marquis'.[3] The beautiful girl's 'real' name, however, is also
symbolic: 'Margaret' – an analogue for female suffering from Goethe's
Faust, which Maturin also used in *Melmoth the Wanderer*, in the relationship between Melmoth and Immalee/Isidora.

This text is acutely aware of this symbolism in its choice of visual analogue and uses it to broach the theme of possession. Cleve is projecting
all the way – a chiaroscuro image of his own perverse desires and fantasies. The 'phantom' is about to be translated – at the ultimate cost –
into reality. Cleve must possess it. The selfish and destructive projection
of masculine substance is absolutely paramount in this long opening
intrigue of the novel. Le Fanu's apparently rambling, but actually rather
sardonic narrator's voice already makes the possibility clear, in his ironic
use of the painting, a secondary layer of representation, that there is
nothing there for Cleve to project on to – it has already vanished into a
'phantom'.

But there are no limits, it seems, to what bull-necked romanticism can
achieve. Cleve is staring at 'the Guido' from the heights of the Verney pew
'whose flooring', the narrator does not neglect to tell us, 'is raised a full
foot higher than the surrounding level'. The Verneys own the landscape,
including the ancient priory of Malory itself, the place in which this
beauty is currently living, which is an ancient monastic site. It is natural
for the latest Verney, young Cleve, to want to extend his possession.

We watch Cleve manoeuvre himself closer and closer to her. He
decides to make use of his childhood friend, the old lady, Rebecca
Mervyn, who happens to live next door in the Steward's House. The

Figure 5 'The phantom of Beatrice', Portrait of Beatrice Cenci, attributed to Guido Reni.

Gothic discourse is used, in the course of these internal and external manoeuvrings, to cross this plot with the second one:

There too, in the Steward's House, a veritable relic of the ancient Friary, lived dreamy old Rebecca Mervyn; he wondered how he had forgotten to ask whether she was still there. She had seemed to his boyish fancy one of those delightful German ambiguities – half human, half ghost; her silent presents of toffy, and faint wintry smile and wandering gaze, used to thrill him with a "pleasing terror". He liked her, and yet he would have been afraid to sit alone in her latticed room with that silent lady, after twilight. Poor old Rebecca! It was eight years since he had last seen her tall, sad, silent form – silent, except when she thought herself alone, and used to whisper and babble as she looked with a wild and careworn gaze over the sea, toward the mighty mountains that built it round, line over line, till swell and peak are lost in misty distance. He used to think of the Lady of Branksome Tower, and half believe that old Rebecca was whispering with the spirits of the woods and cataracts, the lonely headlands, over the water.

Cleve refers here to Scott's 'The Lay of the Last Minstrel' in his comparison of Rebecca to the Lady of Branksome tower. The text uses this haunted picture of an apparently mad old woman to braid one plot into the other. Both begin from the uncanny image of a woman. And this picture of Rebecca also introduces the theme of water and the story of Undine, which is a presence in both plots, metonymised from the 'Cyclopean' landscape of the Menai straits. Undine is the heroine of De la Motte Fouqué's popular fairy story, a beautiful water spirit, whose immortality is purchased, as it were, at the price of not having a soul. She desires a soul, and 'falls' into mortality, acquiring suffering at the same time. Translated in the 1830s, the story became popular as an opera and a ballet in the nineteenth century.

The two tenants are neighbours. How convenient that the self-seeking Cleve remembers old Rebecca, who lives in the Steward's House on Verney charity – the graciousness of Cleve's aunt – a visit to whom might allow him to glimpse, and even get close to, by some pious fraud, the Guido next door.

Old Rebecca is aptly named. It seems that she is the deserted wife of Arthur Mervyn, who has taken her name: Arthur whose real name is Verney, is the true heir to the Verney estates who, after conceiving a child with her, was forced to 'levant', or flee to Constantinople, to avoid his debts. He has promised her to return. Arthur Mervyn, alias Verney, it seems, has died out there, but proof of this is necessary before Cleve's garrulous and talentless Uncle Kiffyn can actually inherit the baronetcy and become Viscount Verney. Rebecca is permanently turned towards the sea, as if expecting something.

We get a glimpse here of the second plot, but the true outlines of it are withheld from us. Rebecca is a variant of Undine with a soul – while Margaret is still without; they are deliberately paralleled – and we are to learn what this means.

'Vindictive adoration'

Eventually, by Chapter X, Cleve does manage to get near the new tenants of Malory, and the fateful meeting is woven with a foreboding and humorous use of the Gothic and the Picturesque. From Ware, across the straits, he spots them going in a boat to the ruins of Penruthyn Priory, another medieval site further along the coast, set in a 'that wild and lonely park called the Warren' (47). He contrives to appear, just as the two ladies are in the act of studying the ruin. Cleve treats them to a 'graceful little lecture on the building' and the beautiful girl ignores him. Cleve is piqued. The intimate and personal implied narrator makes no secret of not liking Cleve. The narrative voice bends towards him, parodying his vain and egotistical point of view:

> The young lady looked from building to building as he described them, but with no more interest in the speaker, it seemed to him, than if the bellman of Cardyllian had been reading it from a handbill. He had never done anything so well in the House of Commons, and here it was accepted as a piece of commonplace. The worst of it was there was no finesse in this. It was in perfect good faith that this beautiful young lady was treating him like a footman.
>
> Cleve was intensely piqued. Had she been less lovely, his passion might have recoiled into disgust; as it was, with a sort of vindictive adoration, he vowed that he would yet compel her to hang upon his words as angels' music, to think of him, to watch for him, to love him with all that wild and fiery soul which an intuition assured him was hers.[4]

'Vindictive adoration' is a brilliant oxymoron for this male confusion of love and possession. The perversity is established on both sides. At this point the Gothic language of the sublime and the picturesque weaves itself into the romance plot, as they stare at the 'dim and ponderous Saxon chapel':

> 'How strange! How rude it is, and irregular; not large, and yet how imposing!' murmured the girl, as she looked round with a

momentary awe and delight. It was the first remark she had made, which it was possible for Cleve Verney to answer.

'That's so true! considering how small it is, it does inspire a wonderful awe,' said he, catching at the opportunity. 'It's very dark, to be sure, and that goes a long way; but its style is so rough and Cyclopean, that it overcomes one with a feeling of immense antiquity; and antiquity is always solemn, a gift from the people so remote and mysterious, as those who built this chapel, is affecting.'

At this point Cleve Verney paused; either his ideas failed him, or he felt that they were leading him into an oration. But he saw that the young lady looked at him as he spoke, with some interest, and he felt more elated than he had done for many a day.[5]

The text keeps its distance from the characters. Cleve's bad faith – his projection of desire, his exploitation of his position as an *owner* – is quite clearly exposed, as is Margaret's comical indifference to him. The bathos of his pause on 'affecting' and what he perceives a shift in her attention are all part of the joke. She responds to the sublimity of the 'Cyclopean' chapel, and sits, framed for a moment, in an oak stall, as he looks back, to take the architecture in. Again, the pictorial motif is insisted on:

The young lady had seated herself in a sort of oak stall, and was looking up at the groining of the round ribbed arches, at some distance. The effect was singular. She was placed in deep chiaroscuro, a strong gleam of light entering through a circular aperture in the side wall, illuminated her head and face with a vivid and isolated effect; her rich chestnut hair was now disclosed, her bonnet having fallen back as she gazed upward, and the beautiful oval face was disclosed in the surrounding shadow with the sudden brilliancy and isolation of a picture in a phantasmagoria.[6]

The 'Guido' returns to the surface of the text. I have already remarked on the 'secret history' nature of the 'Cyclopean', the ironic shift it initiates from a present, a contemporary incident, into the past, the darkness and monstrosity it signifies beneath the surface of contemporary reality. Le Fanu transfers it here from Ireland to Wales, but it signals no less the return of an uncanny loss of substance in the scene before us (the 'phantasmagoria', a technical term for the early cinema, is fifty or sixty years earlier) and a revenge of the inner, and monstrous, past.

At the level of the romance plot, the framing suggests that Cleve's vision of her as a portrait of Beatrice Cenci, the cynosure of the perverse – the aggressively vulnerable, so to speak – is a fiction, a trick of the cultural light, though he does recall that her mother was Italian. And yet his 'vindictive adoration' is precisely going to destroy her. The trap of 'seeing' (i.e. imagining) is set for Cleve and the narrator uses the language of what will be a central term in Le Fanu's uncanny ('the tail of his eye') to convey its fictive, unreal nature:

> Cleve either felt or fancied, seeing, as the Italians say, with the tail of his eye, that she was now, for a moment, looking at him, believing herself unseen. If this were so, was it not the beginning of a triumph ? It made him strangely happy.[7]

The narrator butts in at this point, reminding us of the sense and sensibility tradition; but now attributing it to a kind of mesmerism, which reveals how self-consciously linked in this text the notion of a contrast between town and country, the picturesque theme, the dreamy narrative of 'romance', is to modern questions of auto-suggestion:

> If Cleve had seen those sights in town, I can't say whether their effect would have been at all similar; but beautiful scenery, like music, predisposes to emotion. Its contemplation is the unconscious abandonment of the mind to sentiment, and once excite tenderness and melancholy, and the transition to love is easy upon small provocations. In the country our visions flit more palpably before us; there is nothing there, as amid the clatter and vulgarities of the town, to break our dreams. The beautiful rural stillness is monotony itself, and monotony is the spell and the condition of all mesmeric impressions.[8]

The plot of 'romance' is a more than slightly uncanny, robotic affair, in which all kinds of perverse emotions are present, both destructive and self-destructive.

However, in this particular instance, the text will show the mutual self-enslavement of the two figures, not just Cleve's projective 'mesmerism'. Ironically, he insists on the two ladies reading the epitaph of one Martha Nokes, the faithful servant of the Verneys in the time of George I, who 'had no less than twenty-three substantial offers of marriage, all which she declined, preferring her single state to the many cares and trials of wedded life, and willing also to remain to the end of her days in the service of the family of Verney ...'. This is hardly a tactful or deft approach from a would-be suitor. On Cleve's part, it is meant to be an advertisement of the Verney largesse (they have placed this plaque), but it misfires, first in silence, and then in Margaret's laughter at the thought of the eccentric old spinster, with whom she seems to feel some sympathy.

But we learn something of Margaret's own contradictory emotional condition in the next chapter, when it emerges, as a result of her proud spirit, that she is not only perfectly well aware that Cleve's uncle has persecuted her ruined father, Sir Booth Fanshawe, for debt, but that Sir Booth is indeed secretly living with them at Malory. Beatrice gives Father away to the enemy. Margaret gives Cleve a speech which is at once a helpless plea, and a highhanded set of instructions, in which she intimates that they implicitly require the service of Cleve's silence and complicity on the matter, at least to give them time to help the old man escape:

> There was a kind of contradiction here, or rather one of those discords which our sense of harmony requires, and mysteriously delights in – for while her language was toned with something of the anguish of pleading, her mien and look were those of a person dictating terms to the vanquished. Had she but known all, they might have been inspired by the workings of his heart. Her colour had returned more brilliantly, her large eyes gleamed, and her beautiful eyebrow wore that anguine curve, which is the only approach to a scowl which painters accord to angels. Thus, though her tones were pathetic, she stood like a beautiful image of Victory.[9]

The point of view hovers, keeping the narrative at bay here, keeping the contradiction of her powerful helplessness as an aesthetic thing. She appears to be purely innocent, entirely unaware of his feelings for her. So the notion that he is projecting an image upon her is kept before the reader, while the significantly Gothic term 'anguine' (snaky, or even 'snake-in-the-grass-y'), which is already code for the uncanny powers of the diabolical seducer in Le Fanu's writing, is converted here into the witty picture of an almost-scowling, painted angel. Margaret is made unconsciously to model again for a Renaissance or Baroque picture, the framing device recalling the habits of the Italian masters like Botticelli who used local girls and youths for their angels. But if this is not enough, the narrator then switches from the head to the body, invoking the posture and force-lines in the exquisite drapery of the (headless) Winged Victory of Samothrace.

We finish this section with Cleve's insistent attempts to use his complicity to gain further visiting concessions. He will do anything to win her, even confront and try to appease the irascible old Sir Booth (with whose boat he has already inadvertently collided, unbeknown to them), an approach to the problem which, to Margaret's horror, he goes so far as to suggest. This is a tactical error, we see, of great magnitude, which causes her to withdraw into silence and become a recluse. Cleve is left to make pleasantries with the old lady, her cousin, Miss Anne Sheckleton, who is acting as Margaret's companion and, as far as he is concerned, go-between. He sees them off from Penruthyn Priory, finally, with an ominously cold handshake from Margaret, whose relationship with her father is likened a little later to the Erl King and his daughter (61), a joking allusion which keeps alive the Franco-German Gothic/Romantic register and the feeling that Cleve, in pursuing his 'Guido', is teetering on the brink of something uncanny, transgressive, and dangerous. But more dangerous, as it happens, to Margaret than Cleve.

The rhetoric of darkness

The rhetoric of darkness in the novel covers a wide variety of contexts. It is used to fuel the rather Dickensian satire of Cleve's parliamentary ambitions, for example. When Lawyer Larkin reveals to him that he thinks he can prove that Uncle Kiffyn's elder brother, Arthur Mervyn is dead, Cleve sees the point immediately and we get the following passage which modulates into a kind of Gothic gloating at the expense of the muscular young heir:

> 'If the Old Man of the Mountains be really out of the way, it's an important event for us ?'
> And a dark smile lighted the young man's face, as he thought of the long train of splendid consequences that would awake at his death-bed, and begin to march before his funeral.
> Ambition, they say, is the giant passion. But giants are placable and sleep at times. The spirit of emulation – the lust of distinction – *hominum volitare per ora* – *digito monstrarier* – in a wider, and still widening sphere – until all the world knows something about you – and so on and on – the same selfish aspiration, and at best, the same barren progress, till at last it has arrived – you are a thoroughly advertised and conspicuous mediocrity, still wishing, and often tired, in the midst of drudgery and importance and *éclat*, and then – on a sudden, the *other* thing comes – the first of the days of darkness which are many:

> > 'Thy house shall be of clay,
> > A clot under thy head;
> > Until the latter day,
> > The grave shall be thy bed.'[10]

The *memento mori* undertow in this exploitation of a personal and digres-
sive narrator (a sort of anonymous version of Charles de Cresseron) constantly invades the lightness of tone of the romance, leaving it stranded
in its own brightness. But this menacing undertone of Gothic satire is
not the only tone. Even Cleve unconsciously understands a relation
between love and death, as the narrator makes clear:

> But beside all this delicious rape-cake and man-gold of politics, Cleve
> Verney had his transient perceptions of the flowers and fruits, as
> we say, that spring elsewhere. There are fancy, the regrets, the
> yearnings – something recluse in the human soul, which will have its
> day, a day, though brief it may be, of entire domination.[11]

Modern readers are tempted to exclaim: 'Ah, the return of the repressed'.
A contemporary example (though a more socio-political one) might be
the study of this kind of breaking down and breaking through of desire
in Dickens's *Hard Times*, in his Carlylean perception of the 'wolfish turn'
reality will make, if it is covered up or suppressed constantly. The notion
of 'entire domination' is fascinatingly self-conscious in its picture of
desire's role in the psyche, and ominous for these lovers. Here the notion
of 'something recluse in the human soul' links Cleve to Margaret, and
the contradiction of her desires. 'Recluse', used as an adjective, meaning
'closed up', links with the 'anchorite' theme, and plays into the idea of
Margaret's self-imposed isolation.

The text reports Cleve's campaign in detail. Margaret's cousin has
happened to let drop that her pet squirrel has died, and almost
immediately there appears at Malory a 'little Welsh Murillo' (65), a gypsy-
looking boy, with a cage containing two squirrels, who understands not a
word of English. Margaret, who doesn't understand this, ironically enters
into a playful invocation of (Gothic) 'romance' which this text frames:

> 'You've climbed the wall, little gypsy,' said the beautiful lady, with a
> shake of her head and a little frown, traising her finger threateningly.
> 'What ! You saw nothing? This is a lonely place; don't you know there
> are ghosts here and fairies in Malory? And I'm one of them, perhaps,'
> she continued, softening a little, for he looked at her with round eyes
> of wonder and awe.[12]

Later, she thinks of him as a 'sprite'. But all this has a material explanation:
the sprite is a lad from the Verney estate, whose innocence is used to forward Cleve's campaign, and when she learns of this, Margaret is both

ashamed and angry that he can take such liberties with them, because they are 'fallen, ruined people' (67). She bridles and flares up, and when Cousin Anne defends him, on the grounds that he has 'contrived that a purchase should be thrown in [her] way' we suddenly see her 'perversity' appear:

> ... and I know, for my part, I'm very much obliged to him – *if* he has done it – and I think he admires you too much to run a risk of offending you.
>   'What ?'
>   'I do – I think he admires you.'
>   The girl stood up again, and glanced at the mirror, I think, pleased, for a moment – and then took her candle, but paused by the table, looking thoughtfully. Was she paler than usual ? or was it only that the light of the candle in her hand was thrown upward on her features? Then she said in a spoken meditation –
>   'There are dreams that have in them, I think, the germs of insanity; and the sooner we dissipate them, don't you think, the better and wiser?'
>   She smiled, nodded, and went away.
>   Whose dreams did she mean? Cleve Verney's, Miss Sheckleton's, or – could it be, her own?[13]

The narrator withdraws here into teasing mode, pretending, like Charles in earlier romances, that he does know what she is thinking. Her first thought is to glance in the mirror and feel pleasure; but then the 'perversity', the 'anchorite' fantasy overcomes her, she grows pale, and makes that strange remark about the relationship between dreams and insanity. Le Fanu is perhaps thinking of his pretty wife, and some of the strange 'germs' in Susan that resulted in their final ordeal in the 1850s. But the text keeps its shape after this hint, and succeeds, I think, in exploiting the floating space of doubt between the reader and itself, so that the enigma of desire's 'perversity' applies to all three characters involved in the drama of this romance.

The narrator makes the complexity of this contradictory emotion of Margaret's quite clear: from this point, she starts to act out the part of a heroine of romance in an earlier Gothic novel, but self-abducted and self-incarcerated in her gloomy and ghostly conventual site of Malory:

> Outside the precincts of Malory Margaret Fanshawe would not go. Old Miss Sheckleton had urged her. Perhaps it was a girlish perversity; perhaps she really disliked the idea of again meeting or making an

acquaintance. At all events, she was against any more excursions. Thus the days were dull at Malory, and even Miss Sheckleton was weary of her imprisonment.

It is a nice thing to hit the exact point of reserve and difficulty at which an interest of a certain sort is piqued, without danger of being extinguished. Perhaps it is seldom compassed by art, and a fluke generally does it. I am absolutely certain there was no design here. But there is a spirit of contrariety – a product of pride, of a sensitiveness almost morbid, of a reserve gliding into duplicity, a duplicity without calculation – which yet operates like design.[14]

Subtle stuff indeed. She is clearly not playing hard to get, in a shallow calculating way. In fact, she is a split self – this is the stuff of which the Gothic study of the double is made, here placed on a relative scale of 'romance'. Mariana is firmly ensconced in the moated grange, and her own impetuousness turns against her mirrored self. The snaky hints – the 'anguine' presence in 'a reserve gliding into duplicity' are painterly metaphors for a morbid psychology. We see that the most 'innocent' gestures can trigger serious consequences. Le Fanu will use this trigger again in *The Rose and The Key*, where he traces the exploitation of this already established expectation (about girls) by Maud Vernon's mother, the ruthless and terrifying Barbara Vernon.[15]

Cleve, who is no more used to waiting than Louis XIV, is piqued every time he gazes across the straits at the 'dusky woods of Malory', but he can, for the moment, go no further. We are treated instead to news of the Constantinople plot. It seems that Uncle Arthur Mervyn, alias Verney, has indeed died, and the obsequious Lawyer Larkin has found 'one reliable witness to depose to his death' out in Turkey. It is the notion of 'darkness' which crosses over from one plot to another:

> 'Where, Mr Larkin, did my poor uncle die?' enquired Cleve, with a little effort at the word 'uncle.'
> 'In Constantinople, Sir – a very obscure quarter. His habits, Mr Verney, were very strange; he lived like a rat – I beg your pardon, I should say a *rabbit* in a burrow. Darkness, Sir, obscurity – known, I believe, personally to but two individuals, one of whom died – what a thing life is! – but a few months before him, leaving, I may say, but one reliable witness to depose to his death ...'[16]

'Darkness' means secrecy, obscurity, the undertow of menace, and the fear of the devil: the term traverses a whole gamut of levels and responses.

Here, the conceit of the plot is made evident, but none of us, including Larkin, can understand it at this point. It is a psychic version of Charles and Joseph Surface, the Two Brothers Plot. There is in fact only Arthur out in Turkey. Arthur's friend never existed, and Arthur, who wants to come back to England for reasons we also don't at this stage understand, is now impersonating the remaining 'reliable witness' to his own death, one Mr Dingwell, an eccentric yankee, knowing the desperate desire to inherit (and therefore the gullibility) of his brother, Kiffyn.

Cleve's delight knows no bounds and, excited and restless at the news, he takes to his boat, the *Wave*. The glow of the picturesque is thoroughly ironic, presented as pure projection:

> Two sedatives, however, were at his disposal – cigars and the sea – and to them he betook himself. Away went the *Wave* over the sparkling sea, with a light breeze, towards the purple dome of Pendillion, streaked with dull yellow rock and towering softly in the distance. Delightful sea-breeze, fragrant cigars, and gently rising, misty woods of Malory, with their romantic interest – and all seen under the glory of this great news from the East. The cutter seemed to dance and writhe along the waves in elation and delight, and the spray flew up like showers of brilliants from the hands of friendly Undines sporting round her bows.[17]

The Undines, associated, both literally and metaphorically, with precious stones, are part of the rhetoric of darkness here, because (besides their crude reflection of Cleve's vision of his future wealth) they allude to the story of the destroyed girl, an image of the freedom and beauty which is about to be thrown away. Money frames romance in the ambiguity of this description, but not from the character's point of view.

Cleve makes, of course, for Malory, and there he has a vision, which again challenges this sardonically realist perspective, and reasserts the presence of Gothic romance and fairytale in the text, as the only way to describe Cleve's desire:

> Walking slowly, and now and then pausing, he looked among the glittering trunks and down the opening aisles of the wood. But there was no sign of life. The weeds trembled and nodded in the shadow, and now and then a brown leaf fell. It was like the wood of the 'Sleeping Beauty.' The dusky sunlight touched it drowsily, and all the air was silent and slumbrous.

The path makes a turn round a thick clump of trees, and as he passed this, on a sudden he saw the beautiful young lady standing near the bank, her hat thrown on the ground, the thick folds of her chestnut hair all golden in the misty sunlight. Never so like the Guido before. The large eyes, the delicate oval, and pearly tints, and the small vermillion mouth, its full lips parted, he could see the sunlight glitter on the edge of the little teeth within.

A thrill – a kind of shiver – passed through him, as if at sight of a beautiful spectre.[18]

The spectral nature of this vision corresponds to the bits of Cleve that are out of sight of his rapaciously materialist ambition, the objective correlative of the 'recluse' part of the soul. It is clear that the language of 'haunting' describes a kind of unconscious behaviour here, a perversity, which crystallises in his 'vindictive adoration', hence the appropriateness of the painting and the details of its features. Melville, following the Gothic novel, describes it thus:

> He wore that nameless look
> About the mouth – so hard to brook –
> Which in the Cenci portrait shows ...
> A trembling over of small throes
> In weak swollen lips, which to restrain
> Desire is none, nor any rein.[19]

Cleve is able to get back on terms with them and meets the two ladies again at the priory of Penruthyn, where he faces them with a stone tablet which is purely Gothic – the very image of death and the maiden which has been hovering beneath the picturesque and the social all through this text:

'It is elaborately carved, and is dated, you see, 1411. If you look near you will see that the original epitaph has been chipped off near the middle, and the word "*Eheu,*" which is Latin for "alas!" cut deeply into the stone.'

'What a hideous skull !' exclaimed the young lady, looking at the strange carving of that emblem, which projected at the summit of the tablet.

'Yes, what a diabolical expression! Isn't it?' said Cleve.

'Are those not *tears*?' continued Miss Fanshawe, curiously.

'No, look more nearly and you will see. They are worms – great worms – crawling from the eyes, and knotting themselves, as you see,' answered Cleve.

'Yes,' said the lady, with a slight shudder, 'and what a wicked grin the artist has given to the mouth. It is wonderfully powerful! What rage and misery! It is an awful image! Is that a tongue?'

'A tongue of fire. It represents a flame issuing from between the teeth; and on the scroll beneath, which looks, you see, like parchment shrivelled in fire, are the words in Latin, "Where their worm dieth not, and the fire is not quenched;" and here is the epitaph – "Hic sunt ruinae, forma letifera, cor mortuum, lubrica lingua demonis, digitus proditor, nunc gehennae favilla. Plorate. Plaudite." It is Latin, and the meaning is, "Here are ruins, fatal beauty, a dead heart, the slimy tongue of the demon, a traitor finger, now ashes of gehenna. Lament. Applaud." '[20]

Margaret is confronted by the image of her own destruction ('fatal beauty, a dead heart, the slimy tongue of the demon'), but fails to recognise it. In fact, it becomes a coup for Cleve in his courtship of her. Echoing Lilias Walsingham, she declares: 'It is a very good horror' (96). There is a certain gloating in his exposure of her to this; it comes in the context of a 'bitter yearning' (94) that swells up in his heart, when he sees how unconscious she still is of him, after all his efforts to win her. She seems to him to be 'half-unconscious of what she is doing, quite unconscious of everyone near her' (94). This need for acknowledgement (partly) explains the iconoclasm of his desire; his attempts to break the spell and then, in revenge, possess her.

At any rate, after this contact, Cleve somehow hangs on, returning to Malory, and declares himself to her. The picturesque theme continues, the extreme and grotesque burst of Gothic in the chapel sinking back into a tissue of running allusions to Gothic romance: he approaches at one point 'the iron gate, where, as at a convent grille, the old and young recluse stood' (101). The upshot is that Margaret, like Immalee, capitulates; pathetically, she begs him to promise never to change, warning that if he does, she will die. The narrator, after scorning such promises, withdraws his labour and refuses to tell us what passed between them. All he can venture is a notion of the Fall: 'Undine has received a soul, and is changed.' (125).

In his new-found confidence Cleve makes the mistake of approaching the irascible old Sir Booth Fanshawe, Margaret's father, and letting him know that he knows he is there. He gets short shrift with the old man, whom his uncle is persecuting for debt. Sir Booth, having enjoined him never to have the effrontery to visit again, leaves the area and forbids Cleve contact with his daughter. It is some time before Cleve manages even to trace them. In the end, he journeys to Caen, where Sir Booth is renting a dilapidated château:

> Here is an old wood, cut in a quincunx; old ponds stocked with carp; great old stables gone to decay; and the chateau itself is indescribably picturesque, and sad.
>
> It is the Chateau de Cresseron – withdrawn in historic seclusion, amid the glories and regrets of memory, quite out of the tide of modern traffic. [21]

This passage connects Irish, French, English, history to the 'anchoritic' romance theme. It is a dream of Le Fanu's own ancestral home – the home of the Huguenot family before Charles de Cresseron went over from Caen to Ireland with James II. The narrator of this text resembles Charles, and uses the same personalised disclaimers, the same paradox of witnessing something he was not present at. Instead, in this novel, Le Fanu chooses to name the place: the ghostly, picturesque setting of the home of this family ghost, for his romance.

This whole encounter is a moonlit stage-set. Margaret rejects him afresh ('That beautiful cruel girl!'), and he wishes he had never heard 'that mermaid voice' (which pins Undine to Shakespeare). He confronts her, and Anne Sheckleton, devoted matchmaker as she is, leaves them alone. Margaret capitulates again, when faced with his urgent devotion. The narrator makes an interestingly agonised aside on 'perversity':

> Lovers' promises or lovers' cruelties – which oaths are more enduring? Where now were Margaret's vows? Oh! inexhaustible fountain of pity, and beautiful mutability of woman's heart! In the passion avowed, so often something of simulation; in the feeling disowned, so often the true and beautiful life.[22]

The scene from this point on loses its substance. His voice as he pleads with her is 'a voice in a dream, and a form seen there, in that dream-land in which we meet the dead, without wonder, forgetting time and separation' (196). And when they begin to talk, their shadows gliding side by side along the poolside, to the handsome old Miss Sheckleton's eyes the moonlight makes the scene 'look filmy as a fairy castle'. This filminess is a key part of the rhetoric of the Gothic in *Uncle Silas* and *Carmilla*. She watches, unobserved and pleased, 'this picture of Lorenzo and Jessica' – with a 'mixture of melancholy and delight and fear' (197).

Of course, what we are watching is Margaret's destruction. Cleve marries her, and she becomes pregnant. He is a member of parliament, and feels he cannot reveal their marriage, because of the ruin of her family, and the fact that his own has still yet not inherited the baronetcy. So she is kept in a redbrick suburban cottage, away from the world. The scene in which he visits her and the baby is painful and bears out the feeling of deadness:

> 'And where's the good of seeing me here, dear Margaret? Just consider, I always come to you anxious; there's always a risk, besides, of discovery.'
>
> 'Where you are to me is a paradise.'
>
> 'Oh, darling, do *not* talk rubbish. This vulgar, odious little place! No place can be *either – quite*, of course, where *you* are. But you must see that it is a 'paradise' – and he laughed peevishly – 'of red brick, and lilacs, and laburnums – a paradise for old Mr Dowlas the tallow-chandler.'
>
> There was a little tremor in Margaret's lip, and the water stood in her large eyes; her hand was, as it were, on the coffin-edge; she was looking in the face of a dead romance. [23]

The Gothic touch is light, but unmistakeable here – the coffin-edge. As she stares at Cleve's face, Margaret stares down into the coffin: we don't see what she sees there, but its significance is purely anticipated. The materials of this scene are indeed those of realism: one could imagine how George Moore, a few years later, would draw out its sordid decline in chapter after squabbling chapter. But Le Fanu's text insists on using the dreaminess of a plot which we experience, alongside Margaret, as a painful riddle, an almost mystical kind of *déjà vu*. The cruelty and pain of the scene are tragic, because inevitable, not because they illustrate 'how life is', or the peculiarly modern nature of this death of love.

As they talk, skirting round the issue of 'murder', the pain increases, with the analogy between a love and a life:

> 'No, of course, love is eternal,' said Margaret.
>
> 'Just so; the King never dies. Les roix meurent-ils? Quelquefois, Madame. Alas, theory and fact conflict. Love is eternal in the abstract; but nothing is more mortal than a particular love,' said Cleve.
>
> 'If you think so, I wonder you ever wished to marry,' said Margaret, and a faint tinge flushed her cheeks.

'I thought so, and yet I did wish to marry,' said Cleve. 'It is perishable, but I can't live without it,' and he patted her cheek, and laughed a rather cold little laugh.

'No, love never dies,' said Margaret, with a gleam of her old fierce spirit. 'But it may be killed.'

'It is terrible to kill anything,' said Cleve.

'To kill love,' she answered, 'is the worst murder of all.'

'A veritable murder,' he acquiesced with a smile and slight shrug; 'once killed, it never revives.'

'You like talking awfully, as if I might lose your love,' said she haughtily; 'as if, were I to vex you, you never could forgive.'

'Forgiveness has nothing to do with it, my poor little woman. I no more called my love into being than I did myself; and should it die, either naturally or violently, I could no more call it to life, than I could Cleopatra or Napoleon Bonaparte. It is a principle, don't you see? that comes as direct as life from heaven. We can't create it, we can't restore it; and really about love it is worse than mortal, because, as I said, I am sure it has *no* resurrection – no, it has no resurrection.'

'That seems to me a reason,' she said, fixing her large eyes upon his with a wild resentment, 'why you should cherish it *very* much while it lives.'

'And *don't* I, darling ?' he said, placing his arms round her neck, and drawing her fondly to his breast, and in the thrill of that momentary effusion was something of the old feeling, when to lose her would have been despair, to gain her heaven, and it seemed as if the scent of the woods of Malory, and of the soft sea breeze, was round them for a moment.[24]

From the reader's point of view, this toying with murder is indeed strange and cruel, because it has already started to happen. They are talking in a cruel dream about something which has already begun. Cleve (whose name is a perpetual denial of the marriage service – he does not 'cleave' to her at all) is thinking of bigamy with a society heiress, Caroline Oldys. He has prevented his uncle Kiffyn from marrying Caroline by blackmailing the clergyman who would have married them, in order to give himself the option. Since no one knows about his clandestine marriage to Margaret, and the baby, an arrangement with which he is already bored, his Uncle is actively looking for a wife for him. The mnemonic whiff of the picturesque in the final image ('the scent of the woods of Malory, and of the soft sea breeze') is seen from his own egotistical point of view – Margaret is already looking in the coffin.

Tenants of Malory transposes this Gothic nightmare (*'no* resurrection', vastation, complete loss of substance) into the language of 'romance', appropriating its central metaphors as a description of the emotional (and the economic) life. Margaret has already been consoled by her cousin Anne, a once-beautiful old lady spinster, whose love was lost, when she was young, among the Canadian snows. Typically, the narrator is out of earshot: 'I cannot hear what she is saying, but the young lady looks up, and kisses her thin cheek, and lays her head upon her old shoulder' (212). He does, however, venture a strange 'archaeological' expansion of what she might have been saying, which denies the efficacy of 'plot' in this universal terror of mutability and depression ('black Care'):

> In a few concise and somewhat dry sentences, as old prison stones bear the records which thin hands, long since turned to dust, have carved, the world's corridors and corners bear the tracings of others that were busy two thousand years ago; and the inscriptions that tell the trite story of human fears and sadness, cut sharp and deep in the rock, tell simply and briefly how Death was the King of Terrors, and the shortness of life the bitter wonder, and black Care the companion of the wayfarers who marched by the same route to the same goal, so long ago. These gigantic griefs and horrors are all in a nutshell. A few words tell them. Their terror is in their truth. There is no use in expanding them; they are sublimely simple. Among the shadowy men and women that people these pages, I see them everywhere – plots too big and complicated to be got, by any compression, with the few pages and narrow covers of the book of their lives: Care, in her old black weeds, and Death, with stealthy foot and blow like thunder.[25]

This whole plot of 'romance' is deliberately truncated, a kind of memorial tablet; this text merely overwrites the graffiti of all grave sites, even at the time of the gospels, two thousand years ago. The plot of this novel (betrayal, depression, and death) is already 'in a nutshell' – framed, and studied. This text is therefore a *study* of a romance, not just a rendition, or expansion, of a universal story. The touches of allegory in the characters – Undine, and Rebecca Mervyn as a version of 'black Care' (and Cousin Anne as a benign survivor of this plot, ironically anxious to promote it again in her beautiful cousin) – are here explicitly referred to. All the narrator needs to do is remind us, give us the sign of the plot, not all the realistic detailed consequences themselves. It is the algebra of perversity we need, not the 'felt life' of Margaret's undoing by romance. And that algebra is, traditionally, a nightmare – a pilgrimage into the dark, without the consolation – the resurrection of the dead – so pathetically and courageously striven for, and so perversely almost-missed, by Maud in *Uncle Silas*.

This explains the perfunctory treatment of Margaret after this point. Once her hand is on the coffin-side, the story of her romance is a repetition. She is always represented deliberately and experimentally to the reader, as a perverse sterotype, through the Gothic, painterly metaphor of 'the Guido' – Cleve's Guido – as the possession of his gaze. Her substance was never there. She exits from the plot at this point, and is allowed to die. In fact the narrator dismisses her.

The rationale of this representation is that it is held at bay – it is a study of romance. The point about 'possession' (material possession of the spiritual is an impossibility, possession of the object of desire is an impossibility) is the driving centre of the romance 'plot', not the actual story of Cleve and Margaret. It is term in a central comparison with the 'two brothers plot', which then gives the whole text its hybridity.

The two brothers (in one) plot

The other half of the double plot of *The Tenants of Malory*, which intersects with the 'romance' plot of Margaret and Cleve, is a variation of the plots of the three earlier novels, and is to recur in *Haunted Lives*, and *Checkmate*.[26] Arthur Verney decides to impersonate his friend and perform the role of 'reliable witness' to his own death. The rascally lawyer Larkin, in cahoots with the shady Jewish moneylending firm of Goldshed and Levi, is milking the foolish Kiffyn Verney for vastly inflated expenses, by bringing 'Mr Dingwell' (alias Arthur Verney, the true heir), an eccentric American gentleman from New York who has supposedly been living in Constantinople, over to England to testify in court to the death of the baronet, so that Kiffyn can inherit. Larkin knows that Kiffyn Verney will pay anything for this proof of his brother's death. So they install him in cheap lodgings in Rosemary Court, a block of rack-rented tenements owned by Goldshed and Levi. In doing so, 'Mr Dingwell', who is a marvellously sinister comic character, acts as a counter-vampire on the vampires, squeezing money out of them for a rakehelly existence in London. His speech in his pea-green dressing gown and his scarlet fez to his bewildered landlady, Sarah Rumble, is a series of pointed Gothic jokes about resurrection:

> 'Look at me – don't I look like a vampire? I tell you, Ma'am, I've been buried, and they would not let me rest in my grave, and they've called me up by their infernal incantations, and here I am, Ma'am, an

evoked spirit. I have not read that piece of paper. How do they intro-
duce me – as Mr Dingwell, or Mr Dingwell's ghost? I'm wound up in
a sort of way; but I'm deficient in blood, Ma'am, and in heat. You'll
have to keep the fire up always like *this*, Mrs Rumble. You'd better
mind, or you'll have a bit too much like a corpse to be pleasant. Egad!
I frighten myself in the glass, Ma'am. That is what they call transfu-
sion of blood *now*, Ma'am, and a very sensible thing it is. Pray don't
you think so?'
  'I do suppose what you say's correct, Sir.'
  'When a fellow comes out of the grave, Ma'am, – that's sherry in
that bottle; be kind enough to fill this glass – he's chilly and wants
blood, Mrs Rumble. A gallon or so, transfused into my veins wouldn't
hurt me. You can't *make* blood fast enough for the wear and tear of
life, especially in a place like merry England, as the poets call it – and
merry England is as damp all over as one of your charnel vaults under
your dirty churches. Egad ! it's enough to make a poor ghost like me
turn vampire, and drain those rosy little brats of yours – ha, ha,
ha! ...'[27]

Arthur is clearly enjoying himself here at Mrs Rumble's and Larkin's
expense. The sadistic fantasy is perfectly matched to the plot impersonation, and theatrically develops the idea of the hypocrite into the split
self or Gothic double. Dingwell is himself a deliberate parody by Arthur,
of agency, of Larkin and Co. An allusion he makes to Sheridan confirms
this relationship between the theatrical type of the hypocrite, the
divided self, and the parody of the agent as an actor. The consummate
Larkin smoothes him down, after an outburst of temper, when it looks
as if they are not going to give him his weekly allowance, which he is
screwing out of them, and they are screwing, in their turn, out of Kiffyn
Verney, the prospective heir of Arthur's own baronetcy. So, effectively,
Arthur is willing to blackmail his own estate, in order to expose them:

  '... I wish, Mr Dingwell, I *were* the party; you and I would not, I venture to think, be long in settling it between us.'
  'No, to be sure, you're all such liberal fellows – it's always some one
else that puts us under the screw,' laughed Mr Dingwell discordantly,
with his face still flush, and his hand trembling visibly, 'you never
have the stock yourselves – not you, – there's always, Mr Sheridan
tells us, you know, in that capital play of his, a d——d uncon-
scionable fellow in the background, and in Shakespeare's play
Shylock, you remember, he hasn't the money himself, but Tubal, a

wealthy Hebrew of his tribe, will furnish him. Hey! I suppose they gave the immortal Shakespeare a squeeze in his day; he understood 'em. But Shylock and Tubal are both dead and rotten long ago. It's a comfort you can't escape death, with all your cunning, d——n you."[28]

Here *The School for Scandal* slips into the anti-Semitism of *The Merchant of Venice*, both of which pre-texts are treated as glances on the 'theatre' of Arthur-as-Dingwell, and his counterplot, which he almost gives away in his real rage. So the 'Lorenzo and Jessica' scene at the Chateau de Cresseron is an allusion which links the two plots of the novel like a Shakespeare play. It also of course links the anti-Semitism of Shakespeare and Sheridan to Le Fanu's scene here. The unnerving violence of the racism which Arthur is supposed to be impersonating, at this point breaks out completely into the text, and makes it very difficult to invoke the novel's form: one can only say what the aesthetic effect is meant to be, not that it achieves anything more than a breakdown into stereotype.

Dingwell's outburst has in a number of different ways stretched the comic device of Arthur Verney's disguise to breaking point, as we can see in the violence of the earlier part of this scene, when he almost hits Mr Levi with the poker:

> 'If you don't treat me, as I say, with common fairness, I'll go to young Mr Verney myself, and put you out of the baby-house altogether.'
> '*What* babby-houshe?' demanded Mr Levi, glowering, and hanging the corners of his great half-open mouth with a sullen ferocity.
> 'Your castle – in the air – your d——d plot, Sir.'
> 'If you mean you're going to turn stag,' began the Jew.
> '*There* – do – pray, Mr Levi – you – you *mistake*," interposed Mr Larkin, imploringly, who had heard tales of this Mr Dingwell's mad temper.
> 'I say,' continued Levi, 'if you are going to split–'
> 'Split, Sir!' cried Mr Dingwell with a malignant frown, and drawing his mouth together into a puckered ring, as he looked askance at the Jew. 'What the devil do you mean by *split*, Sir? 'Gad ! Sir, I'd split your black head for you, you little Jew miscreant!'
> Mr Larkin saw with a qualm that the sinews of that evil face were quivering with an insane fury, and that even under its sun-darkened skin it had turned pale, while the old man's hand was instinctively extended towards the poker, of which he was thinking, and which was uncomfortably near.[29]

The argot is an open sign of criminality to Arthur, who is genuinely enraged by it. To whom is his face 'evil'? Larkin and Levi alone? Or is it the reader? The energy of the text here betrays itself, because Arthur has really become the part he is playing of choleric Dingwell. The Gothic melodrama of spleen against the money society, which he is acting out in the text (with the full approval of his author) almost gives him away, when his passion is roused.[30]

Later, when Dingwell appears to be dying, another allusion to Sheridan's central allegory of the double in *A School for Scandal* confirms the relation between the two brothers' plot and the anti-Semitism of this text:

> For the recovery of Mr Dingwell were offered up, in one synagogue at least, prayers as fervent as any ever made for that of our early friend, Charles Surface, and it was plain that never was patriarch, saint or hero, mourned as the venerable Mr Dingwell would be, by at least three estimable men, if the fates were to make away with him on this critical occasion.[31]

Josiah Larkin, the hypocritical dissenter (ex-Methodist, and *real* Joseph Surface-figure), is made an honorary Jew here, alongside Levi and Goldshed, and this coven of extortionists is termed a 'synagogue', as 'the firm' mourns to see its investment slipping away.

For the Gothic of this plot is, without doubt, violently anti-Semitic. Chapter XXVII, entitled 'Judaeus Apella' – the 'circumcised Jew' (a quotation from Horace, which Le Fanu used before in *The House by the Churchyard*) is a very unpleasant and unreconstructed piece of rhetoric, whose Gothic image makes a monster of sadistic cruelty out of East-London Jew, Mr Levi, who pauses, on the last stage of his journey to Malory to interrogate Rebecca Mervyn concerning the whereabouts of her son, to torment a beetle in the grass:

> The little man, put his stick, point downward, before him. The beetle rounded it carefully, and plodded on inflexibly in the same direction. Then he of the black eyes and the long nose knocked him gently in the face, and again and again, jerking him this way or that. Still, like a prize-fighter he rallied between the rounds, and drove right on in his old line. Then the little man gave him a sharper knock, which sent him a couple of feet away, on his back: right and left sprawled and groped the short legs of the beetle, but alas! in vain. He could not right himself. He tried to lurch himself over, but in vain. Now and then came a frantic gallop with his little feet; it was beating the air. This was pleasant to the man with the piercing eyes, who stopped over, smiling with his wide mouth, and showing his white fangs.[32]

Perhaps Le Fanu was criticised for this passage. There is one copy of the text of this chapter, on which, in the margin, Le Fanu himself appears to have written: 'I regret writing this' in the margin. The narrator addresses the beetle, as it struggles to reach the end of its journey:

> Alas! there is no sympathy with your instinct, with the purpose of your life, with your labours and hopes. An inverted sympathy is *there*; a sympathy with the difficulty – with 'the Adversary' – with death. The little man with the sharp black eyes brought the point of his stick near the beetle's back, having seen enough of his pilgrimage, and squelched him.
>
> Which is pleasantest, building castles in the air for ourselves, or dungeons in pandaemonium for our enemies? It is well for one half of the human race that the other has not the disposal of them. More rare, more grotesque, more exquisitely fiendish, is the sport with the mysteries of agony, that lust of torture, that constitute the desire and fruition of some monstrous souls.[33]

Le Fanu does not appear to have been got at, like Dickens was, before he wrote *Our Mutual Friend*. Perhaps the Jewish community in Britain didn't notice him. But nothing could be more blatant than this. Through some neo-Darwinist fantasy, the sadistic cruelty of Benjamin Levi is attributable here to his wolfish race: he of the 'the sharp black eyes', the 'long nose', and the 'white fangs'.

The second half of the novel is a carnival of savage theatrical comedy, which matches the 'perversity' of the romance theme in the Cleve–Margaret plot. Dingwell persecutes poor Sarah Rumble and her children. Dingwell causes the downfall of everyone. His final confrontation with his younger brother, Kiffyn Verney, is a purely theatrical reversal, which leaves the would-be hypocrite bereft of all his agents and even of the bell-rope that would save him:

> The man was speaking in quite another voice now, and in the most awful tones Lord Verney had ever heard in his life, and to his alarmed and sickly eyes it seemed as if the dusky figure of his visitor were dilating in the dark like an evoked Genii.
>
> 'I – I think about it – it's quite unaccountable – all this.' Lord Verney was looking at the stranger as he spoke, and groping with his left hand for the old-fashioned bell-rope which used to hang near him in the library at Verney house, forgetting that there was no bell of any sort within his reach at that moment.
>
> 'I'm not going to take poor dear Arthur's mallet out of my pocket, for the least tap of it would make all England ring and *roar*, Sir. No, I'll

make no noise; you and, Sir, *tête-à-tête*. I'll have no go-between; no
Larkin, no Levi, no Cleve; you and I'll settle it alone. Your brother was
a great Grecian – they used to call him *Odysseus*. Do you remember ?
I said I was the Greek merchant? We made an exchange together. You
must pay. What shall I call myself, for Dingwell isn't my name. I'll
take a new one – Το μεν πρωτον Οντιν 'εαυτον επικαλει – επειδανδε
διεφευγε και εξω ην βελουω Οδυσσυν ονομαζεσθαι εφη. In English –
at first he called himself Outis – *Nobody*; but so soon as he had escaped,
and was out of the javelin's reach, he said that he was named
Odysseus – *Ulysses*, and here he is. This is the return of Ulysses !'

There had been a sudden change in Mr Dingwell's Yankee intonation.
The nasal tones were heard no more. He approached the window, and
said, with a laugh, pulling the shutter more open –

'Why, Kiffyn, you fool, don't you know me?'[34]

Charles Surface confronts Joseph Surface, in a comic resurrection, a carnivalesque version of the return of Ulysses. But Sheridan's scheme has
been inverted: Arthur Verney is actually more like a theatrical version of
the hypocrite, Joseph Surface, than the open-handed benevolent aristocrat; and he is the very image of perversity, a kind of violent cosmic
joker. He doesn't believe in God, but describes himself as *Porcus e grege
epicuri*: a pig from the epicurian herd. Not really Ulysses, but one of
Circe's prisoners. He wants no tomb – on his headstone 'just the date of
his decease, and the simple description, "Check-mate"'. The narrator
comments: 'But whether he meant to himself or his creditors I'm not
able to say.' Having found his son, Tom Sedley, who will be the true heir
to the Verney estate, he neatly foils both Kiffyn and Cleve, on the one
hand, and Larkin and Co., on the other. His final defeat of them is to
commit suicide by poisoning himself and thus foil Larkin's plot, even
while the latter makes valiant efforts at the last minute to prosecute him
for fraudulently impersonating someone else and bearing false witness.
However, he witnesses to his own death in the end, by killing himself.
The 'checkmate' is clearly to himself, as well as to his creditors, and it
links to Le Fanu's novel of that name, which also involves a double
figure, in Walter Longcluse, otherwise known as Yelland Mace.

The logic of this plot is that it puts Arthur Verney in the same 'perverse' position as Margaret Fanshaw in the 'romance' plot – just as her
perversity exposes Cleve's selfish projection of desire and manic need to
possess the object of that desire at any cost, so Arthur's perversely secret
'return of Ulysses' from the Levant exposes Larkin's sordid conspiracy to
defraud Kiffyn Verney by unscrupulously promoting him as the heir to
the Verney estate, in order to milk him of legal expenses; and exposes

Kiffyn Verney himself as seeking to squeeze out the true heir to the baronetcy, Arthur, and then the offspring of his marriage with Rebecca Mervyn, Cleve's friend, young Tom Sedley.

A black kind of Gothic satire overlaps with romance: Margaret's father, the choleric Sir Booth Fanshawe, a sworn enemy of the Verneys, whom Kiffyn is persecuting for debt at the opening of the novel, is a version of Arthur Verney himself, hunted from pillar to post, his tenancy of Malory strictly temporary, ready to move at short notice to the Continent in order to avoid prison. Essentially, this is the position Arthur is in: he could not have returned to England as himself, or his creditors would have instantly thrown him into debtor's prison. So he comes back as another: one, 'Mr Dingwell', who testifies to his death and thus precipitates the conspiracy against his own estate. It is the old 'test' idea of the comedies, metmorphosed into a mad, existential tautology. In his absence, Kiffyn has taken over Ware and lives there as the local lord, when the estate actually belongs to Arthur who seems to be trapped in Constantinople, having persuaded Rebecca to wait for him. She then waits (ludicrously, from a realist point of view) for twenty years.

Both Margaret and Arthur die, leaving Cleve and Kiffyn, the second-raters, to their well-earned obscurity, while Tom Sedley, Arthur and Rebecca's son, becomes the Viscount Verney.

7
Doubleplot II: *Haunted Lives*

Layering

Haunted Lives (1868) is a scherzo on the romance plot of *Tenants of Malory*, which, however, develops the textual dynamics of the earlier novel in an interestingly theatrical way. It is very close in some ways to the much more developed picture of madness and passion, the 'germs of insanity', which lurk in the first manifestations of 'perversity' in the (much better known) *The Rose and the Key* (1871), which of course turns into a fully fledged, Gothic madhouse conspiracy. *Haunted Lives*, which has never seen the light of day since it was first published in 1868, is a deliciously teasing, maddening development of the 'morbidity' and 'perversity' theme, which transfers, as far as it is possible to do so, the sado-masochistic encounter of desire between lovers into the space between the reader and the text, via a compressed and multiply framed, fairytale Gothic romance version of the Two Brothers Plot.

Here the full chaperone figure, Max (in *The Rose and the Key*) or Anne Sheckleton, the attractive old spinster, perhaps herself disappointed in love, who acts as the go-between in *The Tenants*, is reduced to the figure of Julia Wardell, Laura Gray's conveniently stupid and imperceptient companion, a reduction which provides the novelist with a technical challenge; it leaves the central theatrical encounter between the lovers the only ground on which they can communicate (or miscommunicate) with one another, with the exception of the narrator's own agency. The use of this agency is blatantly selfconscious, carrying the notion of a divided self into the divided *position* of the narrator, in a variation of the ghostly Charles de Cresseron in *Wylder's Hand*, and torments those who are reading for the plot, an aspect which may have caused readers bristling with the expectations and standards of realism to simply feel that the book is a bad novel. But if we see in it the pattern of exploratory hybrid forms of the Gothic romance, I think it has a certain power. This is Le Fanu's closest study of perversity to date.

The novel is set in what was then the suburb of Old Brompton probably sometime between the early 1830s and, at the latest, 1842 – it is difficult to put a date to its action, which is enfolded in tissues of anachronism. One of the characters, De Beaumirail is confined to the Fleet prison for debt, which was knocked down in the Gordon riots in the 1770s, but which was rebuilt and not finally closed until 1842.[1] Old Brompton is, however, a significant nineteenth-century setting: Laura's anchorite fantasy in the novel takes place on the site of the Brompton oratory, perhaps in a deliberate piece of anachronism, *before* Newman built the oratory after he 'went over' to Rome in 1845. In 1852, the London oratory wanted to move from the Bayswater ex-gin-palace it was in, and 'had', in the words of Newman's biographer, 'fallen for the charms of Brompton'. In 1853, they moved there.[2]

This is a layered text. There are in addition several references to operas in the novel, and these cannot have been earlier than the early 1830s, so it seems that there are several layers:

(1) the theatrical Sheridanesque, eighteenth-century plot of the 'double', modulated into a Gothic key: Guy De Beaumirail, a rake-hell debtor who is temporarily let out from the Fleet, impersonates a dead man, 'Mr Dacre', in order to negotiate his release from (and his revenge on) Laura Challys Gray, the young woman who originally had the power to let him out, and refused it, because he had seduced and destroyed her favourite sister;

(2) the early 1840s, and old Brompton: the period after Catholic Emancipation but before the rise of the Oxford Movement, when the old Gothic was finished and a plethora of romantic operas came on the London stage of the Franco-German variety, like Bellini's *La Sonnambula, Undine,* and Meyerbeer's *Robert Le Diable,* and so on. This anachronism forms a kind of twilight area that 'reads back' the continuous popularity of these operas and melodramas in the later Victorian period, into the earlier, pre-Victorian era – Old Brompton is pastoralised, perversely, and deliberately, as part of Laura's 'anchoritic fantasy' in the novel, as if it were the site of an old convent, thus appropriating the register of the Gothic Romance;

(3) as a ghostly (and a ghastly) version of Elizabeth's court (Laura is sy bol-ically, or metaphorically, Elizabeth, the Virgin Queen, the Petrarchan cynosure, as her name suggests ...), in which one of the plotters in

the conspiracy against her, the most benign and independent from the others, is named Parker, after Archbishop Parker, who represents Establishment (i.e. Anglican Protestant, but politically 'liberal') hypocrisy, in an unholy alliance with Gillespie (Scottish dissent), Larkin (Methodism), and Levi, the Jew, in order to get the Essex-figure, de Beaumirail, off his sentence; and

(4) the Neo-Darwinian, post-Newman (*Apologia*), post-Papal Aggression, era of 1868, when the book was published.

The ghost of a ghost narrates

All of these layers of coding come into play in this text, which, with relentless camp and a sinister lightness of tone, pursues the notion of perversity as a true description of the psyche of the lover. The strange narrative method must be put into the equation at the very beginning, because it enacts the theme of the divided 'modern' self, on another level. We begin with the combined technique of omniscience and first-person narration, in the person of Charles Mannering (not Charles de Cresseron, a ghost of a ghost), and a cousin of Laura Challys Gray, the beautiful golden-ringleted, high-born, proud, heroine, whose attempt to live without compromise, as a young, rich, unmarried woman in her new house in Old Brompton, is to come to such fairytale grief.

The novel opens with the anonymous narrator's double-take; he invents himself in a kind of daydream, in front of the reader's eyes:

Beautiful cousin, Laura Challys Gray ! A pretty music rings in your name, for me – with those sad notes that come from the distant past, and die in the far future.

I close my eyes, and I see you, your violet eyes, and rich brown tresses, with their golden folds, the delicate oval of your face, and your crimson lips. Oh ! pretty Laura – odd, wayward, misunderstood, full of faults – with many perfections, I am sure, that others possessed not – I am going to jot down my recollections of you, and what I know of a story as odd as your character.

In this house, at the open drawing-room window, Charles Mannering – a tall young man, with a face kind, frank, and also sensitive – was standing, looking westward, where the sun was nearing the horizon, with the glow of a coming sunset. I think there is a pleasant sentiment in the artificial rurality of such a scene, and he could fancy, among the urns and roses under the distant groups of ruddy chimneys, melting in the misty light of evening, a pretty powdered Daphne ogling her piping Philander across her crook.[3]

The tone is unstable, passing from sentimental to camp (Daphne and Philander). Formally, the third person narrator is virtually indistinguishable, by a coy sleight of hand, from the first-person witness. Charles Mannering is a cousin of Laura's. So, we are invited to rationalise the effect by introducing the gap between the two voices, as a fiction of 'family history'. But the split self is embedded in the very act of narration. In fact, Charles narrates himself, in the third-person:

> He liked being employed, too, by his pretty cousin. Here was a commission which had given him a world of trouble – to find her just such a house in the old-fashioned suburbs of London as he had lighted upon.[4]

We can read this from the point of view of the writer, or the character, once we have seen the narrative joke – that the voice, in a sense curiously unassigned, is talking about itself. To put it another way: Charles is talking about himself, in the third person:

> Miss Laura Challys Gray was still standing between the voluminous silk curtains, looking out through one of the tall windows, as he entered the room. In shadow and reflected lights there is sometimes a transparent effect which heightens beauty; and I think he never saw her look so lovely as when she turned towards him from the light, as he entered. I pause for a moment to recall that pretty image.
>
> She had removed her little bonnet, which dangled by its ribbon at one side from her slender fingers. Her rich brown hair, so wonderfully voluminous, in the shadow showed its golden glimmer where the dusky sunset touched it. Her large violet eyes, under the long curve of their lashes, were turned upon him. Nearly in shadow, her beautiful lips, with a light just touched in crimson, parted, and very grave. What a beautiful oval that little face was, and how richly her shadowy brown hair parted low above her brows. As she looked at him this pretty face was thoughtful and nun-like, and after a little silence she said, with a very imposing seriousness:–
>
> 'I think I shall like this out-of-the-way house, and the fifteen trees, and the half-acre of grass.'[5]

This strangely elaborated effect binds the split self to the act of narration: 'I pause to tell you what he saw, because I was there, watching her through his eyes.' Both of them are in love with her, but one is a writer and must 'pause' – halt the process of narration – to 'remember' (describe). The apparent contradiction of the witnessing effect, as in the earlier case of Charles de Cresseron, is flaunted in front of the reader, until he or she is forced to perform that very Victorian, drawing-room conflation of 'I' and 'he' with which Dickens's novels are filled, from Pecksniff to Jaggers, from Bradley Headstone to Jasper. But here the split is written into a game with the reader. So the text insists on making the switch from character to the intrusive narrator:

> As he walked up the short straight avenue, dark with the shadow of old elms, it was still a quarter of an hour to the appointed time. Already Miss Challys Gray had been busy, and under her beautifying influence tall flowers were nodding and quivering in the great stone pots along the balustrade that ran before the windows, and on the drawing-room window-sills were other tinier flowers, and there he saw her as *I* always see her – looking from the shadow of the open window.[6]

And she is 'nun-like', a thematic observation which comes not only from Charles, but from the narrator, his alter-ego, the writerly witness behind the witness: because this ghostly narrator, perhaps a sort of Charles in old age, is mockingly aware that there is a connection between Brompton, Laura's plan, on arriving in London from her family estate of 'Gray forest', to renounce love and live without it, and her little queen's (I, 7) demeanour:

> 'I think I shall like it,' she repeated a little imperiously, as much as to say, 'It is your place to listen at present, and mine to speak.' 'It looks old, and homely, and secluded. It has a monastic air; and has not the slightest pretension to elegance, and is perfectly dull – *thank* you. You have acquitted yourself, as far as I can see, to admiration.'[7]

Here is where the imperious Queen Elizabeth fantasy enters, mercilessly mocked by her semi-conscious courtier, Charles Mannering. Laura is twenty two, proud and high-born, very beautiful, and means to 'live as pleases her best, and die an old maid.' (I,8):

> 'A passionless recluse?' he continued.
> 'Wrong again. No, not passionless. With one passion very fixed – very wicked. What do you look at? Why do you laugh?' she

demanded a little fiercely. 'I say very wicked, not because it *is* wicked, but because the cant of the Pharisee and the cant of the world concur in calling it so. I don't choose to reason: I suppose I could if I chose, but I have no taste for arguing. I leave that to philosophers like you, who always lose their tempers when they engage in it. I read my Bible, and that is my church. I have no notion of being bullied by clergymen. I have gone into various places of worship, both at home and abroad, and I'm not particular about forms. None of them please me exactly, and none of them displease me altogether.'

'Ah! Miss Challys,' said he, raising his finger, and shaking his head, with a smile, however, 'you are the same wild girl – Undine, before she acquired her soul.'[8]

The Undine analogy is ominous, as we have seen in previous novels. Her dream of uncommitted liberty is very difficult for a Victorian woman. But Laura is full of spirit, and she can defy and tease, in return, her Cousin Charles, her witness and the agent, so to speak, of the retrospective narrator who is, on another aesthetic level from both of them, writing behind his back, as he teases her:

'But you talked of a passion just now. It can't be *the* passion?' suggested he.
'Now, that's so like your sex! You poor weak men, when you hear passion spoken of, can imagine nothing but the insipid sentiment you call love. Come, rouse your energies, and be a – woman.'[9]

Laura has all the means to be independent. Her profound distrust of men comes from the past behaviour of the man who languishes in the Fleet prison across London, Guy de Beaumirail, a debtor in the grip of his creditors, of whom she is a principal one.

Her first task, it seems, is to review his case and make a decision as to whether she agrees to release him. The text sets up the image: she really is surrounded by counsellors, like Queen Elizabeth. For the men who surround her, her decision is a foregone conclusion; her mercy, as a woman of twenty-two, is taken for granted. But to their astonishment and consternation, she declines and condemns him to perpetual durance. These early chapter headings are jokes: 'Brothers of Mercy', which refers sarcastically, via a glance at the conventual theme: 'Sisters of Mercy', to the unholy alliance of creditors which seeks to get De Beaumirail out of jail, so that they can squeeze him properly; and 'Ad Misericordiam' ('In accordance with mercy'). Afterwards, she explains her motives to Mr Parker, the gentle clergyman, who reveals himself to be a distant relative of de Beaumirail:

> 'I have lost my father; I have lost my sister; I stand alone in the world, sir. My father suffered from a complaint under which he might have lived for many years to come, but his life was cut short by the excitement and anxiety of a wanton attack upon his property. My sister died when I was very young, seven years ago. They called it consumption – it was a broken heart. The lawsuit which hurried my father's death was instituted by a man who snatched at that desperate chance to redeem his fortunes from the ruin in which his selfish prodigality had plunged him. My sister's heart was broken by the same unscrupulous man, who first won her love, and then deserted her, and that cold, frivolous villain was Guy De Beaumirail.'[10]

It is important for the fairytale plot, that this judgement should be reasoned, absolute, and implacable; it then acts as the first prohibition or taboo, in a fairytale. She tells the clergyman Parker, in good stern Anglican fashion, that his recommendation of mercy is 'imbecile' and 'wicked' and 'a distortion of our reasonable faith'. She declares, with more than a touch of Enlightenment rebellion: 'If I thought you represented Christianity truly, I should cease to be a Christian.' (I, 43)

Charles is not present in this scene – only the narrator, who doesn't draw attention to himself. Charles is piqued because he has been ignored, and he stays away for a day or so. But she summons him, regally, and they make up their friendship. At this point, the question of how she will amuse herself here in London arises, and Charles suggests a number of diversions which involve actually going outside the walls of Guildford House. Laura defends herself against what she sees as his picture of her as an immature and capricious female who doesn't know herself:

> '… besides, you fancy my plans are all whims and caprices. When the truth is, I have no spirits – no energy – and a positive dislike of nearly everyone – and a genuine horror of all that sort of thing you fancy I secretly like. I can't prevent your thinking – if so, it must be – that I am telling stories; but, remember this, I never told a lie in my life, and anyone who tells me an untruth, I *never* forgive; and that sort of thing would, you know, of itself disqualify me for all the amenities of human society.'[11]

The heiress who rejects the world takes up her absolute and absolutely 'perverse' position, which includes a fairytale prohibition – that no lies can enter her world, without the liar being banished from it. She thus disqualifies herself from loving the lie which is about to enter and dominate her little world, in the shape of a ghostly or fictive dead man. She is bound to be 'haunted'. This is again the narrative signal from Propp's Russian folktale structure: a pattern of prohibition and transgression.[12]

Charles seeks to divert her again, and at this point she confesses her vulnerability to him. In doing so, she introduces the first sign of the Gothic:

> 'I have felt so oddly – I'm sure it's nervous – a kind of fancy that I am – how shall I describe it? – watched – well, not exactly watched – a kind of feeling that I am going to meet somebody – I don't know whom – whom I have never seen, perhaps, except in a dream, or somehow,' she laughed, 'in a pre-existent state, a kind of expectation mixed very largely with fear. And, of course, you and I know the whole thing is purely nervous.'[13]

The fairytale/supernatural discourse, insisted on as 'modern' in the 1860s and therefore reduced to a question of incipient morbid psychology, enters the text here. We are invited to read this 'superstitiously' (i.e. in reverse), as usual, as a truly ominous anticipation in the manner of Propp. But she is articulating the plot of the novel here, the grotesque and implausible train of events which is indeed to occur, in this apparently unpromising setting of surburban Old Brompton (despite, at another level, the associations of Romish 'superstition', which shadow Laura's conventual fantasy). The fairytale, its prohibitions all in place, and archly enshrined in an urban setting, is under way: Undine, soulless, innocent, has taken up her position at the door, inviting across the threshold mortality (in the shape of erotic passion) through her very denial of its reality.

Necromantics: the trap

Now that he knows Laura has condemned him to the Fleet for the rest of his days, Guy De Beaumirail decides to carry out the conspiracy to marry her and grab her estate anyway, as a matter of revenge. The Fleet ran a notoriously complicated system of parole, largely based on bribes. He is a Cinderella: he persuades the unholy alliance (Messrs Larkin, Levi, and Gillespie) to invest in bribing the jailor to let him out every day, so that he can woo Laura and eventually marry her. To do this, he impersonates a dead man, one 'Mr Alfred Dacre'.

The scene in which this alter ego first appears is at a theatre, in which some operatic favourites are being performed. The male–female roles have been reversed. Laura is in the box, surveying the audience through her opera-glasses when she catches sight of an 'elegant-looking young man, with dark hair, moustache, and a small peaked beard in the Italian style, an oval face and large soft eyes, and delicately pencilled eyebrows':

> This face was very feminine. There was colour in the cheeks, and a soft lustre in those large eyes, with their long lashes, and a soft carmine touched the lips. The waving hair lay low upon a very white forehead. Altogether the tints and formation of the face were feminine and delicate, and there was something of fire and animation, too, that gave it that kind of beauty that belonged to the great Italian tenor in his young days.[14]

This is De Beaumirail, let out of jail, in drag, or, rather, dressed (and fully made-up) as a consumptive Italian tenor, an icon of theatrical femininity. The image, in its transposition of art and nature, anticipates Oscar Wilde and Thomas Mann's Gustave Aschenbach. 'Carmine' here is make-up, though the innocent Laura does not understand this. The 'great Italian tenor' is here ambiguously generic or specific. Later, Lady Ardenbroke identifies him as 'Mario the Tenore'.

The opera they are watching is Meyerbeer's *Robert le Diable*, a Victorian favourite in London from the early 1830s onwards, which forms the title of this chapter of the novel. This eclectic musical piece has a sinister Gothic aspect to it; it is in part an adaptation of Weber's *Der Freischutz*, (which forms a sub-text in *Uncle Silas*), and it seems also to have allusions to Maturin's tragedy *Bertram*.[15] The opera is set in thirteenth-century Sicily to which Robert, Duke of Normandy, exiled because of his evil doings, has gravitated, because he has fallen in love with the Sicilian princess, Isabella. Robert's Father, Bertram, is the Devil. Robert is a gambler, who has lost all his possessions, including the armour which would have allowed him to enter the tournament and win the hand of Isabella. In Act III occurs the famous scene in which Bertram, having pledged Robert, his son, to join a company of evil spirits, conjures from their graves a quantity of nuns who have broken their vows, who entice Robert to remove a magic cypress branch from the grave of St Rosalie with which to woo Isabella.

It is this scene which Laura is watching when she becomes most powerfully aware of the sinister and dominating presence of 'Mr Dacre' in the audience. First, she experiences a kind of anti-sublime, an interval of visionary dreariness comparable to the opening of the 'Fall of the House of Usher'. Play and audience, imagination and reality, are reversed:

> This night there were selections from two operas. The scenes from 'La Sonnambula' had closed. In the internal between it and those that followed from 'Robert le Diable', the people in Miss Gray's box who had talked now and then during the singing, grew perversely silent. Most persons whose spirits are at all capricious have at times experienced in a theatre something like the sensation which that young lady on a sudden felt just now. A sudden air of desolateness seemed to overspread the stage; an idea of cavernous solitudes beyond, half lighted and silent, made the scene joyless and unreal; the illusion failed; imagination and the spirits collapsed altogether; the music sounded jaded and forlorn; the lights grew less light, and fancy and enjoyment chilled.[16]

This is a moment of 'perversity', of semi-reflexivity, a moment at which she intuitively realises that the source of this feeling of joyless unreality is in the audience, not on the stage. De Beaumirail, alias 'Mr Dacre' (not yet named) is cast as Robert the Devil, the genuinely horrible Gillespie by his side is his father, the Devil, Bertram; but what Laura cannot know is that she is cast as his Isabella, and that she herself is a part of the sublime scene she is apparently watching:

> This 'Robert the Diable' did not find in that house a spectator so predisposed to receive in good faith the whole melodramatic impression of that great church-yard scene. The peaks and shafts of the ruined abbey, glimmering in moonlight, the terrible necromantic basso, and the sheeted phantoms, all but a moving picture – had yet a relation to real emotions which circumstances and fancy had already set in motion within her; and Miss Gray, to whom accident made the opera and all such scenic glamour still new, gazed on in the sort of eerie rapture with which she might have read, for the first time, in the solitude of her room, the ghostly scene in the 'Lay of the Last Minstrel' in the aisle of Melrose Abbey.[17]

The 'necromantic basso' is Bertram, the Devil (the double of Gillespie in the auditorium). Walter Scott's sublime (a more modern version of Ann Radcliffe's) is used to convey the 'eerie rapture' of the solitary reader of the scene in which Michael Scott's grave is opened, which, in its turn is a metaphor for Laura's morbid, transfixed state of mind. There are three layers of representation in these passages: (1) the characters in the novel, Laura Gray and De Beaumirail ('beauty to be wondered at'); (2) the opera characters, Isabella and Robert, the son of the Devil; and (3) 'Laura Gray', the anchorite of Brompton, dimly aware of herself as already playing a part in a drama that is unfolding around her, and 'Mr Alfred Dacre', the creature born of a diabolical conspiracy to seduce her for her money. In this drama, it is Alfred Dacre who possesses the character of the snake, the ur-seducer, as Laura acknowledges when she looks for 'those lines and curves of cruelty which gave, in her eyes, to his beauty an anguine and dangerous character – subtle, sinuous, baleful ...' (I, 137), 'Anguine' is a key item of vocabulary here, that shifts between levels: Eve has become dimly aware of her snake's ('female') beauty.

Laura progressively enters the trap. Her cousin Lord Ardenbroke (who has betrayed her, helping De Beaumirail out, by pretending to recognise 'Mr Dacre' at the theatre) tries feebly to warn her about the fiction of 'Mr Dacre' by making a set of ('Old Gothic') jokes about the raising of spirits. Feeling guilty, he even tells Laura the unvarnished truth, that 'Mr Dacre' is a 'Doppelganger':

> Lord Ardenbroke was laughing, but he looked uncomfortable.
> 'Place a pentagram at the door, as Dr Faustus did – a pentagram which Mephistopheles could not pass, you remember.'
> 'I do remember; but I should like to know what you mean,' said Miss Laura Gray.
> 'I mean this – simply shut your door against him,' he answered.
> 'Why?' persisted Laura.
> 'I can't define my reason; but he is a 'double' – a Doppelganger – he is, I assure you. He is an unreality.'[18]

The novel reveals itself in this conversation to be a commentary *on* the Gothic tradition, as much as a 'gothic novel'. This is the case with all these romances of the 1860s: they are hybrid, not just between folk-tale, for example, and Old Gothic, but also between novel and commentary. Even if we had not watched the Gothic plot of the Double being constructed, the idea of 'suspense' in the revelation of that double identity would be absurd, for the reader, after this. This is the story-telling that lays bare its means.

But not to the *ingénue*, Laura. Ardenbroke, visibly embarrassed, is the representative of the patriarchy here, still excluding the female from any proper information, much as Austin treated Maud in *Uncle Silas*.

Masquerade

The second stage of this story is like the 'middle eight' in a song: it modulates via the jealousy of Charles Mannering who sees that 'Mr Alfred Dacre' is a fake, and alludes to Sheridan's *The Critic* in describing him:

> He looked towards the window where Laura Gray was sitting, but she was not looking toward him, on the contrary, through the window, 'following no doubt,' thought Charles, 'in spirit, the departed Don Whiskerandos, who has passed beneath those files of elms.'[19]

Charles follows 'Mr Dacre' to the Fleet prison, and we follow Charles, but his jealousy gets the better of him, distorting his angle of vision. He doesn't realise that 'Dacre' and de Beaumirail are one and the same, because the fact that this deception is practised every day renders it an open secret into which everyone at the prison, including the warden and guards, enters; what he overhears is in fact, to the narrator and reader, the shared pretence that 'Mr Dacre' is visiting Mr De Beaumirail. But Charles simply thinks he has discovered a conspiracy against Laura between the two men. So near and yet so far: jealousy renders Charles too literal-minded to guess the obvious truth of impersonation:

> He, Charles Mannering, would find out all about him. He had no idea of mere masks and disguises, *mimae, balatrones*, winning their way by sheer impudence and insinuation, with their disguises still on, into such houses as Challys Gray's. He was huffed and wounded, and in no mood to mince matters with Mr Dacre. The sooner, in his present temper, he thought, they went to the heart of the question, and understood one another, the better.[20]

This initiates the subplot, in effect, because 'Mr Dacre' realises that one-dimensional Charles is in his way, and engineers a duel with him in which he expertly shoots him, and obliges him to hide himself while he recovers from his wound at the remote Silver Dragon inn, thus earning him the narrator's mock-chivalrous title of 'the Knight of the Silver Dragon'.

After the duel, Dacre soliloquises to himself, railing against his divided self. This is the point at which the romance discourse is undercut by the colder current of the 'modern' register – a complex mixture of morbid psychology and neo-Darwinist speculation about sex and competition. 'Mr Dacre' (i.e. De Beaumirail, speaking about himself in a third person) speaks the part of the Byronic devil, who longs to be a real ('unsplit') devil:

> 'Green – green – green,' murmured Mr Dacre enigmatically, as he looked out of the carriage window; 'tiresome thing green is; paradise – simplicity – verdure – moonshine; yes, I like the other world better; yellow stucco – red brick – gas light – and d——d clever fellows – devils. The angelic life is insupportable insipidity.'
>
> And with a sigh and a shrug he threw himself back in his seat, and his discourse went rambling on.
>
> 'I wish I were altogether a devil; I'm perplexed and made inefficient by stupid yearnings after Eden; a divided being is self-torture, not a grain of conscience, or *all* conscience, – anything between is loss of force and deep-seated incurable pain.'[21]

This perverse psychology is very reminiscent of Melmoth and Immalee in Maturin's great Gothic classic, or indeed of Byron himself – the tempter tempted. Or of the original of these – Milton's Satan – who remains for a moment, 'stupidly good', when faced with Eve, in Milton's *Paradise Lost*.[22]

But his reflections grind on and the whole sexual basis of love is quite clearly reduced to sexual competition. The Devil is a Neo-Darwinist:

> 'It is the nature of the lioness,' he suddenly resumed, returning from music to metaphysics; 'an instinct for picking out the grandest mate, whether they like him or not, and so with a vain-glory strangely humble, to make him their boast, and their sex's envy their happiness. Yes, mesdemoiselles, if the lioness is not satisfied with her suitor, when they take their moonlight walk together in the jungle, she roars and roars, despite the uneasiness of her lover, till from a distant jungle comes an answering roar, and nearer, and nearer, and nearer – and so a battle – and she secures the benefit of competition and the finer animal for a mate; and what young ladies, is your courtesy at St. James's – your coming out and all that? Is it not your way of roaring and inviting from all circumjacent jungles those lions whom it may concern?'[23]

The lion, having disposed of his rival, Charles, is about, coldly, to make his play for the lioness, Laura.

But Laura herself desires no such thing, and has no intention of doing any roaring. This is a *Clarissa*-plot: the Virgin Queen and the Rakehell

Seducer are the immovable object and the irresistible force. Neither can have the other, and they know it. And yet both are divided (and therefore 'haunted') selves. He sings and enchants her through the ear, leaving her 'smiling, with a dilated eye and pale cheek' (II, 210–11). Yet she resists him, beautifully, remaining within the metaphor of her reasoned piety:

> 'Do you believe in possession, Miss Gray?'
> 'A very cheerful question, Mr Dacre.'
> 'But do you ?' he urged.
> 'Of course I believe it, and so must you, for it's in the Bible.'
> I don't know that Mr Dacre quite admitted that logic. He was too well-bred, however, to dispute the authority to which Miss Gray bowed.
> 'Double identities and all that,' he resumed. 'When you mean and don't mean – when you are quite in earnest, yet ridicule your own earnestness – when you admire and yet despise yourself – and perhaps love and also hate some other person.'
> 'I have never been in that delightful state of confusion,' says Miss Gray, with a laugh.[24]

With Charles thoroughly out of the way, he can get on with his project. His casual tone is a blind, as we know. He tempts her, and longs to confess to her, at the same time. Indeed he is confessing to the reader, and the torment is narratively exquisite. De Beaumirail's cruelty is already beginning to weaken in these scenes:

> In another minute he was driving away under the old trees. His odd, half-bitter smile had subsided. He looked back at the drawing-room windows in which the light was shining. He wished to see her there, even her shadow; but a bough of a great tree hid the window, and he leaned back and said –
> 'Yes; it is a deep game, or – a *very* shallow one. This mechanism then is wound up – springs, wheels, levers – rather a nice piece of work. It must run on and down, and play its figures and strike the hours. By Heaven, I haven't thought for days; I never think now – my head swims and whirls so pleasantly. I hear, I see, I enjoy, but I never think. What a pretty creature she is – the prettiest creature in the world. It is a great pity.'[25]

The mechanism of the plan is perfect, but we begin to see that De Beaumirail hasn't much time. He is dying all along, of what is eventually described to Laura, in a joke that anticipates Joyce's romantic witticism, as 'some affection of the heart'.[26] And it is this fact, which lies behind the cosmetic pallor of Mr Alfred Dacre, as he makes his seductive play for her. He deliberately misunderstands her anger, pretending that it is directed towards himself:

> 'Certainly not; oh, Mr Dacre! my true and brave friend, how could you think so?'
> She spoke with a kind of enthusiasm that thrilled him. And, at the same time, extended her hand, which he took. He was very cold; he looked as pale as a dying man, and he gazed in her face with his eyes full of a strange fire. Was it confusion – was it love – was it remorse? It was so intense she could not endure it. She felt a shudder in his hand; and, with a short sigh, like a gasp, he raised her hand to his lips, and passionately kissed it.
> 'What have I done? Forgive me, Miss Gray, I am very unhappy; I fancied you were – offended with me, and in the rapture of our acquittal, I forgot myself, and the immeasurable fate that separates us.'
> She drew back her hand from him. He did not attempt to retain it. She had blushed intensely, but treated this stage act as the wildness of a moment. So estimating, it was perhaps more dignified to ignore it as she did.[27]

Typically the narrator withdraws into her confused perception of his emotion, and substitutes for it a series of coded jokes ('as pale as a dying man') in which love and death, and the stage character 'Mr Dacre', and his original, De Beaumirail, are elided. This is Death and the Maiden. But though she blushes, the Maiden, through high-born *naiveté*, does not behave like a Maiden, but like a Virgin Queen, and amusingly treats his gesture as 'a stage act', which is precisely what it is. What she fails to see is that her gallant courtier's stage gesture is more than that: the 'cold' seducer is a dying man, who is really falling in love with her.

The result is that, in order to save her, he (De Beaumirail) conceives a counterplot against the conspiracy whose principal agent and protagonist he himself is (i.e. 'Mr Dacre'). He expresses it to Laura, with characteristic indirectness, a little later:

> 'Have you never read in that tiny romance, Lewis's "Bravo of Venice", how Flodoardo – I beg pardon for naming myself with so perfect a hero – associates, under the name of Abelino, with the assassins who hold the city in awe and enlists in the conspiracy against its government, for the purpose of delivering them all to the executioner?

Now, my little counter-plot is near its crisis, only don't disturb my operations, and do give me a few days more.'[28]

Monk Lewis's Old Gothic tale of political conspiracy comes in very handy here: the improvised lie De Beaumirail tells her here, simply to gain time, is in fact the truth. He intends from this moment, not to carry out the conspiracy to marry her, but to run away from his creditors to Paris, and save her. He has no use for time any more, and yet the only way he can tell her the truth is through a mask. She, on her side, has no choice but to be in love with the mask, not the man. The man De Beaumirail, for her, is unthinkable, and at this stage she has never entertained the idea of pardoning him.

So both are 'haunted' by a real passion that is a ghost. The final phase of this three-decker, operatic recitative, recapitulates what 'haunted' – the metaphor derived from the old Gothic romance – means. For 'Mr Dacre':

'If I allowed that fancy to run away with me, I might be in love with that girl before I could tell how it came to pass. As it is, that pretty phantom haunts me more than consists with my cold and scientific ideas. In some respects all the worse, in others all the better. The adventure interests me more pleasantly as I proceed.'[29]

and Laura is also the object of a 'phantom', like the heroine of the Gothic romance:

So much for monastic peace. What of her conventual platonics? Had not a stranger stolen into her heart? Was there not a phantom in her pretty head – a fancy hardly suspected till now, and now almost detected as – a passion?[30]

The conceit of 'haunting' involves, by analogy, a series of conflicts: between the Old Gothic and the Modern Novel, between superstition and sceptical materialism, the heart and the head, and between Victorian Doubt and Faith.

The narrative is a series of masks, a masquerade, in which the two central characters are locked into a series of confessions that are shaped by illusionary interlocuters. Laura's great speech about the taboo subject of De Beaumirail is made to 'Mr Dacre':

'I've often wished that I were a man, that I might let him go free, and fought him – to strike down that cold villain with a pistol shot, or die by his – and let him lay death upon death, and go to judgement with a double murder. Ardenbroke and you – and you and Ardenbroke – with your metaphysics and your partisanship, and your cruelty! To break a girl's heart is but the breaking of a china tea-cup. What's a woman? The plaything of your insolence. What her love? A song to laugh over. The feather of your vanity. But *I* say, the noblest treasure that ever God poured out on earth! Oh, manhood! Oh for the time when men were men, and honoured the creatures whom nature committed to her protection. But, oh, that's all old-fashioned now – entirely mistaken – and men are wiser; and women must be patient – yes, patient – till God's justice comes to rule the world.'[31]

So much for the rational justice she invokes at the beginning of the novel. This is the passion of nobility revealing a passion *for* nobility. This is Elizabeth down at Tilbury docks addressing the fleet, a passionate outcry against the betrayal of her sex, the dissolution of masculinity, and the decadence of all ideals of chivalry, all romance. Elsewhere she is compared to someone 'representing' (i.e. acting) Charlotte Corday.

The dramatic irony of this is that she can only articulate it to a fiction, and De Beaumirail can only hear it through the ears of 'Mr Dacre', a mask. Only the phantom can respond.

The equivalent awakening for De Beaumirail, masked entirely, even for the reader, under the appellations 'Dacre' and 'he', is the final death of his narcissism. How incredible, he thinks, that he – of all people – could have been driven off course by this wild romance:

In this there was, of course, something of that self conceit in which, like other young men, he was principled. But in his heart the ruling idolatry is declining – 'the great god Pan is dead' – and a truer and holier worship is superseding that selfish superstition which had burnt a perpetual incense, and offered up so many sacrifices before his own handsome image.[32]

The adoption of the alter ego, 'Mr Dacre', has allowed the cold, cynical seducer, De Beaumirail, access to Laura's nobility, and that access has caused him to love (quite hopelessly, as it happens, since he is dying) outside himself. Even though his counterplot against himself fails (foiled by his watchers), he takes great delight in dying, and wrecking his own plot against her. Here the narrator uses Plutarch's contrast between a dying Paganism and a new era, as an analogy for the transitional state of the Masculine Self: Narcissism is the old religion, a form of superstition, and Love, the new, but it is a *Liebestod*, a love that can only be revealed in death.

For her part, through loving the nobility and sensitivity of 'Alfred Dacre', Laura comes to realise her own passion for another, and she spontaneously forgives her enemy, De Beaumirail in jail, while entirely under the illusion that he is a separate and evil person (which, in a sense, he is).

Too late, of course. He has died, so Mr Parker tells her, of 'some affection of the heart' (III, 255). But in his death, she learns she has been deceived, even by the good Parker, and that all along the loathesome seducer was her beautiful, sensitive, feminine, anguine, 'Alfred Dacre', her own special snake.

Theirs are to remain 'haunted lives', lives, that is, haunted by the phantom of an overwhelming, mutual and impossible love like the 'eerie rapture' of the old romance, read in solitude.

Cultural paranoia and the Old Gothic

I've been simplifying this discussion at several points just to get its main lines clear. This sophisticated, operatic piece is writing full of extraordinary, sublime, and sometimes awkward contradictions. These are not least apparent at the first level of representation, the handling of the conspiracy against Laura by De Beaumirail's creditors. The familiar 'firm' of Larkin and Levi, (with the addition of Gillespie, a Scottish Presbyterian) represents the coarse Materialism, the cosmopolitan money society which Le Fanu first identified, as we have seen, in his early Irish fiction, as a fatal result of the Williamite Settlement: here, a mixture of dissenting Protestantism and Jewish commercialism, makes up a company of hypocritical Whig speculators, comically defeated by their fall-guy, De Beaumirail's counter-plot.

I have been arguing that most of the text uses the rhetoric of the Old Gothic as a framing device. But the language of the text also inserts into this framing process not simply illusory 'possession' by passion, ('haunting') but also social paranoia and violence. The conspiracy against Laura involves a certain amount of objective pressure on her, through letters and through the invasion of her house. Here is where the Old Gothic is most fully recycled.

Before he falls in love with his enemy, Laura, De Beaumirail is uninclined, but also quite unable, to control the conspirators who are backing him. The much-vaunted monastic isolation of Laura's house in Old Brompton leaves her vulnerable to the vulgarity of an attack.

De Beaumirail, as 'Mr Dacre', is careful to insinuate this possibility of a conspiracy against her, in order to propel her into his arms. And this is precisely what happens: the outrage of a trespass from the world beyond, the social world. Thinking about the conspiracy, Laura is suddenly faced through the window with the vision of a horrific figure out in the darkness staring back at her:

> With an instinctive wish to escape from the room and accomplish her errand as quickly as might be, she hastened to the table near the window, and as if her approach had evoked it, suddenly the figure of a small, rather long-limbed man, appeared at the same large window, and laying his arm above his eyes, to shade them from the reflected light, he looked for some seconds into the room.[33]

The ambiguity of 'as if her approach had evoked it' makes it seem at first subjective, a ghost. But he is out there, waiting for her. Somehow, the fact that he can't see her, and the way he shades his eyes, makes him even more sinister. It's a kind of blind man's buff.

Police report meets Gothic romance here. This sinister figure is straight out of a novel, but he is indeed waiting for her, because there really is a conspiracy, orchestrated by her friend 'Mr Dacre' who is inside the house at this moment, and is the real 'enemy within'.

Le Fanu, however, is not content with mere subtlety: he forces the issue of 'the Other', in the rhetorical expansion of this uncanny moment, and we see the combination of the anti-Semitism and the Neo-Darwinism of this text emerge, alongside its Gothic:

> The light coming from behind touched his face oddly. The outlines of the figure were apish, and there was, well as she could see, something sinister, which stared into the room with great eyeballs and a gaping mouth.
>
> She stood quite motionless, and chill, as if she saw a ghost. She could not tell whether this man, with his face close to the glass, and his features distorted by the faint odd light and deep shadow, saw her or not. One thing she felt – that he might be one of those persecuting agents who were spying out all her ways, and weaving about her a new, with what object or how much malignity she could not guess.[34]

The 'gaping mouth' takes us back to Madame de la Rougierre in *Silas*. A moment later, Laura stares over the bannisters and she sees the hall-door partly open. He steps in, 'peering jealously round him as he did' (I, 225).

Semi-hallucinated as it is, the reader knows perfectly well that this is a (Gothicised) portrait of the Jew, Mr Levi. The implication is rather similar to the picture of Hyde in Stevenson's classic. It is pure Lombroso: the invading Jew is an atavistic regression.[35] Later, when she interrogates the servant who answered the door to him, Laura receives the servant's version of him, which again emphasises this notion of regression to a lower form of life:

> When Miss Gray came down she questioned the servant who had opened the door to the unknown visitor of last night. When did he come? A few minutes before Mr Dacre left. Did he know or ring at the door; or how was it? He came with a postman's knock. Would the servant know him again? Yes, he was a low-sized, vicious-looking little wasp of a Jew. ... That was the narrative.[36]

The picture is carefully put down to the violent prejudice of a servant, but it is corroborative. What Laura misses here, is the significance of the association with 'Mr Dacre' who she thinks at this point is on her side. In fact, it's a set-up, and Laura has just dismissed her real friend, good old faithful Cousin Charles Mannering, after a disagreement. So, she's alone to face this threat, with only 'Mr Dacre' to help her.

The invasion here by the Monstrous Other, on the level of plot, is a fake. But the contradictory implication is that it is no less *culturally* sinister for that. When we meet him later, Levi is not a monster, he is a largely, but not entirely, comic figure: an East-End Jew, quite unable to pronounce an 's' without making it 'sh', who is an adept at the science of boxing, and is coolly able to contain the desperately violent attempt to escape made by De Beaumirail. This scene is reminiscent of the sudden extraordinary outburst of violence in *Uncle Silas*, when Dudley, another adept at the science, knocks out Captain Oakley's teeth.

There is a class aspect in this anti-Semitism. In the centre of the novel, 'Mr Dacre' arranges for Laura and Julia Wardell to visit a synagogue, ostensibly to listen to the singing, but in reality to 'identify' Mr Levi as a 'co-conspirator' with his alter ego, de Beaumirail, thus distracting her and gaining himself credit. On that visit, Laura relishes the 'Oriental seclusion of the lattice', occupying the position of a woman behind a grille, finding herself able to see but unable to be seen – a charade, since 'Dacre' has pre-arranged it all – and at first she thinks of the music as sublime. Mr Levi, it turns out, is a sullen little tenor and she recognises him, as she is meant to. The music immediately loses its sublimity for her and becomes a Gothic masquerade:

> Henceforward the vocal music, rich in harmony, finer still in the quality of the voices that mingled in it, had ceased to enchant her. Like sweet and solemn music heard through a terrible dream, it confused her sensations, but her spirit no longer took part in it. She could think of nothing but the chance of again seeing, and with more certain observation, that odious face which she was so nearly certain she recognised.
>
> Now, again, the chanting was suspended. The reader and his choir returned in the same order to their former places, and as they marched slowly down this face turned fully to the gallery, she did see the face that had looked in at the study window and peered into the hall, and that pale, black-browed man, with the large sullen mouth, and the great lurid eyes, chanting the time-honoured Jewish liturgy, was actually one – perhaps the chief – of those miscreant conspirators who were persecuting her with so satanic a persistency, and had actually attempted to murder Alfred Dacre.[37]

We know that Le Fanu regretted his earlier, anti-Semitic excesses. The real nobility and sublimity of the Jewish ceremony and liturgy (and with them, the authority and purity of the Rabbi) are acknowledged, in passing, here. The vulgar upstart Mr Levi is presented as just a red-herring: for Laura he is the arch-threat, but for the reader the real conspirator is nearer home, among the Anglo-Saxon community. The attempt on Dacre's life is another fake, to give him credibility, and here Laura has exactly the reactions she is meant to have: naive 'horror' (II, 57). However, there is no doubt that the Orientalist fear is added at this point to the Gothic notion of a Monstrous Other, however self-conscious the framing process becomes, however much the plot frames Laura's visit as an extension of the 'firm's' conspiracy.

8
'Carmilla': 'I'll let you be in my dream, if I can be in yours'

The question of whose dream we are in (and whether life is 'dream' or not) is a crux in the narrative of 'Carmilla'. For the reader, the complication of this question is comparable to the difficulty felt by the reader in *Wuthering Heights*, when Cathy is crying out to Lockwood: 'Let me in!' – on what level is 'reality' supposed to be? Nina Auerbach has pointed recently to the distinctive nature of the friendship between the victim and the vampire in 'Carmilla', compared with other nineteenth-century vampire stories; she is thinking of the intense, erotically charged conventions of Victorian girls' friendships which had no need to be chaperoned. The two girls in the story 'dream the same dream at the same time'.[1] It is Laura's longing for a 'friend' or 'another half' which takes us back to Captain Walton at the beginning of *Frankenstein* and the disastrous results of that longing for the authenticating presence of the other, which Frankenstein himself is also reproducing when he determines to create his creature. Behind this, lies the whole tradition back to Aristophanes' speech in Plato's *Symposium*, and the notion that friendship is the completion of the self, that the two halves form a mirror for each other.[2]

But 'Carmilla' is also a parody of this rhetorical tradition: and the use of these tropes of idealised mutual witnessing is ironically reversed. This is a powerfully ambiguous text, which represents several taboos at once. Its major theme is 'possession', and is a development from the romances I have been discussing earlier. Lesbian seduction is famously one aspect of the theme of 'possession'; but the textual presentation of this motif, manifested on a number of levels, is inseparable from the seduction of the reader.

Superstition and truth: the reversal

The initial account of Laura's 'dream' occurs when she is six years old.
She begins by insisting that it was not a dream, though the official line
is that it was a dream. The reader is immediately placed at the centre of
the contradiction. The narrator says clearly that she 'awoke':

> I can't have been more than six years old, when one night I
> awoke ... I was vexed and insulted at finding myself, as I conceived,
> neglected, and I began to whimper, preparatory to a hearty bout of
> roaring; when to my surprise, I saw a solemn, but very pretty face
> looking at me from the side of the bed. It was that of a young lady
> who was kneeling, with her hands under the coverlet. I looked at her
> with a kind of pleased wonder, and ceased whimpering. She caressed
> me with her hands, and lay down beside me on the bed, and drew me
> towards her, smiling; I felt immediately delightfully soothed, and fell
> asleep again. I was wakened by a sensation as if two needles ran into
> my breast very deep at the same moment, and I cried loudly. The lady
> started back, with her eyes fixed on me, and then slipped down upon
> the floor, and, as I thought, hid her self under the bed.[3]

Several things are textually established at the outset. One is that the narrator is awake; and two, that she is caressed into sleep, and then bitten
by the vampire, an event which wakes her again. The child is adamant
that this is not a dream. The adults are in confusion and there is some
corroboration of the narrator's testimony inserted into the text which
the reader must absorb:

> I was not for the first time frightened, and I yelled with all my might
> and main. Nurse, nursery-maid, housekeeper, all came running in,
> and hearing my story, they made light of it, soothing me all they
> could meanwhile. But, child as I was, I could perceive that their faces
> were pale with an unwonted look of anxiety, and I saw them look
> under the bed, and about the room, and peep under the tables and
> pluck open cupboards; and the housekeeper whispered to the nurse:
> 'Lay your hand along that hollow in the bed; some one *did* lie there,
> so sure as you did not; the place is still warm.'[4]

These people are servants, and servants are superstitious (with good reason, in this area), so the reader is invited to hold two contrary things in
mind at this stage. This difficulty is exacerbated by the clear contradiction

between the child's perception and the 'official' version, which we watch being created:

> I remember my father coming up and standing at the bedside, and talking cheerfully, and asking the nurse a number of questions, and laughing very heartily at one of the answers; and patting me on the shoulder and kissing me, and telling me not to be frightened, and that it was nothing but a dream and could not hurt me.
>
> But I was not comforted, for I knew the visit of the strange woman was *not* a dream; and I was *awfully* frightened.
>
> I was a little consoled by the nursery-maid's assuring me that it was she who had come and looked at me, and lain down beside me in the bed, and that I must have been half-dreaming not to have known her face. But this, though supported by the nurse, did not quite satisfy me.[5]

Truth is already deeply at stake here for the reader. Father laughs 'very heartily at one of the answers' – presumably the 'superstitious' account, which we think is the truth. The nursery-maid is lying when she says it is she who lay on the bed. The nurse's initial counter-testimony to the official line has also been 'adjusted' as the quasi-legal evidentiary term 'supported' suggests here. But we suspect that pressure has been brought to bear in this denial of her former 'superstitious' testimony. So the whole drama of this incident takes place in the language of testimony, and the reader, drawn by a kind of three-dimensional irony into the corroborative net, is aligned on the child's side against the grown-ups.

The only thing that puts Laura's fears to rest is the priest in his black cassock. Who has called him, we don't know; perhaps it's the women who pray together with them. He teaches Laura a prayer which her nurse makes her include for years in her prayers. At any rate, he is the antidote to the grown-up masculine Enlightenment version of what has happened and he brings a welcome oblivion to the narrator. The scene is atmospheric as she emphasises the combination of his feminine qualities and the ancient furniture:

> I remember so well the thoughtful sweet face of that white-haired old man, in his black cassock, as he stood in that rude, lofty, brown room, with the clumsy furniture of a fashion three hundred years old about him, and the scanty light entering its atmosphere through the small lattice. He kneeled, and the three women with him, and he prayed aloud with an earnest quavering voice for, what appeared to me, a long time.[6]

The ritual is pathetic, almost comic, (the 'earnest, quavering voice') especially when we think that we, as readers, have been obliged to inhabit the position of 'superstition'; but it is communal and a secret acknowledgement of the truth which comforts the child and empties time of its pressure and crisis; and yet there is just a hint of a reversal in the metaphor with which she finishes this opening section:

> He kneeled, and the three women with him, and he prayed aloud with an earnest quavering voice for, what appeared to me, a long time. I forget all my life preceding that event, and for some time after it is all obscure also, but the scenes I have just described stand vivid as the isolated pictures of the phantasmagoria surrounded by darkness.[7]

The content of this last figurative expression is obvious. Light is truth, and darkness falsity or oblivion. The 'phantasmagoria' here stands for resurrected truth, an accurate memory of an experience. And yet the vehicle of the metaphor (the allusion to the early cinema) is that of representation, and more, illusion and fantasy; so that the reader feels the undertow of reversal, the advent of the magic mirror: it is the light which has become phantasmagoric and the darkness which is reality. The truth is that she has been bitten, and reality has already begun to reverse itself; in the mirror of Friendship, time has already begun to 'leak'.

When 'Carmilla' appears twelve years later, pitched out of the coach in a fraudulent accident, she is placed in a room in the Schloss which contains 'a sombre piece of tapestry opposite the foot of the bed, representing Cleopatra with the asp to her bosom'. This emblem of erotic suicide echoes the feeling of being bitten by the vampire, the two needles that run into the breast, which Laura has already experienced as a child. As she approaches the bed for her first encounter with the mysterious guest, Laura is plunged immediately back into the old conflict between her own interior sense of truth ('superstition') which she has clung to as a horrified memory, and the official (parental) version of reality. The text foregrounds this sense of inner eye-witness testimony. But it is Carmilla, now, who claims to have had the dream (when we know it was reality) and we watch with horror as this simple bold rhetorical strategy immediately works on Laura:

> What was it that, as I reached the bed-side and had just begun my little greeting, struck me dumb in a moment, and made me recoil a step or two from before her? I will tell you.

I saw the very face which had visited me in my childhood at night, which remained so fixed in my memory, and on which I had for so many years ruminated with horror, when no one suspected of what I was thinking.

It was pretty, even beautiful; and when I first beheld it, wore the same melancholy expression.

But this almost instantly lighted into a strange fixed smile of recognition.

There was a silence of fully a minute, and then at length *she* spoke; *I* could not.

'How wonderful!' she exclaimed, 'Twelve years ago, I saw your face in a dream, and it has haunted me ever since'.[8]

Carmilla seizes the dream, and in doing so, possesses Laura's reality. We watch the helpless Laura like watching a terrible wildlife film in which the predator mirrors the movements of the prey. The ploy is as openly fraudulent to the reader as later the ruse of the 'accident' which has brought her to Laura's gate, and the ruffianly company of solid apparitions by whom she is surrounded like film 'extras'. This however is epistemological mesmerism, not simply physical: the reader, too, cannot escape the paradox of the mirror. The 'strange, fixed smile of recognition' is very dangerous, but ironically it relaxes, as Laura, though still trying to preserve the dignity of a posture of doubt, enters the corroborative space even as she tries to counter Carmilla's possession of it and assert her own identity:

'Wonderful indeed !' I repeated, overcoming with an effort the horror that had for a time suspended my utterances. 'Twelve years ago, in vision or reality, *I* certainly saw you. I could not forget your face. It has remained before my eyes ever since.'

Her smile had softened. Whatever I had fancied strange in it was gone, and it and her dimpling cheeks were now delightfully pretty and intelligent.[9]

If we look at the structure of the two utterances. Laura can only mirror Carmilla's speech now. The deadly smile relaxes because her prey is caught (she would simply get this over and done with if Laura, this reluctant Petrarchan cynosure, were a peasant girl) and we are left with the perfect camouflage, the insect mimicry, of her coy, young-girl simulacrum. The apparent scepticism of 'in vision or reality' is a touchingly frail irony, from one whose inner horror has been in conflict with outer reality for twelve years.

Laura, marvellously vulnerable to the sense of having an 'other half', the ideal of adolescent friendship, has to be persuaded finally that she is in Carmilla's dream by a process of mutual witnessing which places the reader in as difficult a position as she or he is in *Alice Through the Looking Glass*, because it implies that if both were in each other's dream, then it was reality.[10] But the mirror into which she is about to be seduced is also a reversal, a representation: as Carroll puts it, 'Live into Evil'.[11] Laura is being persuaded of this proposition and the reader is forced to watch, while desperately applying the Alice Raikes test of going *behind* the mirror-rhetoric:

> I took her hand as I spoke. I was a little shy, as lonely people are, but the situation made me eloquent, and even bold. She pressed my hand, she laid hers upon it, and her eyes glowed, as, looking hastily into mine, she smiled again, and blushed.[12]

No give-away 'Gothic' pallor here, but the perfect mimicry of shyness – 'hastily', however, is ambiguous: either it means 'shyly', or it suggests a quick check. We become aware of the doubled narrative point of view.

Carmilla then makes her main rhetorical bid for control of Laura. It works by confirming Laura's memory from a reversed or mirror-image perspective (so Laura can apparently perform the experiment of transposing it into her own remembered experience – the reader does it alongside her), and thus corroborating it. The text insists on direct speech at his point:

> She answered my welcome very prettily. I sat down beside her, still wondering; and she said:
> 'I must tell you my vision about you; it is so very strange that you and I should have had, each of the other so vivid a dream, that each should have seen, I you and you me, looking as we do now, when of course we were mere children. I was a child, about six years old, and I awoke from a confused and troubled dream, and found myself in a room, unlike my nursery, wainscoted clumsily in some dark wood, and with cupboards, and bedsteads, and chairs and benches placed about it. The beds were, I thought, all empty, and the room itself without anyone but myself in it; and I, after looking about me for some time, and admiring especially an iron candlestick, with two branches, which I should certainly know again, crept under one of the beds to reach the window; but as I got from under the bed, I heard someone crying; and looking up, while I was upon my knees, I saw *you* – as I see you now; a beautiful young lady with golden hair and

large blue eyes, and lips – your lips – you, as you are here. Your looks won me; I climbed on the bed and put my arms about you, and I think we both fell asleep. I was aroused by a scream; you were sitting up screaming. I was frightened, and slipped down upon the ground, and, it seemed to me, lost consciousness for a moment; and when I came to myself I was again in my nursery at home. Your face I have never forgotten since. I could not be misled by mere resemblance. You *are* the lady whom I then saw.'[13]

The speech traps both character and reader who listen to it. But the reader naturally tries to gain a point of vantage. To understand the irony of the text, we must see that this speech is a pack of lies from beginning to end. The reason why Carmilla is so convincing in her testimony about the details – and this challenge is presented with deliberate legalism to character *and* reader – is that she was *there*, not that she dreamt it. It presents reality as fake dream, mimicked from Laura's own actual reactions, and positions it as a corroboration of what Laura herself saw and felt. In fact it *is* what she saw and felt, observed, selected, and then simply reversed: so Carmilla reveals that she was a child of six in *her* dream, and Laura was a young woman as she is now, the exact reversal of what Laura herself saw.

There is a point of slippage: the reader leaps into the gap opened up by the sudden surge of speech ('I saw *you* – most assuredly you – as I see you now; a beautiful young lady, with golden hair and large blue eyes, and lips – your lips – you, as you are here ...'). The corroborative insistence on Laura's identity fails to conceal the oddity of this – the fact that Carmilla can't resist the rush of flattery and erotic suggestion, even as she confirms Laura's identity to her. She is almost too hasty and takes a perceptible risk. She is genuinely distracted for a second by the oral; and threatens for a moment the polished mirror she has created in which to reflect Laura to herself. Later we learn that it is the lips which cause the small mark which vampires make on the breast of their victims. Hence the irony of 'I could not be misled by mere resemblance'. Laura is not a resemblance at all; it is Carmilla who resembles her.

The trap for the reader is that in order to 'see through' Carmilla's speech like this, and reverse its testimony, we are forced to accept her vampire existence as 'reality'. Otherwise we couldn't expose her testimony as lies. (We cry: 'Don't listen to her: six indeed ! Carmilla is least as old as 1698 ... .')

Laura is now well and truly caught in the mechanism of mutual corroboration. She now calls what she spent her childhood insisting was not a dream 'my corresponding vision'. What we get is Carmilla's brilliantly fake reaction, again simply mimicking back Laura's own feelings, building on the 'correspondence', which now consolidates 'a right to your intimacy':

> It was now my turn to relate my corresponding vision, which I did, to the undisguised wonder of my new acquaintance.
>
> 'I don't know which should be most afraid of the other,' she said, again smiling – 'If you were less pretty I think I should be very much afraid of you, but being as you are, and you and I both so young, I feel only that I have made your acquaintance twelve years ago, and have already a right to your intimacy; at all events it does seem as if we were destined, from our earliest childhood, to be friends. I wonder whether you feel as strangely drawn towards me as I do to you; I have never had a friend – shall I find one now?' She sighed, and her fine dark eyes gazed passionately on me.[14]

This last sigh and gaze are indeed hard to resist. It is brilliant theatre, especially the idea of 'Carmilla' being 'afraid' of Laura – her mirror-mimickry here almost revealing that she herself is not as pretty as she seems (as Laura herself has once or twice implied with hindsight). And the idea that they dreamed each other before they met is of course the traditional Platonic 'affinity' of romantic friendship which we can regard as persuasive on Laura.

By the time we come to the following morning, the reversal is complete. Laura, distracted by the complex dynamics of friendship that have been built upon it, accepts the translation of her former memory, which as a six-year old she fought so stoutly against, into 'dream':

> Next day came and we met again. I was delighted with my companion; that is to say, in many respects.
>
> Her looks lost nothing in daylight – she was certainly the most beautiful creature I had ever seen, and the unpleasant remembrance of the face presented in my early dream, had lost the effect of the first unexpected recognition.
>
> She confessed that she had experienced a similar shock on seeing me, and precisely the same faint antipathy that had mingled with my admiration of her. We now laughed together over our momentary horrors.[15]

We are given some indication of a double focus in the narration here: throughout the scene Laura takes us to the limit of what she couldn't understand at the time and suggests that there was a level on which she couldn't yet accept Carmilla as a friend. But, as the irony of the last paragraph's perfect camouflage suggests, Laura herself has passed into the mirror now; she has colluded in the process of converting her own past, her own memory, into 'dream', a phantasmagoria, a representation of itself, through Carmilla's fraudulent use of the 'mirror' of mutual witnessing.

The anguine line

The reader's position in this is caught between narrative and text; and tainted by the discomfort of paradox. We have to systematically reverse the story's rhetoric, because it is a kind of insect mimicry. We are watching the gradual installation of the parasite within the host. Carmilla is a mimic human being, who, we begin to suspect, can only carry out two or three actions, perfectly adapted to the particular prey-in-hand.

There is an interesting prototype of this kind of effect in a story which Le Fanu published in 1851 called 'The Evil Guest', in which the impersonal narrator's voice performs that reversal for us:

> The young Frenchwoman rose, with downcast eyes and a happy, dimpling smile; and, as Mrs Marston drew her affectionately toward her, and kissed her, she timidly returned the embrace of her kind patroness. For a moment her graceful arms encircled her, and she whispered to her, 'Dear madame, how happy – how very happy you make me.'
>
> Had Ithuriel touched with his spear the beautiful young woman, thus for a moment, as it seemed, lost in a trance of gratitude and love, would that angelic form have stood the test unscathed ? A spectator, marking the scene, might have observed a strange gleam in her eyes – a strange expression in her face – an influence, for a moment, *not* angelic, like an shadow of some passing spirit, cross her visibly, as she leaned over the gentle lady's neck, and murmured, 'Dear madame, how happy – how very happy you make me.' Such a spectator, as he looked at that gentle lady, might have seen, for one dreamy moment, a lithe and painted serpent, coiled round and round, and hissing in her ear.[16]

Here we can see the way Carmilla is developed out of the stock type of the hypocrite. Madamoiselle de Barras is a seducer, but a betrayer, who is treating this relationship purely instrumentally to get at depressed, unconfident Mrs Marston's husband: she is an adultress, not a lesbian. But the point is, she is psychopathically cold and 'anguine'. Carmilla belongs to the anguine line: this is the pathos of Laura's realisation: that what the isolated girl thinks of as warm and close and self-confirming – a true acknowledgement of her self – is merely cold and dead. What Laura longs for above all is candour: transparent self-revelation from the other, as she gives it herself.

The Anguine Line develops alongside the Two Brothers Plot in Le Fanu. The theatrical character of the Hypocrite, as we have seen, has become the unconscious hypocrite, an impossible state of self-division; here it becomes a language for the representation of the obsessively secret desire to possess at all costs, including that of life itself. Laura, like Mrs Marston, mistakes this behaviour for what she thinks of as love. Unlike Mlle de Barras, Carmilla refers teasingly in riddles to the savage nature of her own passion, hovering on the edge of self-revelation, which she knows would ruin everything, so converting it to another set of seductive invitations. She uses the Gothic romance metaphor of the 'anchorite' to describe her rejection of the world, in the perfect egotism of her state:

> 'But I am under vows, no nun half so awfully, and I dare not tell my story yet, even to you. The time is very near when you shall know everything. You will think me cruel, very selfish, but love is always selfish; the more ardent the more selfish. How jealous I am you cannot know. You must come with me, loving me, to death; or else hate me, and still come with me, and *hating* me through death and after. There is no such word as indifference in my apathetic nature.'
>
> 'Now, Carmilla, you are going to talk your wild nonsense again,' I said hastily.[17]

Protagonist Laura (unlike narrator Laura) doesn't understand a word, is afraid of this sort of talk. Le Fanu dramatises these emotions again in his last novel, *Willing To Die*, in which the female narrator, Ethel Ware – a kind of Laura who does understand what this means – declares herself an anchorite, and 'willing to die', for her own obsessive love of Richard Marston, the villain who has betrayed and attempted to destroy her.[18]

But the textual dynamics of this story are much more subtle than those of 'The Evil Guest'. For the reader of 'Carmilla', the author is not like Milton's God who can send the angel Ithuriel to separate reality from illusion. The author has vanished into the frames of the story.[19]

Instead, we are left to sense the presence of another meaning in the details we are offered.

Take, for example the details of the hands. When Laura first sees her, she is kneeling by the side of the bed 'with her hands under the coverlet'. But the primal scene is with the hands *under* the coverlet, secretly caressing. Laura then mimics this action of the hands in Carmilla's hair:

> ... her hair was quite wonderful, I never saw hair so magnificently thick and long when it was down about her shoulders; I have often placed my hands under it, and laughed with wonder at its weight. It was exquisitely fine and soft, and in colour a very rich dark brown, with something of gold. I loved to let it down, tumbling with its own weight, as, in her room, she lay back in her chair talking in her sweet low voice, I used to fold and braid it, and spread it out and play with it. Heavens! If I had but known all![20]

The recoil of Laura's last cry directs us back into the symbolic trap of this sheerly mimic behaviour – the fetish of mutual hair-combing in Victorian girls' friendships – becomes sinister, not simply because it is code for the erotic; if this final exclamation is, as it appears, an anthropomorphic cry, we must no doubt think of the blood of all the young women which has nourished this body and given this hair its weight and colour, its fascination to the hands, even as Laura touches it. The obvious other connotation is the age-old snare of Arachne's web celebrated by Elizabethan poets, and revived in the uncanny story of Stoker, 'The Secret of the Growing Gold', in which the ideal of Anglo-Saxon beauty, the blue-eyed long-haired girl (a type which Laura conforms to, despite her mixed blood) is made uncanny, because her hair goes on growing after death up through the pavement under which she is buried with terrifying hideous vigour, and all the cultural and erotic associations of beauty's Anglo-Saxon stereotype are reversed.

The concealment of the hands then passes back to Carmilla. They are discussing *her* first attack in which she was 'all but assassinated in my bed, wounded *here*,' she touched her breast, 'and never was the same since.':

> 'Were you near dying?'
> 'Yes, very – a cruel love – strange love, that would have taken my life. Love will have its sacrifices. No sacrifice without blood. Let us go to sleep now; I feel so lazy. How can I get up just now and lock my door?

She was lying *with her tiny hands buried in her rich wavy hair, under her cheek*, her little head upon the pillow, and her glittering eyes followed me wherever I moved, with a kind of shy smile which I could not decipher. (my Italics)[21]

The mimicry is clear in the strange repeated stress on the concealment of the hands and the richness of the hair. The initial proof of her really having been there offered by the nurse is by touch: 'Lay your hand along that hollow in the bed; someone *did* lie there, so sure as you did not ...' (247) and it is precisely this 'true' use of the hand which is subverted by Carmilla.

The true nature of the hand, however, is revealed at the end in the encounter between Carmilla and the General Baron, as the mimic mirror shatters and all glimpse the nature of the creature. It is narrated from the point of view of the lonely, still partly infatuated Laura, and the insistence on the 'cynical and ghastly fancy' of the Gothic carving above the doorway frames the image of Carmilla *as* an image, when she enters the shadowy chapel:

Under a narrow, arched doorway, surmounted by one of those demoniacal grotesqes in which the cynical and ghastly fancy of old Gothic carving delights, I saw very gladly the beautiful face and figure of Carmilla enter the shadowy chapel.

I was just about to rise and speak, and nodded smiling, in answer to her peculiarly engaging smile; when with a cry, the old man by my side caught up the woodman's hatchet, and started forward. On seeing him a brutalized change came over her features. It was an instantaneous and horrible transformation, as she made a crouching step backwards. Before I could utter a scream, he struck at her with all his force, but she dived under his blow, and unscathed, caught him in her tiny grasp by the wrist. He struggled for a moment to release his arm, but the hand opened, the axe fell to the ground, and the girl was gone.[22]

Here the hand shoots out of the mirror to grasp the General's wrist and leave *his* hand numb, perhaps for ever: the touch of the two limbs an emblem of contact between reality and unreality. One of the last details which Baron Vordenburg reveals is that the *real* hand which defeats the hand of the 'oupire' is a form of destiny (perhaps Providence) whose medium is writing. His ancestor, the 'passionate and favoured lover of Mircalla', the original Moravian nobleman, having concealed her tomb, was possessed by horror, and, as a result, left written indications of its whereabouts:

> 'He made the tracings and notes which have guided me to the very spot, and drew up a confession of the deception that he had practised. If he had intended any further action in this matter, death prevented him; and the *hand of a remote descendant* has, too late for many, directed the pursuit to the lair of the beast.'
>
> We talked a little more, and among other things he said was this:
>
> 'One sign of the vampire is the power of the hand. The slender hand of Mircalla closed like a vice of steel on the general's wrist when he raised the hatchet to strike. But its power is not confined to its grasp; it leaves a numbness in the limb it seizes, which is slowly, if ever, recovered from.'[23]

Here are the true and false 'hands' textually juxtaposed and distinguished in a final reversal. The hand that reveals itself in true testimony (confession) is a pun (on writing, i.e. representation): the concealed hand of Mircalla has only a single material sense. This plot is the reverse of *Wylder's Hand*. There, the physical survival of the hand from the grave refuted fake writing. Here, the medium of writing is orthodox: it 'points' beyond the grave – the metaphor is of a true and providential resurrection – and reclaims time from undead seriality in a mirror-world of mimicry. But the little mark of scepticism is also telling: the sign comes too late for many.

Enlightenment: natural history and the monstrous

I've been using terms from natural history as metaphors in the above discussion, which may strike one as an unhistorical and 'modern' superimposition, but I don't think it is. First published in the late 1860s, this particular story inserts itself into a climate in which the debates about Darwinism and the pressure on the Protestant Establishment were at their height. Indeed, as we have seen, Alfred Dacre's speculations about sexuality in *Haunted Lives* are purely Darwinian. But there is an interesting deflection of the question of natural history, because the action of 'Carmilla' is set back into the pre-Darwinian period at the end of the eighteenth century. This is a characteristic double-take on Le Fanu's part; backdating is complex (for Victorian readers, too) because it immediately gives a double reflex – it presents the 1790s to the 1870s, the Enlightenment period of the philosophes to the era of *The Descent of Man*.

We know that Carmilla is a shape-changer, and this idea has a place in Swedenborg's thinking about 'spirits'.[24] She anticipates Val Lewton's *Cat People*, which is the nearest thing I can think of in feeling to her particular menace. But Carmilla is only 'figured' (by the terrified perceptions of Laura) as a black cat:

> But I soon saw that it was a sooty-black animal that resembled a monstrous cat. It appeared to me about four or five feet long, for it measured fully the length of the hearth-rug as it passed over; and it continued toing and froing with the lithe sinister restlessness of a beast in a cage. I could not cry out, although as you may suppose, I was terrified. Its pace was growing faster, and the room rapidly darker and darker, and at length so dark that I could no longer see anything of it but its eyes. I felt it spring lightly on to the bed. The two broad eyes approached my face, and suddenly I felt a stinging pain as if two large needles darted, an inch or two apart, deep into my breast. I waked with a scream.[25]

Having been persuaded, as we have seen, that her earlier experience was a 'dream', Laura's perceptions of the animal resembling a cat are also in what is now firmly (to her, i.e. protagonist-Laura) a dream, and the cat seems metonymically to darken the chamber to its own colour until she can no longer see it. She sees the glowing eyes of something. She then 'feels' something spring lightly on to the bed and the pain 'wakes' her when she sees Carmilla in what appears to be her 'real' form.

Le Fanu uses the form of a double telling, as he does so often in his shorter fiction, which acts out the legal form of attestation. General Spielsdorf, whose corroborative testimony reveals to Laura's ineffectual father the danger that Laura is in, and who has not been bitten, sees this 'figure' in a much more abstract form when it attacks his niece:

> I saw a large black object, very ill-defined, crawl, as it seemed to me, over the foot of the bed, and swiftly spread itself up to the poor girl's throat, where it swelled, in a moment, into a great palpitating mass.[26]

This is much more horrible and reveals Laura's corrupted version of what attacks her to be an anthropomorphic semblance. General Spielsdorf is in no doubt of his own reality and the reality of the thing attacking his ward, Bertha. Here we get the sense of a nameless, shapeless black mass 'palpitating' at the throat, almost like a time-lapse sequence of a huge swelling external cancer.

He sees it as a 'black creature which suddenly contracted toward the foot of the bed' (311) but it's an indeterminate form, nothing so homely as a black panther. Again, the corroborative logic determines the course of the horror: what the reader is invited to do is compare this with Laura's version of the experience, and although there are powerful similarities, there are differences of stress here, which make us look again at the transparency of the I-narration.

The thread through all this equivocation about animal form is the question of whether the vampire is or is not a part of the natural world. This debate is explicit in the text. Hesselius's editor in his note at the beginning of the story quotes tantalisingly from the learned Doctor's notes on it which describe it as 'involving, not improbably, some of the profoundest arcana of our dual existence, and its intermediates'. This last crucial qualification is often taken to be a reference to Swedenborg's *Arcana Coelestia* and it's certainly true that Swedenborg's philosophy is a machine for eroding the distinction between the spiritual and the material. Spirits for him often take the form of animals (fera). But I want to add to this: the idea of the 'intermediates' of our dual existence has another, quite different function in the story, and this meaning is a part of Enlightenment discourse about natural history and the concomitant question for people at both points of the historical spectrum straddled by the tale's backdating, the question of religious belief.

Carmilla is also represented persistently as a kind of fish in this text. The allusions to natural history intensify with the entry of the hunchback mountebank who is himself a living allegory of an 'intermediate' form:

> It was the figure of a hunchback, with the sharp lean features that generally accompany deformity. He wore a pointed black beard, and he was smiling from ear to ear, showing his white fangs. He was dressed in buff, black, and scarlet, and crossed with more straps and belts that I could count, and from which hung all manner of things. Behind, he carried a magic-lantern, and two boxes, which I well knew, in one of which was a salamander, and in the other a mandrake. These monsters used to make my father laugh. They were compounded of parts of monkeys, parrots, squirrels, fish, and hedgehogs, dried and stiched together with great neatness and startling effect. He had a fiddle, a box of conjuring apparatus, a pair of foils and masks attached to his belt, several other mysterious cases dangling about him, and a black staff with copper ferrules in his hand. His companion was a rough spare dog, that followed at his heels, but

stopped short suspiciously at the drawbridge, and in a little while began to howl dismally.[27]

This is the precise carnivalesque anti-body to Carmilla. He is as medieval as a Shakespearian fool, as grotesque and predatory as Autolychus, and as allegorical of montrosity as 'Rumour, full of tongues' is of whispering. His mongrel detects the presence of a vampire immediately and refuses, appropriately (one thinks of the mastiff in 'Christabel'), to cross the threshold. His figure makes visible the presence of monstrosity; of something that is the outside, or the opposite, of the Enlightenment grid of species-classification. Laura's father laughs again at superstition, and one is instantly chilled.

The mountebank's diagnosis is precise. He knows the left–right reversal has taken place here; that the dextra has been replaced by the sinister and he sees his commercial opportunity:

> 'Will your ladyships be pleased to buy an amulet against the oupire, which is going like the wolf, I hear, through these woods,' he said, dropping his hat on the pavement. 'They are dying of it right and left, and here is a charm that never fails; only pinned to the pillow, and you may laugh in his face.'
>
> These charms consisted of oblong slips of vellum, with cabalistic ciphers and diagrams upon them.
>
> Carmilla instantly purchased one and so did I.[28]

Carmilla buys a charm against herself, a bluff, and Laura, doomed to mimic, however real she feels the threat, follows suit. But the mountebank, staring up from the courtyard below, has now seen something about Carmilla and this provides him with an another instant commercial pitch. Here the written text imprisons us perversely (a technique used throughout) in the limitations of Laura's eye-witness testimony – sarcastically, she makes us guess at the expression on the exposed Carmilla's face:

> He was looking up, and we were smiling down upon him, amused; at least, I can answer for myself. His piercing black eye, as he looked up in our faces, seemed to detect something that fixed for a moment his curiosity:
>
> In an instant he unrolled a leather case, full of all manner of odd little steel instruments.
>
> 'See here, my lady,' he said, displaying it, and addressing me, 'I profess, among other things less useful, the art of dentistry. Plague

take the dog!' he interpolated. 'Silence, beast!' He howls so that your ladyships can scarcely hear a word. Your noble friend, the young lady at your right, has the sharpest tooth – long, thin, pointed, like an awl, like a needle; ha, ha! With my sharp and long sight, as I look up, I have seen it distinctly; now if it happens to hurt the young lady, and I think it must, here am I, here are my file, my punch, my nippers; I will make it round and blunt, if her ladyship pleases; no longer the *tooth of a fish*, but of a beautiful young lady as she is. Hey? Is the young lady displeased? Have I been too bold? Have I offended her?'[29] (my Italics)

This is a teasing sequence which puts the reader in a very interestingly helpless position. We rely on the (already corrupted) innocence of Laura. His 'mistake' is evidently no mistake, but she can only indicate this, narratively, in retrospect: unlike Laura the protagonist (not Laura the writer), he can see Carmilla as she really is. So the reader understands the irony of his 'superstitious' address to his dog: 'beast', because the dog is registering the presence of the monstrous. Is this all a mime? Let the reader examine: does the monstrous, needle-like, fish-tooth actually show itself at all, or this all part of the pedlar's tease: 'Come on show yourself – oupire! – I know you're there!'

Eventually his baiting has its effect and her aristocratic fury, which scarcely masks her bestial brutality, emerges in full feudal violence:

'How dares that mountebank insult us so? Where is your father? I shall demand redress from him. My father would have had the wretch tied up to the pump, and flogged with a cart-whip, and burnt to the bones with the castle brand'.[30]

But it's too late: she's been exposed to the reader as a sort of fish. Later she will describe the action of her memory, in recalling the first attack made on herself, 'as divers see what is going on above them, through a medium, dense, rippling, but transparent. There occurred that night what has confused the picture and made its colours faint' (277). Mirror-life is a watery affair: this is what real narcissism, i.e. when you fall into the pool and have no mirror, feels like. Fish of course are cold-blooded. Her vampire existence is also later, in the final, 'explanatory', chapter, twice referred to as 'amphibious' by Baron Vordenburg (317, 318), which is, when seen in this context, perhaps not as metaphorical as one might have assumed.

There follows a thoroughly Victorian conversation in which Laura's father, who has, throughout, been laughing at 'superstition' reveals his own weak spot. Describing the peasant reaction to another set of attacks, he plays the Enlightenment aristocrat. But, in a witty reversal, the vampire turns out to be the true rationalist: Carmilla exposes his rationalism as skin-deep:

> 'All this,' said my father, 'is strictly referable to natural causes. These poor people infect one another with their superstitions, and so repeat in imagination the images of terror that have infested their neighbours.'
> 'But that very circumstance frightens one horribly,' said Carmilla.
> 'How so?' inquired my father.
> 'I am so afraid of fancying I see such things; I think it would be as bad as reality.'
> 'We are in God's hands; nothing can happen without his permission, and all will end well for those who love Him. He is our faithful creator; He has made us all, and will take care of us.'
> 'Creator! *Nature!*' said the young lady in answer to my gentle father.
> 'And this disease that invades the country is natural. All things proceed from nature – don't they? All things in the heaven, in earth, and under the earth, act and live as nature ordains? I think so'.[31]

As so often in Le Fanu, the narrative surface, which is being held at bay anyway, slips away into another code. The Vampire is deliberately made to talk like Voltaire, contemptuously echoing the bible ('in heaven, in earth, and under the earth': Rev. 5:3) and scoffing at the hypocrisy of Christian attempts to proscribe superstition. Yet the irony in the passage is double, because Carmilla's 'fear of fancying I see such things' which perfectly articulates the silent Laura's female condition, is not felt by herself: narratively, this is another of the devil's tricks, hiding behind the cloak of 'modernity', appealing to Enlightenment doctrine. This is if one thinks of the backdated action as occurring in the later eighteenth century, say the 1790s; but if one thinks of this conversation in the context of the 1870s, then surely it refers quite directly to the most important debate of all in the Victorian period: Darwin versus the Christians. (And we get all the late Victorian fears of 'degeneration' entering the text.) Carmilla exists on both levels here: she is appealing to womanly 'sensitivity'; and then showing her hand as the hard-edged and aggressive Atheist she is, and totally impatient of male 'authority'.

It is in this context that the text makes us consider the celebrated lesbian erotics. The mirror demands sinister, left-handed beauty, live into evil. Carmilla is one of the great seducers in literature, playing on Laura's fear, and borrowing the rhetoric of the Elizabethan sonneteers, which she places in the Enlightenment context, seeing all sexuality, including perverse sexuality, as purely natural:

> 'Why does your papa like to frighten us?' said the pretty girl, with a sigh and little shudder.
>
> 'He doesn't dear 'Carmilla', it is the very furthest thing from his mind.'
>
> 'Are you afraid, dearest?'
>
> 'I should be very much if I fancied there was any real danger of my being attacked as those poor people were.'
>
> 'You are afraid to die?'
>
> 'Yes, every one is.'
>
> 'But to die as lovers may – to die together, so that they may live together. Girls are caterpillars while they live in the world, to be finally butterflies when the summer comes; but in the meantime there are grubs and larvae, don't you see – each with their peculiar propensities, necessities and structure. So says Monsieur Buffon, in his big book, in the next room.' (271)

This is a profane parody of Christian paradox ('to die together, so that they may live together'). 'Die' becomes a double-entendre here, couched in a romantic *Liebestod*: the conversation takes place with Carmilla's arm passed lovingly round Laura's waist, as she titillates her fear in order to allay it. She speaks of the mutual ecstasy of orgasm, but orgasm then, in a reminiscence of baroque literalism, becomes an analogy for natural death, as a stage like adolescence, from which you awake transformed. Predation is glossed over: in this rhetoric, all is mutual. She passes seamlessly on, appropriating the Greek idea of the soul (psyche) on the way, and re-literalising it as natural history, ruthlessly cleansing it of its Christian connotations ('caterpillars' into 'grubs and larvae'). Nothing is more 'natural' than the apparently 'monstrous'.

One familiar context for making sense of the elements of this speech is Swedenborgianism which is a kind of natural history of the soul. Swedenborg was brought up as a scientist at the court of Queen Christiana of Sweden. Le Fanu uses him in *Silas* as a vehicle of chiaroscuro, the spectralising of perception; and the reverse, a study of the way obsessions can get out of your mind and assume material form. Carmilla is a Swedenborgian demon, who denies the conventional boundaries of matter and spirit. However, it's not Swedenborg but a different figure, Buffon, who is explicitly invoked here, and the overt, scientific tradition of natural history, rather than its occult shadow. Even in the eighteenth century, the time of the narrative, Buffon was a symbol of the Enlightenment, an aristocrat and colleague of Diderot and Voltaire, whose 'big book', as 'Carmilla' refers to the great *Natural History*, spoke openly of sexuality in man and animals and was an object of opposition by the Church, so much so that Buffon, like Galileo, was forced to make an accommodation, the degree of whose sincerity is still a source of debate among scholars. Later, the natural history, bowdlerised for the young, became a favourite Victorian picture book. Darwin said that Buffon was his forerunner.

But just as the empiricist Bacon's desire to catalogue the monstrosities of nature became notorious, so Buffon too has an ambiguous reputation. One sees the Sadeian side of the Enlightenment emerging and the possibility of a prurient readership with it. Here is how a couple of authoritative recent commentators describe it:

> The customs of others are of interest only to the man who considers his own customs to be relative, not, in most cases, absolute norms from which all others have degenerated. Buffon felt, therefore, only too often a need to sustain his readers' interest by presenting the most exotic and "colorful" details he could find, and many sections of the *Histoire Naturelle de l'Homme* are consequently little more than catalogues of marvels and horrors. Reports, authenticiated or unathenticated of human monsters, ... All the varieties of sexual mutilation, were exhaustively categoried; "One can imagine nothing bizarre or absurd of this nature," Buffon assured his readers, "that men somewhere have not put into practice, either through passion, or through superstition."[32]

Under the category 'monstres par renversement ou fausse position des parties' he discusses among others, for example, the case of M. Mery in 1688 in the royal 'hotel' of les Invalides whose internal organs were all reversed: 'celles qui, dans l'ordre commun de la nature occupent le côté droit étant situées au côté gauche, et celles du côté gauche l'étant au droit'.[33]

This sequence of the narrative finishes with Laura's father's shallow scoffing again at 'superstition'. The subject of the males' conversation is not given, as usual, but the text treats it ironically. The doctor is the effeminate, urban type – modern, and civilised, and he has spoken seriously of the oupire:

> Later in the day the doctor came and was closeted with papa for some time. He was a skilful man, of sixty and upwards. He wore powder, and shaved his pale face as smooth as a pumpkin. He and papa

emerged from the room together, and I heard papa laugh, and say as they came out:

'Well I do wonder at a wise man like you. What do you say to hip-pogriffs and dragons?'

'The doctor was smiling, and made answer, shaking his head –

'Nevertheless life and death are mysterious states, and we know lit-tle of the resources of either.'

And so they walked on, and and I heard no more. I did not then know what the doctor had been broaching, but I think I guess it now.[34]

The 'amphibious' is outside Father's ken, even though it's right there in front of him: he persists in his pyrronhism, baiting the doctor as a man of science, applying the dichotomous grid of classification between the human and the animal, between reason and unreason, which had already become scientifically discredited as a shield for Christianity when this story was published. So the reader's inability to inhabit Laura's father's position is reinforced again here. The last coy remark from Laura sets her writerly self against the limited point of view of the eye-witness, only to conceal from the reader the revelation of what the 'guess' is.

Representation and death: the parody of 'development'

Live is Evil. Passing into the mirror is linked to a self-conscious focus on representation throughout the story – the loss of 'substance'. But it's allegorical: not a kind of Lyotardism or Baudrillardism before its time. The vampire vanishes into protective anagrams as a kind of camouflage: Carmilla is Millarca; Millarca is the Mircalla of 1698, the commence-ment of the Williamite years of the Protestant settlement in Ireland. When General Spielsdorf is told about the portrait of Millarca painted in 1698, and asked if he would like to see it, he declines, saying that there is no need – he believes he has 'seen the original' (306). This is presented as a paradox in the text. In one sense he is right, another wrong: there is no original. The original survived the portrait, just as Uncle Silas does. The Karnsteins repeat the sterile genealogy of a landowning class, which is nothing more than a heritage of suicide, destroying itself by preying upon the peasantry and then suicidally upon itself. In fact the whole blood-line has committed suicide, and stolen its own future. It is a con-spiracy to substitute repetition for development.[35]

The blood-line of the Karnsteins is a closed loop: the whole thing has descended through the mother's blood and the daughters are related through the maternal line. Both Carmilla herself and Laura have the same blood, because Laura's mother was a Karnstein. When we meet the mirror-image story of General Spielsdorf, which extends the principle of corroboration into a whole narrative sequence, we learn that his deceased wife is a relative of Laura's deceased mother – she too is 'maternally descended from the Karnsteins' – which makes Spieldorf's story of Bertha only a serial variation of Laura's own first-hand testimony. Bertha Rheinfeld, General Spielsdorf's 'ward', and the victim before Laura, may be the daughter of his wife's sister, rather than his own or his brother's sister. If this were true, there would be consanguinity between the victims and the vampire in each 'case' that is not an attack on the peasants. This becomes explicit when Laura discusses the portrait with Carmilla: Father tries in vain to pay her a compliment, but she's not listening:

> The young lady did not acknowledge this pretty speech, did not seem to hear it. She was leaning back in her seat, her fine eyes under their long lashes gazing on me in contemplation, and she smiled in a kind of rapture.
>
> 'And now you can read quite plainly the name that is written in the corner. it is not Marcia; it looks as if it was done in gold. The name is Mircalla, Countess Karnstein, and this is a little coronet over it, and underneath AD 1698. I am descended from the Karnsteins; that is, mamma was.'
>
> 'Ah!' said the lady, languidly, 'so am I, I think, a very long descent, very ancient. Are there any Karnsteins living now?'
>
> 'None who bear the name, I believe. The family were ruined, I believe, in some civil wars long ago, but the ruins of the castle are only about three miles away.'
>
> 'How interesting,' she said, languidly.[36]

This is very teasing: Laura's point of view is at its most formal and apparently knowing here, even calling Carmilla 'the lady' at one point, as if she were much older, even though she has begun by calling her the 'young lady'. Is this sarcasm, or because she wishes to stress something older in the way Carmilla speaks? Carmilla is at her most dangerous when she is 'languid' – she appears erotic, but the vampire is also seeking information about further prey – further Karnstein blood. The name has been lost, but the blood remains, flowing through the maternal line in various lateral branches. Le Fanu's earlier social allegory of the corrupt legacy of the Williamite period peeps out here, grafted on to the vampire genealogy in Laura's innocent reference to the 'civil wars'.

Blood flows in a loop, not a line: Carmilla is her own mother and all the other mothers that stretch back to the *ur*-suicide, the demon who haunted the first mother. At the very beginning, the lineage passed into a kind of dream of itself. The genealogy is a matriarchal nightmare; that is, the action of the story we read is the bad dream of an *ur*-Mother, acted out through its agent-daughters. The text acts out a terrifying, suffocating aspect of Virginia Woolf's: 'We think back through our mothers.' This is, I think, the only way to explain the puzzling scene in the pivotal chapter 'Descending' (i.e. into 'Avernus' or Hades), in which we find the following passage in Laura's account of her dreams as she wades across a kind of physiological Styx:

> Certain vague and strange sensations visited me in my sleep. The pre-vailing one was of that pleasant, peculiar, cold thrill which we feel in bathing, when we move against the current of a river. This was soon accompanied by dreams that seemed interminable, and were so vague that I could never recollect their scenery and persons, or any one connected portion of their action. But they left an awful impres-sion, and a sense of exhaustion, as if I had passed through a long period of great mental exertion and danger. After all these dreams there remained on waking a remembrance of having been in a place very nearly dark, and of having spoken to people I could not see; and especially of one clear voice, of a female's, very deep, that spoke as if at a distance, slowly, and producing always the same sensation of indescribable solemnity and fear.[37]

This voice is not presented as if it were Carmilla's voice. This is the voice of the *ur*-Karnstein-Mother, the original sinner and suicide, who takes the form of a demonically furious black woman, the director of the other demoniac 'movie-extras' in the 'coach accident', founder of this nightmare parody of a lineage, who ultimately possesses the dream in which both 'Carmilla' and Laura now exist. They are her agents.[38]

Hence the reversed point of view from which this scene is narrated. Laura clearly no longer owns her own 'dreams': of course, they are not 'dreams'. As the blood flows steadily and slowly out of her, she appears to herself to be merely dreaming. But there is still a struggle going on for ownership of 'the dream':

> I am going to tell you now of a dream that led immediately to an odd discovery.

One night, instead of the voice I was accustomed to hear in the dark, I heard one, sweet and tender, and at the same time terrible, which said, 'Your mother warns you to beware of the assassin.' At the same time a light unexpectedly sprang up, and I saw Carmilla, standing, near the foot of my bed, in her white nightdress, bathed from her chin to her feet, in one great stain of blood.

I wakened with a shriek, *possessed with the one idea that Carmilla was being murdered.*[39] (my Italics)

This is a brilliant stroke: dream and reality are systematically reversed in Laura's point of view. Even the warning which comes from (a real memory of?) her own deceased mother (a Karnstein, but not bitten) tears aside the sham curtain of the spell to reveal Carmilla's activity as it really is – even this – which will have one type of reader momentarily cheering – is misread by Laura's 'fallen' point of view, because she has been seduced into abandoning her own self, 'possessed' by the idea that Carmilla is the one who is really frail and in danger.

Postscript

One of Le Fanu's obsessive narrative motifs is the picture that gets down out of its frame; a moment of profane resurrection, since to be a representation, to be framed, is to be dead. Profane resurrection – revenancy – is the religious theme of Le Fanu's works – the master-trope of his narratives – the thing that makes him Gothic. But for him this Gothic motif is a formal principle which describes the act of reading: the imagination itself is a form of resurrection. It brings before the 'superstitious' eyes of the reader a set of significations which challenge and stimulate what *The Purcell Papers* refers to as 'the precious gift of credulity', often expressed as profound unease, or even horror, while remaining as textual (i.e. framed, dead) as the marks of paint upon a canvas.

For Le Fanu, from the outset, a story thus has two levels – the narrative (resurrected) and the textual (dead). Ethel Ware, at the beginning of his last novel, is careful to distinguish two types of rhetoric: her role as a first-person witness from her management of the 'historical' text of her story:

> What I have learned from others, and did not witness, that which I narrate, in part, from the hints of living witnesses, and, in part, conjecturally, I shall record in the historic third person; and I shall write it down with as much confidence and particularity as if I had actually seen it; in that respect in imitation, I believe, of all great historians, modern and ancient. But the scenes in which I have been an actor, that which my eyes have seen and my ears heard, I will relate accordingly.[1]

The convention of omniscience, for Ethel, is necessary but a remote fiction. It is the textual frame. The real, 'inner' narrative is the act of live witnessing. The adapted Calvinism of this strange writer means that the past – however, traumatic, buried, or remote the events in which it is shrouded – never goes away. But to achieve life again it must be witnessed. It needs an epiphanic, not a historical form. The analogy is with the last judgement. Yet clearly, those events can never be present in the same sense. A narrative of those events thus presents a puzzle: they are 'called up', summoned by a witness, or, more often, a chain of witnesses, often piecemeal. The reader is the implied final witness, judge and jury, in this process of resurrection or re-presentation, which often, in practice, takes the form of the textualising of oral testimony. The text implies a space between itself and a reader. Its own provenance, and process of its transmission to a reader, its very means of textuality, is an integral part of its subject matter; as above, it forms a kind of tableau which is added to the process of reading and which inevitably conditions it. The text itself is thus layered, fissured, framed. So the origin of the text – a narrative, but perhaps a spoken one – is often worked (narratively) into its textual existence, as we scan that text – either through an outer (paratextual) frame, a series of (intratextual) narrators, a running allusion to another (intertextual) form of representation or through the split nature of the narrative voice (between conventional (i.e. fictional) omniscience, and first-hand witnessing. It is these chiaroscuro spaces, where narrative and text tease each other's limits, and the boundaries between truth and fiction are crossed, which this book has been committed to enter.

By these means, Le Fanu's narratives are held at bay (stylised, forbidden mimetic force) by their very textuality. The reader's 'superstition' (fear of the gods of meaning), invited, mocked, diverted, parodied, is intensely aroused and as intensely disconfirmed, by these textual operations. The condition of reading is to be 'all in the dark' (one of Le Fanu's favourite phrases, and the title of a late hybrid novel) until the reader receives, through a peephole generated by the overlap of intersecting frames, an 'image', the palingenesis of a narrative. 'Darkness', for Le Fanu, is a complex term: it connotes 'secrecy', 'conspiracy', 'ignorance', 'barbarism', 'violence', 'horror', 'superstition', 'portentousness' and even 'allegory' or anything that has a secret meaning, after Edmund Spenser's description of his poem *The Faerie Queene* as a 'continued allegory or darke conceit'. As we have seen, it is also present in another title: 'In a Glass Darkly', which twists St Paul's metaphor for the nature of perception after death, that we shall see 'through a glass darkly', converting 'glass' to 'mirror' and trapping us on this side of it.

Above all, 'darkness', with shades of all these senses, is the readerly condition. In this condition we are like children, peasants, prehistoric creatures, anchorites, or anyone at the fantasmagoria in the Strand: we are possessed by unregenerate curiosity and expectation, 'the secret lust of human souls', as Maud refers to it. But we can only receive a narrative, finally, through a text; we are simultaneously (like Milton's readers in *Paradise Lost*) adult, and 'fallen' readers, both products of, and protagonists in, the story we are reading, aware of the serpent of textuality, the process of re-presentation.

It is my contention in this study that Le Fanu presents us with a quite explicit paradox, as we read him: our internalisation of the conventions and rules of narrative gives it life and movement – 'resurrects' it – while our awareness of the text *as* a text – a signifying medium – leaves it as dead as the marks on a canvas, or the blotches that make up the graphic surface of a photo. One of the pleasures of reading this author is the teasing relationship between the two wings of this paradox – a bird that produces a strange, crooked, but (for me) sublime flight. Where does the 'authority' lie, in the act of reading? Is it with the 'precious gift of credulity', or with its opposite, the textual frame, which absorbs and deadens all content into the letter – the material stratum, the fragmentation of its secret narrative of its own (and therefore our) origins? Le Fanu's pun on 'Hand', which begins in *The House by the Churchyard* and ends in 'Carmilla', straddles both these levels.

But what of the demonic in this process? What relation does Evil have to the 'darkness' of the reader's condition? We have to turn again, first, to St Paul: 'The letter killeth, the spirit giveth life.' The dead letter (*litera scripta*) is textuality; the spirit, the imagination, the 'precious gift of credulity'. But the epiphany of horror has its roots in a rebellion against the materialising force of the 'letter'. The conditions of this resurrection lie buried, stirring, within the 'perversity' of the reader's own self. Compare Roland Barthes' rebellious conflation of guilt and perversity against the letter:

> The author of these lines has always felt a deep dissatisfaction with himself at being unable to keep from making the same mistakes in retyping a text. These mistakes are commonly omissions or additions; diabolic, the letter is *too much* or *too little*; the wiliest mistake, however, and the commonest as well, is metathesis: how many times (doubtless animated by an unconscious irritation against the words which were familiar to me and of which I consequently felt myself to be a prisoner) have I not typed *sturcture* (instead of *structure*), *susbtitute* (instead of *substitute*), or *trasncription* (instead of *transcription*)? Each of these mistakes, by dint of repetition, takes on a bizarre physiognomy, personal and malevolent – it signifies to me that there is

something inside me that resists the word and punishes it by distorting it. In a way, evil begins with the word, with the intelligible series of letters.[2]

For Le Fanu, I am arguing, textuality represents the 'fallen', post-Enlightenment default position – its automatic (conditioned) habit of doubt panders to our sense of truth and authority. Paradoxically, this leaves the reader helpless: the perpetual satisfaction of that habit of doubt leads, by a tortuous *via negativa*, to credulity, and thus to chiaroscuro, the epiphany of horror in the dark. Narrative assimilated to testimony – the prime mover of 'resurrection' – is like Barthes' mistakes; it renders the letter momentarily evil and distorted, a distorted physiognomy, a profane, transgressive resurrection. As Lewis Carroll points out in *Through The Looking Glass*, 'live' (adjective or verb) when exposed to the mirror becomes 'evil'. Le Fanu's Gothic is that rhetorical mirror.

Notes

Introduction

1. For the political and historical sophistication of the Irish point of view on Le Fanu and his Anglo-Irish Ascendancy class, and their relations to the occult and uncanny, See W.J. McCormack, *Dissolute Characters* (Manchester, 1993); J. Moynahan, *The Anglo-Irish: The Literary Imagination in a Hyphenated Culture* (Princeton, NJ, 1995); and Roy Foster, *Paddy and Mr Punch* (London, Allen Lane, 1993). For recent work in the Gothic in historicising the Uncanny, see Terry Castle, *The Female Thermometer* (Oxford, 1995); Robert Mighall, *A Geography of Victorian Gothic Fiction* (Oxford, 1999) and Andrew Smith, *Gothic Radicalism* (Basingstoke, 1999). Landmark discussions of Victorian 'sensation fiction' which bear on the form of Le Fanu's later work, are Winifred Hughes, *The Maniac in The Cellar* (Princeton, NJ, 1980); and Patrick Brantlinger, 'What is "Sensational" about the "Sensation Novel"?', *Nineteenth Century Literature*, 1982, Vol. 37, No. 1, 1–28.
2. T. Eagleton, *Heathcliff and the Great Hunger* (London, 1995), 196.
3. See Walter C. Edens, *Joseph Sheridan Le Fanu: A Minor Victorian and his Publisher*, Unpublished PhD Thesis (Urbana, Illinois, 1963) for comment on Jewsbury, and a list of reviews in the London papers. According to this logic, Le Fanu's last novel, *Willing To Die* (1873) is often considered his weakest. I must dissent, and, though I haven't the space below to carry out the detailed textual analysis to support this judgement, I hope these chapters will provide a model for reading that novel too. It seems to me a fascinatingly knowing use of the Old Gothic, anti-Catholic convention (a response to the so-called 'Papal Aggression') which is a better novel than Wilkie Collins's *The Black Robe* (1881), on the same theme.
4. James M. Cahalan, *Great Hatred, Little Room: The Irish Historical Novel* (Dublin, 1983), 74.
5. For a refreshing re-reading of Scott's relation to the Gothic, see Fiona Robertson, *Legitimate Histories: Scott, Gothic, and the Authorities of Fiction* (Oxford, 1994).
6. For comment on the reception and politics of *Macbeth*, see the Oxford edition (1993), ed. N.S. Brooke, Introduction.
7. For a new analysis of Ainsworth's relation to Catholicism, see S. Carver, *Abnormal Literature: the Fiction of Harrison Ainsworth, 1821–1848* Unpublished PhD thesis (University of East Anglia, 2000).
8. Just as it did in the earlier eighteenth-century phase of the Old Gothic. See M. Kilgour, *The Rise of the Gothic Novel* (London, 1994), Introduction, 4–5.
9. The phrase and the sense of disappointment are Wayne Hall's, in 'Le Fanu's House by the Marketplace', *Eire-Ireland*, Vol. 21, No. 1, (1986), 55–72. But for 'female Gothic', see Alison Milbank, *Daughters of the House: Modes of Gothic in Victorian Fiction* (Basingstoke, 1992); for a review of more recent feminist analysis of the Gothic, see Kate Ferguson Ellis, 'The Gothic Heroine and

Her Critics', in *A Companion to the Gothic*, ed D. Punter, Oxford, Chapter 20, 257–68.

10. This process of Gothicising is related to changes in taste in the early nineteenth century, and in this case specifically to styles of acting which respond to a darker interpretation. Charles Lamb, for example, recorded a shift in the interpretation of the consummate stage hypocrite, Joseph Surface's character: 'Joseph Surface, to go down now, must be a downright revolting villain – no compromise – his first appearance must shock and give horror …'. Charles Lamb, 'On the Artificial Comedy of the Last Century', in Roy Park (ed.), *Lamb as Critic* (London and Henley, 1980), 65–7.

11. Jan B. Gordon, 'Narrative Enclosure as Textual Ruin: An Archaeology of Gothic Consciousness', *Dickens Studies Annual*, Vol. 11, 1983, 209–39; 225–6.

1 Two Stories: Chiaroscuro and the Politics of Superstition

1. Quoted in Joseph Spence, *The Philosophy of Anglo-Irish Toryism, 1833–52*, 1991, Unpublished PhD dissertation, Birkbeck College, University of London, 328. I am grateful to Professor R. Foster for drawing my attention to this study.

2. The term 'evidentiary' is used in Gilbert and Gubar's *The Madwoman in the Attic* (New Haven, 1979). For accounts of this technique in the Gothic novel, see E.K. Sedgewick, *The Coherence of Gothic Conventions* (London, 1986); M. Kilgour, *The Rise of the Gothic Novel* (Basingstoke, 1998). For the whole question of editorial framing in Scott, see J. Millgate, *Scott's Last Edition* (Edinburgh, 1987); and for a gendering of the question, see J.Wilt, *Secret Leaves* (Chicago, 1985). For relations between oral and written, see P. Fielding, *Writing and Orality: Nationality, Culture, and Nineteenth Century Scottish Fiction* (Oxford, 1996).

3. The same volume of the *Dublin University Magazine*, in January 1838, which carried the first of the Purcell stories, also carried a suspicious article about the loyalty of Catholics and their adherence to the oath, which concludes:

> Mr O'Connell swears that he has no intention of subverting the present church establishment – it is notorious, and it is admitted that he does intend to subvert it. His advocate says, the oath must be received with this mental reservation – I disclaim an intention of subverting the present church establishment, *except by my votes as a member of parliament*, or I will not subvert it *out of mere hostility to the Protestant religion*. The italics being in both cases mental reservations. (*DUM*, 11, January–June 1838, 13.)

Note that the phrase 'mental reservations' is a traditional anti-Jesuit argument.

4. See Spence, op. cit., for the background. For relations between the rhetoric and the framing effects of these stories and their historical context, see K. Sullivan, 'Sheridan Le Fanu: The Purcell Papers, 1838–40', *Irish University Review*, Vol. 2, 1972, 3–19.

5. Le Fanu, *The Purcell Papers*, 3 vols, ed. with an Introduction by Alfred Graves (Dublin, 1880), III, 30. All subsequent quotations are from this edition, unless otherwise specified.

6. ibid., III, 30.

7. For the background, see Jan B. Gordon, op. cit. For some comment on the relation between testimony and fictional form, see V. Sage, *Horror Fiction in the Protestant Tradition*, Chapters 4 and 5.

8. For comment on Defoe, see F. Kermode, *The Genesis of Secrecy* (London, 1979), 113–14; Sage, op. cit., 133–4 and notes.

9. Le Fanu, op. cit., III, 31.

10. Le Fanu, op. cit., III, 38.

11. ibid., III, 39.

12. ibid., III, 40.

13. ibid., III, 40.

14. ibid., III, 40.

15. See S. Rashid, 'Political Economy in the *Dublin University Magazine*, 1833–1840', *Long Room*, nos 14/15 (1977), 16–19. See also, Spence, op. cit., for later background.

16. Le Fanu, op. cit., III, 41–2.

17. For his general tone about such matters, see Scott's correspondence with Maturin about the excesses of his Gothic effects, F. Ratchford and W.H. McCarthy, eds, *The Correspondence of Sir Walter Scott and Charles Robert Maturin* (Austin, Texas, 1837).

18. See P. Coughlan's analysis of Le Fanu's historical layering in 'Doubles, Shadows, Sedan-Chairs and the Past: the "Ghost Stories" of J.S. Le Fanu', in *Critical Approaches to Anglo-Irish Literature*, ed. Michael Allen and Angela Wilcox (Totwa, NJ, 1989).

19. Le Fanu, op. cit., III, 63.

20. Radcliffe, *Udolpho*, 2 vols, (London: 1963), vol. 1, 230.

21. Le Fanu, op. cit., III, 68–9.

22. Le Fanu, ibid., III, 75–7.

23. Le Fanu, ibid., III, 78–9.

24. The connection with Brontë was first pointed out in *The Cambridge History of English Literature* (Cambridge, 1932), Vol. XIII, 407. See also McCormack, *Dissolute Characters* (Manchester, 1993), 133.

25. Le Fanu, op. cit., III, 109. This mirror recurs in Chapter 25 of Charlotte Brontë's *Jane Eyre*, ed. Q.D Leavis (Harmonsworth, 1966), 311–14.

26. See McCormack, op. cit., (1993), 133, for further comments on the treatment of the Williamite connection.

27. See Sullivan op. cit., 12 for comment on the 'vernacular' aspects.

28. This is actually a later story published in 1850, added by Alfred Graves. See Sullivan, op. cit., 6.

29. For broader comment on this split, see Penny Fielding, *Writing and Orality: Nationality, Culture, and Nineteenth Century Scottish Fiction* (Oxford, 1996). The Scottish tradition uses it somewhat differently.

30. Kel Roop, 'Making Light in the Shadow Box: The Artistry of le Fanu', in *Papers on Language and Literature*, 21 (1985), 359–69.

31. Roop, ibid., 359.

32. Roop, ibid., 360.

33. Roop, ibid., 360.

34. Roop, ibid., 369.

35. Roop, ibid., 369.

36. McCormack, op. cit., (1993), 140–1.

37. For some subtle and informative commentary on the relations between biography and history in the story, see McCormack, op. cit., 126.
38. Le Fanu, op. cit., II, 190.
39. For an account of this as a 'meta-political plot', see J. Moynahan, 'The Politics of Anglo-Irish Gothic: Maturin, Le Fanu and the Return of the Repressed', in *Studies in Anglo-Irish Literature*, ed. H. Kosok (Bonn, 1975). This piece makes the play on 'possession' and 'dispossession' which I have used here and below.
40. Le Fanu, op. cit., 195.
41. Le Fanu, op. cit., II, 196–7.
42. Le Fanu, ibid., 197.
43. Le Fanu, ibid., II, 198.
44. The 1851 text is reproduced in *Best Ghost Stories of J.S. Le Fanu*, ed. E.F. Bleiler (New York, 1964), 29–46.
45. Le Fanu, op. cit., II, 224–5.
46. For a remarkable account of a 'house' and a company of aristocrats undergoing this hideous process, see *The Letters of John Wilmot, Earl of Rochester*, ed. J. Treglown (Oxford, 1980), 197–8.

2 Gothic and Romance: Retribution and Reconciliation

1. See Ian Duncan, *Modern Romance and Transformations of the Novel: The Gothic, Scott, Dickens* (Cambridge, 1992). See also on Scott's successors, A. Sanders, *The Victorian Historical Novel, 1840–1880* (London, 1978), 14–31.
2. For equivocations between realist and romantic readings of Scott, see Duncan, op. cit., 62. And see note 12, for bibliography. For the evidence Le Fanu thought of Scott as a romantic writer, see the Preface to *Uncle Silas*, ed. V. Sage (Harmondsworth, 2000), 3–4, and the commentary on this in relation to other Victorian readings of Scott in the Introduction, ix–xiii.
3. Le Fanu, *The Purcell Papers*, III, 217.
4. See his insistence on 'lowering' Maturin's effects in their correspondence, Ratchford and McCarthy, eds, op. cit., passim.
5. Le Fanu, *The Fortunes of Colonel Torlough O'Brien*, Dublin, 1847, 217.
6. In this case, Swift's own. See *The Cock and Anchor*, Ulster editions and Monographs 9, (Gerrard's Cross) 2001, ed. J. Jedrzewski, whose view of the novel is that Le Fanu was writing 'against himself' in this novel. See Intro., xviii.
7. Le Fanu, *The Cock and Anchor* (Dublin, 1845), 2–3.
8. This politicising of the 'picturesque' is an important theme which Purcell has established at the outset of *The Purcell Papers*, in his comments on the analogy between the ancient forests of Ireland, and the depleted condition of the genealogical trees of great Catholic families. Later, the notion of 'waste' is made into a sub-plot in *Uncle Silas*; in his desperate need for money Silas begins to burn his patrimony, the 'grand old timber' on the estate for charcoal. The bitter conditions created by the penal code at this time in Ireland partly explain the tone of this romance and its code of 'unsound timber':

'The social and economic effects of the penal code must have been very considerable. Family life was disrupted in many ways: Catholic fathers were estranged from Protestant heirs; bitter disputes were caused by the activities of 'discoverers' within the family. As the Catholic class diminished in numbers and influence, they were more and more cut off from the social life of the countryside. Uncertainty of tenure discouraged investment in land improvement and led to the cutting of timber for immediate profit.' *A New History of Ireland*, Oxford, 1986, Vol. IV, eds T.W. Moody and W.E. Vaughan, Chapter I, 20.

9. Le Fanu, op. cit., I, 20–1.
10. Le Fanu, ibid., I, 22–3.
11. See Jedrzejewski, Appendix, 476–8.
12. Le Fanu, op. cit., I, 271.
13. Le Fanu, ibid., I, 263.
14. Le Fanu, ibid., I, 267.
15. Jedrzewjski, op. cit., Introduction, xvi–xvii., and 416, note 4. Spence, op. cit., 314. For other aspects of the novel's analysis and its connection to the Gothic of Maturin, see also Spence, 348–9.
16. Le Fanu, op. cit., I, 202.
17. See Paul Hopkins, 'An Unknown Annotated Copy of *The Tenants of Malory*: J. Sheridan Le Fanu Regrets Some Anti-Semitic Expressions', *Long Room*, 30 (1985), 32–5.
18. Two examples I would briefly point to, however. Gordon Chancey, Blarden's lawyer has a dangerously languid nature and sleepy, glittering eyes. These eyes will become those of 'Carmilla', fifty years later. The other example is Black Martha, the demonic female servant of Old Mr Audley. She is the first example in Le Fanu of the 'unconscious hypocrite', whose compulsive, but totally concealed, interior, insists on emerging, in a splendid, purely theatrical soliloquy towards the end of the book. See below for further commentary on this. For a political analysis of this incident, see Spence, op. cit., 348. When Jedrzejewski, calls Le Fanu's characters 'puppets', he is disappointed, using Scott's rounded historical realism as an evaluative criterion, but if seen as a kind of combination of Gothic and political satire, these characters are comic as well as violent and threatening. Their artifice is that of the stage, but shifted into the novel.
19. Le Fanu, op. cit., II, 55–6.
20. The textual presentation of the incident and its equivalent effects in *The Purcell Papers* anticipate Le Fanu's very clear statement to Bentley about how he conceived of a rhetoric of'explanation'in his texts. See Walter C. Edens, op. cit., 238: 'The 3rd Vol. [*The Haunted Baronet*] is a story in equilibrium – between the natural and the *super*-natural. The supernatural phenomena being explainable on natural theories – and people left to choose what solution they please.'
21. Le Fanu is using the biography of Patrick Sarsfield in this novel for 'reconciliatory' purposes. See Piers Wauchope, *Patrick Sarsfield and the Williamite War* (Dublin, 1992). See the incidents at Birr castle (Offaly) reported in this book, which Le Fanu seems to have used as a model for the fictional Glindarragh castle plot, and the generous and just behaviour of O'Brien to his enemies, 50–3, 124, 170,186, and 242.
22. Paul Dangerfield in *The House by the Churchyard* straddles both low and high and is a fake gentleman, with a murderous past. Likewise, Walter Longcluse, in *Checkmate* is another mask for another personality in a past of bloodshed and murder. Both these are Gothic versions of the Double, who begin with

Tisdall, the Ainsworthian ex-highwayman who conceals his past under a mask of pious puritanism. But Bryerly in *Uncle Silas*, and, to a lesser extent, Mr Dawe, in *The Rose and The Key* are inverted 'low' characters.

23. Le Fanu, op. cit., 1.
24. For the relation between this early form of cinema and the Gothic, see Terry Castle, 'The Spectralising of the Other in *The Myseries of Udolpho*', in *The New Eighteenth Century*, eds Felicity Nussbaum and Laura Brown (New York and London, 1987), 231–54. For a more extended account, see also the more detailed and extended background in 'Phantasmagoria and the Metaphorics of Modern Reverie' in *The Female Thermometer: Eighteenth Century Culture and the Invention of the Uncanny*, 140–67. For some further, more recent comment, see Thomas Ruffles, *Life after Death in the Cinema*, unpublished PhD thesis, University of East Anglia, 2001.
25. Le Fanu, ibid., 2.
26. Le Fanu, ibid., 144.
27. Le Fanu, ibid., 3.
28. Le Fanu, ibid., 3.
29. Le Fanu, ibid., 3–4.
30. Le Fanu, ibid., 4.
31. Cf Terry Castle's description of the ambiguities of the fantasmagoria as a badge of the Enlightenment:

> It was never a simple mechanistic model of the mind's workings. Technically speaking, of course, the image did fit nicely with post-Lockeian notions of mental experience; nineteenth century empiricists frequently figured the mind as a kind of magic-lanthern, capable of projecting the image-traces of past sensation onto the internal 'screen' or backcloth of the memory. But the word phantasmagoria, like the magic lanthern itself, inevitably carried with it powerful atavistic associations with magic and the supernatural. To invoke the supposedly mechanistic analogy was *subliminally* to import the language of the uncanny into the realm of mental function. The mind became a phantom-zone – given over, at least potentially, to spectral presences and haunting obsessions. A new kind of daemonic possession became possible. (Castle, (1995) op. cit., 144 (my italics)).

Le Fanu is using the fantasmagoria here in the opposite way, not 'subliminally', but as a conscious and elaborate rhetorical analogy with the craft of the novelist, which allows him to exploit the ambiguities of 'superstition' which Castle describes so beautifully here, for his own (quasi-political) purposes. He frames his novel explicitly as a phantasmagoria in language, which immediately introduces another layer of representation.

3 'Cyclopean History': *The House by the Churchyard*

1. The novel dramatises the contrast between the dark, surviving forces of the past, even going back to the violent intervention of Cromwell, that took place in the seventeenth century and in the later war of succession, and the Whig 'present' of the 1767, when the main action of the book takes place. It

dramatises the symbiotic relationship between a wasted Irish aristocracy and
the race of middlemen – agents, portrayed as in the novel as vampires and
werewolves, who have sucked it dry, and stripped it of its land and power
until, despite the apparent solidity of the eighteenth-century present, that
ascendant class, by the 1760s, had become a ghost of its former self. That loss
has been carried forward into the the 1860s, the decade in which Gladstone
was to disestablish the Irish Church. Nothing in Ireland is as it appears, and
the whole question of the 'substance' of the culture is allegorised in this perpetual process of 'hollowing out', which corresponds to a kind of cultural
uncanny in the book's mordant rhetoric of 'cyclopean' darkness.

2. Le Fanu, *The House by the Churchyard* (London 1861), 3 vols, I, 1–2. The
'Aldermen of Skinner's Alley' were founded in 1690. The practice of minority
politics led Irish Toryism to adopt this violently anti-Catholic loyalist society.
For comment, see Spence, op. cit., 81.
3. Le Fanu, ibid., I, 52.
4. For discussion of this, see Charles Maturin, *Melmoth the Wanderer*
(Harmondsworth, 2000), ed. V. Sage, Introduction, xv–xxii.
5. See Maturin, ibid., Introduction, xxiiff.
6. The 'cyclopean' (sense (1) above) is present here in the 'great flat stone'
which is (apparently outrageously) compared to the 'communion-table', as
part of a humorous reversal of the material and spiritual senses of 'tenement',
in which the curate is the tenant and the family the landholders. Later, Le
Fanu uses this great flat stone as the sign of cyclopean 'presences' in the landscape (*Guy Deverell* and 'Bird of Passage'). This joke, which is the first mention of a 'return' in the text, is grafted here by association on to the notion
of 'horror' as a boyish pleasure in the macabre.
   The motif would have been been quite recognisable to Le Fanu's Victorian
English audience in the 1860s, because of the revival of the Druids. See
Charlotte Gere ed., *Victorian Fairy Painting*, catalogue to the Tate Gallery
Exhibition of 1995.
7. Le Fanu, ibid., I, 10–11.
8. Le Fanu, ibid., I, 16–17.
9. Le Fanu, ibid., I, 27–8.
10. For the conection between the 'cyclopean' and Titanism in the rhetoric of
Irish cultural nationalists like Ferguson, see Spence, op. cit., and Le Fanu, *The
Fortunes of Torlough O'Brien*, ed. cit., 74–5, when he describes the land as
resembling 'some Titanic fortification'. The figure of Ned Ryan (Ned O'The
Hills) in that novel is associated with the land, and it is he who destroys the
villain, Miles Garrett.
11. Le Fanu, ibid., I, 135–6.
12. Le Fanu, ibid., I, 112–13.
13. Le Fanu, ibid., I, 113–14.
14. Le Fanu, ibid., I, 115–16.
15. Le Fanu, ibid., I, 115–16.
16. Le Fanu, ibid., I, 119–20.
17. Le Fanu, ibid., I, 44.
18. Le Fanu, ibid., I, 128.
19. This scene condenses many private meanings for Le Fanu himself by the time
he wrote it. McCormack tells us how George, Susanna's father, used to lay his

hand in a particular way on his daughter's pillow; and of how, after his death, she heard his voice asking her to hasten to him in the tomb. McCormack, *Sheridan Le Fanu and Victorian Ireland*, 133.

20. Le Fanu, op. cit., I, 130–1.
21. The haunting of the hand is also parodied in the sub-plot of Mary Matchwell, self-appointed necromancer, and her rascally lawyer, Dirty Davy, to deprive Nutter, in his absence, of his house, and loyal Mrs Nutter of her home, on a legal ploy. But first, the house has to be invaded. Pretending to be a pedlar on the road outside, Mary whines her transaction at the servant, Moggy. Her 'hard, brown hand, palm open', impersonating that of a beggar, corresponds to the hand of the old Earl of Dunoran. Mary is regarded as a kind of 'devil' and the servants shrink from her 'as if they had seen a ghost'.

   The jokes about soul and body here reveal the parody as part of the same structure of thought as the 'haunting'. It is Moggy's vanity and lust of soul that allows the invasion to take place. The hand of Mary Matchwell, here, impersonating that of a beggar, corresponds to that of the old Earl of Dunoran: once the hand is in, the rest will follow. It is a parody of 'possession', that brings together the Christian metaphor of the house as a body and the boundaries of a property. This whole society, apparently secure and 'merry', is in fact totally, tremulously insecure on material and spiritual levels.
22. Le Fanu, ibid., III, 181–2.
23. Le Fanu, ibid., 182–3.
24. The name suggests Scott, whose mysterious figure of 'Greenmantle' in *Redgauntlet* is also called 'Lilias'.
25. Le Fanu, ibid., II, 5.
26. Le Fanu, ibid., II, 8.
27. Le Fanu, ibid., II, 8–9.
28. Le Fanu, ibid., I, 297. In later editions, Le Fanu changed 'supernatural' to 'dismal'.
29. Le Fanu, ibid., II, 19.
30. Le Fanu, ibid., II, 19–20.
31. Le Fanu, ibid., III, 150–1.
32. Le Fanu, ibid., III, 151–2.
33. Le Fanu, ibid., III, 102.
34. Le Fanu, ibid., III, 122.
35. Le Fanu, ibid., II, 161.
36. Le Fanu, ibid., II, 161–2.
37. Le Fanu, ibid., III, 25–6.
38. Le Fanu, ibid., III, 137–8.
39. Here is Charles on Dangerfield's laugh:

   He smiled a good deal. He was not aware that a smile did not quite become him. The fact is, he has lost a good many side teeth, and it was a hollow and sinister disclosure. He would laugh, too, occasionally, but his laugh was not rich and joyous, like General Chattesworth's, or even Tom Toole's cozy chuckle, or old Dr Walsingham's hilarious ha-ha-ha! He did not know it; but there was a cold, hard ring in it, like the crash and jingle of broken glass. Then his spectacles, shining like ice in the light, never removed for a moment – never even pushed up to his forehead – he ate in them, drank in them, fished in them, joked in them – he prayed in them, and, no doubt, slept in them, and would, it was believed, be buried in them – heightened that sense of mystery and mask which seemed to challenge curiosity and defy scrutiny with a scornful chuckle. (119)

The conflict in this passage is that it keeps the notion of the hybridity of laughter, its life-asserting variety, in view, even while it is clear that the only laughter which concerns us is the lipless grin, which is the type of all laughter. It is, as Beckett's Arsène says, the laugh laughing at the laugh. The bitter laugh that shows through the sweet. And the joke is that Dangerfield does not know that he himself is dead. He is not aware that he is, if you can look clearly enough, the skull beneath the skin. His pallor is 'phosphoric': this again looks forward to Silas, who is also a dead creature.

4 Dreadful Witness: Narrative Perversity and *Wylder's Hand*

1. See *Uncle Silas*, 2000, ed. cit., Introduction, xiv–xv, and note 13, xxxii. The full text of the letter from Bentley which specified such a significant change in Le Fanu's career as an author can be found in Walter C. Edens, op. cit., 164.
2. Le Fanu, *Wylder's Hand* (London, 1863, repr. London, 1978), 163.
3. Le Fanu, ibid., 163.
4. Le Fanu, ibid., 163.
5. Le Fanu, ibid., 22.
6. Friedrich Augustus Retzsch (1779–1859), a Dresden painter, was very much a part of early-nineteenth-century Romantic taste in England. He specialised in etchings which he called 'outlines', which have a peculiar line about them, both erotic and facially grotesque. He illustrated Burger's 'Lenore' (see Figs 1(a) and (b)), Goethe's *Faust*, and between 1828 and 1846, he produced his outlines to Shakespeare, a series of 106 etchings in eight volumes. His work inspired Byron, Shelley, and Dante Gabriel Rosetti. For the 'Phantom Dane', see Figs 2(a) and 2(b).
7. For the connection with the fantasmagoria, see Castle, op. cit. Swedenborg narrates how the angels performed an eye-operation on him, so that he was possessed of spiritual sight. Quoted in *Uncle Silas*, ed. cit., xxxv.
8. Le Fanu, ibid., 136.
9. Usually translated as 'Regeneration', it is, however, not used by St Paul in *Corinthians*, and Wylder seems to be putting the two things together, to comfort Rachel. The term is used in two places: Matthew 19:28; and Titus, 3:5. He is probably thinking of the latter, from the context.
10. Le Fanu, ibid., 192.
11. Le Fanu, ibid., 144.
12. Le Fanu, ibid., 61.
13. Le Fanu, ibid., 75.
14. Le Fanu, ibid., 75.
15. Le Fanu, ibid., 76.

16. Le Fanu, ibid., 205.
17. Le Fanu, ibid., 205.
18. Le Fanu, ibid., 207.
19. Le Fanu, ibid., 69.
20. Le Fanu, ibid., 146–7.
21. Le Fanu, ibid., 254.
22. Le Fanu, ibid., 256–7
23. Le Fanu, ibid., 110.
24. Le Fanu, ibid., 338.
25. Le Fanu, ibid., 387. The 'song' is the first line of Byron's 'Childe Harolde', Canto IV, st.11. Cf also Byron's tragedy 'Marino Faliero'. The 'Lord' refers ostensibly to the legendary historical figure of Marino Faliero, the Doge who was married to the sea, and who was beheaded for conspiracy against the Venetian State. But the quotation inevitably glances at Byron himself, too. Le Fanu, who wrote a verse tragedy called 'Beatrice' which has part of this story of Marino Falieri as its subject-matter, may well be thinking of Hoffmann's 'Doge and Dogaressa' here too, which is a more Gothic and fantastic treatment of the same tale. For the gender ambiguity inherent in the history of representations of Venice, see 'Venetian Views, Venetian Blinds', eds M. Pfister and B. Schaff (Amsterdam, 1999), 22 and note 37.
26. Le Fanu, ibid., 369.
27. Le Fanu, ibid., 79.
28. Le Fanu, ibid.
29. This is an echo of the Titanism motif of the cultural nationalists, which Le Fanu first 'Gothicises' (i.e. makes into a retributory threat) in his early work – in some of the stories from *The Purcell Papers*, for example. See Chapter 3, note 10 above.
30. Le Fanu, ibid., 82.
31. Le Fanu, ibid., 151.
32. Le Fanu, ibid., 19–20.
33. Le Fanu, ibid., 343–4.
34. Le Fanu, ibid., 204.
35. Le Fanu, ibid., 379.
36. Le Fanu, ibid., 385.
37. Le Fanu, ibid., 116.
38. Le Fanu, ibid., 385.

5 Magic Lanthern: *Uncle Silas*, Narrative Indirection and the Layered Text

1. See Wayne Hall, 'Le Fanu's House by the Marketplace', *Eire-Ireland*, 21:1 (Spring, 1968), 59. Quoted in *Uncle Silas*, ed. V. Sage (Harmondsworth, 2000), xxxiii.
2. Le Fanu, ed. cit., 9
3. Le Fanu, ed. cit., 9.
4. Le Fanu, ibid., 12
5. Le Fanu, ed. cit., 12–13.

6. For the background to religious controversy in the novel, see Introduction, ed. cit., xxvi–xxx.
7. This idea of a 'friend' haunts the text. It goes back to Mary Shelley's *Frankenstein* and the idea that we are 'but half made up'. A friend is a witness to the Self. The notion of 'friends' is also a vital part of the dissenting tradition; the other name for the Quakers is 'The Society of Friends'. The text explicitly evokes this context when Silas, in answer to Dudley's panic-stricken question, 'Who's there?' replies with false sweetness 'A friend' – meaning, in the military sense, 'not a foe'. But the sweetness of the white-haired old man's reply is also mediated into the hypocrisy of dissent, as Maud glimpses '... that frail, tall, white figure, the venerable silver locks that resembled those upon the honoured head of John Wesley ...'. Even in the 1860s, from the Established Protestant point of view, Wesley is precisely the 'friend' you do not want. The condensation via 'friend' brings together different levels of isolation. Death is a friend, and, as Austin intimates to Maud in the beginning of the novel, when his friend arrives, 'I must make the excursion the moment he calls.' This transposes the motif of the 'Faustian bargain' in Le Fanu's early stories; of the revenant who calls and will not be denied, in 'Robert Ardagh' and 'Schalken'.
8. Le Fanu, ed. cit., I, 19. For the role of prohibitions in the folktale, see Vladimir Propp, *Morphology of the Folktale* (Moscow, 1922; Bloomington, Indiana, 1968; repr. Bloomington, Indiana, reprinted Austin, Texas, 1990), Chapter 3, 26–7.
9. Le Fanu, ed. cit., I, 14.
10. Le Fanu, ed. cit., 156.
11. Le Fanu, ed. cit., 223. 'Old L'Amour' is a nickname of Milly's for Wyat, Silas's old servant, which alludes to Scott's *The Bride of Lammermoor*, a novel which has a variant Bluebeard plot.
12. Le Fanu, ed. cit., 284.
13. Le Fanu, ed. cit., 435.
14. Anne Radcliffe, *The Mysteries of Udolpho*, 2 vols (London, 1962), Vol. 1, 252.
15. Charles Maturin, *Melmoth the Wanderer* (Harmondsworth, 2000), ed. V. Sage, 24.
16. Le Fanu, ed. cit., 207.
17. Ibid., 421.
18. Maturin, *Melmoth*, ed. cit., 371.
19. Le Fanu, ed. cit., 151.
20. David Hume, *On Religion*, ed. R. Wollheim (New York, 1964). For further background, see Sir Leslie Stephen, *A History of English Thought in the Eighteenth Century*, 2 vols (London, 1927).
21. Le Fanu, ibid., 78.
22. Le Fanu, ibid., 98.
23. Le Fanu, ibid., 102.
24. Le Fanu, ibid., 123.
25. Le Fanu, ibid., 42.
26. Le Fanu, ibid., 133.
27. Le Fanu, ibid., 133.
28. See Sir Leslie Stephen, op. cit., for the eighteenth-century background. For the Victorian aspects of this controversy about resurrection, see Sage, *Uncle Silas*, ed. cit, Introduction, xxvi–xxx.
29. Le Fanu, ed. cit., 431.

30. Le Fanu, ibid., 18.
31. For comment on the contemporary angelic-demonic rhetoric surrounding Sheridan, see E.M. Butler, *Sheridan: A Ghost Story* (London, 1931), 300.
32. Le Fanu, ibid., 365.
33. Le Fanu, ibid., 167.
34. This painting hung over the Le Fanu family mantelpiece. See McCormack, *Dissolute Characters*, 90–1.
35. Le Fanu, ibid., 200.
36. See McCormack, *Dissolute Characters*, *passim*, for the association between Dutch painting in Le Fanu, and the 'dissolution' of realistic notions of character. See also his argument in *Sheridan Le Fanu and Victorian Ireland*, 168 about what he thinks of as 'psychic decomposition': that Silas is the 'dead soul' of his brother, Austin in another resurrected (Swedenborgian) form.
37. Le Fanu, ibid., 41–2.
38. Le Fanu, ibid., 27.
39. The modern interpretation is that it depicts a man in Phrygian (i.e. Asiatic) costume. For a full commentary, see Le Fanu, ed. cit., 448, note 4.
40. Le Fanu, ibid., 103.
41. Le Fanu, ibid., 148.
42. Le Fanu, Purcell Papers, ed. cit., I, 4.
43. Le Fanu, ibid., I, 47–8
44. Le Fanu, ibid., I, 47–8.
45. Le Fanu, ibid, I, 37.
46. Sir Giles Overreach spends most of the play exposing his hypocrisy quite openly to the audience. But when his schemes to marry off his rebelliously pious daughter Margaret (here is a parallel) are thwarted, he suddenly sees his vision of his own death, and it becomes a question of Heaven and Hell. A quite different metaphysical and heroic note is injected into the play at this point. Here one can see why he is a prototype for Silas in Le Fanu's mind: the tension is between the heroic defiance of God, and Hell, and the comic stereotype of the Hypocrite.
47. Le Fanu, 'The Wyvern Mystery' (Luton), 67.
48. Le Fanu, 'Willing To Die' (London), 1874, II, 312.

6 Doubleplot I: *The Tenants of Malory*

1. For further comment on framing effects, see Gerard Genette, *Paratexts*, trans. Jane E. Lewin, (Cambridge, 1997). As a result of his agreement with Bentley not to set subsequent novels in Ireland, Le Fanu uses a number of new 'Cyclopean' settings in Wales, in which the sublime landscape is layered richly with historic 'strata' which threaten revenancy. The Menai Straits is the place where the Druids made their last stand against the soldiers of Imperial Rome; Cor Penmon, at the Eastern tip of Anglesey (renamed 'Malory' in Le Fanu's novels, after the writer of medieval romances, Sir Thomas Malory) is an ancient seat of Celtic learning which consists of the ruins of a sixth century Augustinian priory; Beaumaris Castle is the last of Edward I's sea-fortifications against the unruly Welsh. For Le Fanu's relations

with the area, see Enid Madoc-Jones, 'Sheridan le Fanu and North Wales', *Anglo-Welsh Review*, Vol. 17, no. 40, 167–73.

2. *The Tenants of Malory*, 2nd edn (London, 1876), 4.
3. For discussion of the archetype and the painting, see Mario Praz, *The Romantic Agony*, (Oxford, 1933; repr. 1970), 116–18; 176; 296.
4. Le Fanu, ibid., 49.
5. Le Fanu, ibid., 50.
6. Le Fanu, ibid., 50. For the fantasmagoria, see T. Castle, op. cit., quote in Chapter 2 above, Note 24.
7. Le Fanu, ibid., 50. M.R. James will take up this phrase, 'the tail of the eye' to signal a nasty epiphany.
8. Le Fanu, ibid., 50-1.
9. Le Fanu, ibid., 54.
10. Le Fanu, ibid., 64.
11. Le Fanu, ibid., 64.
12. Le Fanu, ibid., 64–5.
13. Le Fanu, ibid., 67.
14. Le Fanu, ibid., 70.
15. Note the link also between this theme, the setting, and the same theme and setting in *Willing To Die*, in Ethel Ware's anchoritic 'perversity' – with her love for the villain, Richard Marston, she willingly enters into her own death. Maud Vernon on the other hand is unwilling to enter into her death, as she tells Max, her companion, at the beginning of the novel; and this 'perversity' is used as a weapon against her by her mother.
16. Le Fanu, ibid., 74.
17. Le Fanu, ibid.,78.
18. Le Fanu, ibid.,80.
19. Praz, op. cit., 176.
20. Le Fanu, op. cit., 95.
21. Le Fanu, ibid.,190.
22. Le Fanu, ibid.,196.
23. Le Fanu, ibid., 312.
24. Le Fanu, ibid.,313–14.
25. Le Fanu, ibid., 212.
26. I have drawn attention above to the adaptation by Le Fanu of Sheridan's plays – and in particular the plot of *The School for Scandal* – the story of Charles and Joseph Surface – into the Gothic plots of 'doubling' in Le Fanu's later romances. See Introduction note 10 and the last section of Chapter 5. Essentially, the contrast between the arch-hypocrite, Joseph, and the open-handed young aristocratic heir, Charles – both of whom, as their name 'Surface' implies – are essentially superficial and recognisable theatrical and social types – is encoded by Sheridan into a classic study of human folly. The point about Joseph, in particular, relates to the theme and the rhetoric of 'darkness' in Le Fanu's writing. To be 'dark' is Irish for to be 'close'. According to nineteenth-century ways of playing him, Sheridan's Joseph is so consummately hypocritical, so close and secretive about what he really thinks, and what he really *is*, that he scarcely reveals it to himself, and therefore it only emerges in hilariously repressed flashes for the audience too. Le Fanu tilts this essentially comic plot into a Gothic psychopathology, as we have seen,

sometimes – as in this novel – siting the two figures in one body, and allowing the plot of disguise to unfold as a form of paradoxical self-impersonation.

The hypocrite knows himself, of course, always; but does not reveal to others what he knows, and therefore what he is. This is the basis of the tradition
of moral satire that is quite common in eighteenth-century texts, which are
themselves often adaptations of earlier comic forms. Complex variations can
indeed occur – as in *Tom Jones*, for example – on this basically simple for-
mula. If this plot is then tilted into the Gothic plot of the 'Double' – which,
for example, Dickens accomplished quite early on in *Martin Chuzzlewit*, in
his picture of Montague Tigg who became another person, Tigg Montague –
the 'Joseph Surface' figure moves from the position of 'hypocrite', which
comes from the Greek for 'actor', into the position of what Stevenson's Hyde
calls 'a part not a person', an unconscious hypocrite. The self is radically
split. This shift, quite common in the nineteenth-century Gothic, is an
obsessive pattern explored in the hybrid romances of Le Fanu. The pattern
begins in *The House by the Churchyard*, and *Wylder's Hand*; unusually, *Uncle
Silas* actually has the two brothers, Austin (the 'Charles Surface' figure) and
Silas (Joseph, his dark shadow), externalised as characters.

Already, the pattern of leaving the impersonation as an enigma for the plot
to unravel is established in the figure of Paul Dangerfield (alias 'Charles
Archer' – a reverse of 'Charles Surface') in the earlier novel, *The House by the
Churchyard*. Often, the impersonation is that of a dead man, so there is a legal
fraud combined with the Gothic double; and there is a motif of 'resurrection' –
Paul Dangerfield has a 'Pauline' name, and the narrator jokes at one point
that he is actually more like Saul than Paul – so the reference is also to a diabolical parody of 'conversion'.

These elaborations yield a traffic between the idea of hypocrisy and the
split self that goes much further than the traditional moral theatre of
hypocrisy – the impersonation of another becoming the impersonation of
the self. One thinks here of what Dickens is doing in *Edwin Drood*: his intention, according to his daughter Kate, to have the villain confess at the end –
in the third person; and what Poe is doing with his narrators as early as the
1840s. And even what the early Dickens is doing at the most hyperbolic
points of his presentation of Pecksniff.

Le Fanu spreads this move into a study of the fragmented self (which is
already present in the soliloquies of Shakespeare's *Hamlet* and *Richard III* and
so does not need to be naively psychologised, because it has a long tradition
of theatrical representation), into a plot of perjury, impersonation and fraud,
among the buried secrets of the past.

27. Le Fanu, ibid., 177.
28. Le Fanu, op. cit., 187. Arthur is referring to Sheridan's *The Duenna* here.
29. Le Fanu, ibid., 186.
30. One needs to compare this incident with the violence of Bradley Headstone
    in *Our Mutual Friend*, a book which also full of violent and Gothic jokes about
    agency. But Dickens had been restrained by the Jewish community by then,
    and so his Jew, Riah, is a benign old patriarch, who is dead to the dead world
    below the roof-top garden. There is no evidence, to my knowledge, that
    Le Fanu was ever, like Dickens, criticised by the Jewish community. But see
    Paul Hopkins, *op. cit.*, (1985) for detailed comment on the marginalia left by

Le Fanu, regretting that he had written the chapters which include the most anti-Semitic sentiments in the book.

31. Le Fanu, ibid., 344.
32. Le Fanu, ibid., 145.
33. Le Fanu, ibid., 146.
34. Le Fanu, ibid., 388.

7   Doubleplot II: *Haunted Lives*

1. See R. Byrne, *Prisons and Punishments of London* (London: Grafton), 1992, 60–4.
2. 'The London community were in process of transfer to Brompton, then, like Bayswater, a village on the outskirts of the city, at the end of a notoriously muddy road.' *Newman*, 2 vols, L. Meriol Trevor (London, 1962), Vol. 2, *Light In Winter*, 21.
3. *Haunted Lives*, 3 vols (London, 1868), I, 2–3.
4. Le Fanu, ibid., I, 3.
5. Le Fanu, ibid., I, 5.
6. Le Fanu, ibid., I, 16.
7. Le Fanu, ibid., I, 6.
8. Le Fanu, ibid., I, 9.
9. Le Fanu, ibid., I, 11.
10. Le Fanu, ibid., I, 40–1.
11. Le Fanu, ibid., I, 57.
12. For the operation of these structures, see below Chapter 5, note 8. Their relationship is also an allusion to Burger's 'Lenore'. Cf the following passage: 'He stood leaning at the window, and looked out: a shadow of care had overcast him, and it seemed to her, under that gloom, that his face was glowing like that of Leonora's phantom trooper, paler, and thinner, and sterner, from minute to minute.' Ibid., III, 163–4.
13. Le Fanu, ibid., I, 57.
14. Le Fanu, ibid., I, 74
15. See *Uncle Silas*, 2000, ed., Sage, *op. cit.*, 463–4, particularly note 3, 464. For commentary on *Bertram*, see *Melmoth The Wanderer*, ed. Sage, 2000, Introduction, x.
16. Le Fanu, ibid., I, 76–7.
17. Le Fanu, ibid., I, 78–9
18. Fanu, ibid., I, 179.
19. Le Fanu, ibid., I, 230.
20. Le Fanu, ibid., II, 67.
21. Le Fanu, ibid., II, 175–6.
22. For the connection between this kind of 'perverse' moment, and the stage villain, see Satan's soliloquy in Milton, *Paradise Lost*, IV, 358ff.
23. Le Fanu, op. cit., II, 177–8.
24. Le Fanu, ibid., 211.
25. Le Fanu, ibid., II, 217.
26. Le Fanu, ibid., III, 255. Stephen Dedalus's formulation is as follows: '... that cardiac condition which the Italian physiologist Luigi Galvani, using a phrase almost as beautiful as Shelley's [i.e. 'his likening of the imagination to

'a fading coal'], called the 'enchantment of the heart' *Portrait of the Artist*, (London, 1928), 242–3.

27. Le Fanu, ibid., II, 236.
28. Le Fanu, ibid., II, 255–6.
29. Le Fanu, ibid.,III, 14.
30. Le Fanu, ibid., III, 24.
31. Le Fanu, ibid., III, 46–7.
32. Le Fanu, ibid., III, 102.
33. Le Fanu, ibid., I, 224.
34. Le Fanu, ibid., I, 224.
35. For the infuence of Lombroso, see D. Pick, ' "Terrors of the Night,": *Dracula* and "Degeneration" in the Late Nineteenth Century, *Critical Quarterly*, 30 (1988), 71–87.
36. Le Fanu, ibid., I, 242.
37. Le Fanu, ibid., II, 56–7

8 'Carmilla': 'I'll let you be in my dream, if I can be in yours'

1. Nina Auerbach, *Our Vampires, Our Selves*, University of Chicago Press, 1995, 42. For another Carmilla-friendly reading, see also William Veeder, 'Carmilla: The Arts of Repression', *Texas Studies in Literature and Language*, Vol. 22, No. 2, Summer 1980, 197–223.
2. This tradition is recapitulated in Mary Shelley's *Frankenstein*. It is worth remembering that Percy Shelley as a Platonist and a translator of Plato's *Symposium*. I'm indebted in this page to a conversation with Angharad Hill, and her subsequent class presentation, which helped me crystallise the opening argument.
3. 'Carmilla' in *In A Glass Darkly*, ed., with Introduction and Notes by Robert Tracy (Oxford, 1993), 246.
4. *Le Fanu*, ibid., 246–7.
5. Le Fanu, ibid., 247.
6. Le Fanu, ibid., 248.
7. Le Fanu, ibid., 248.
8. Le Fanu, ibid., 259.
9. Le Fanu, ibid., 259.
10. W.J. McCormack points out a cultural link between Lewis Carroll's *Through the Looking Glass* and *In a Glass Darkly* in the trope of mirrors. Carroll's text was published in the same year as 'In a Glass Darkly'; and the latter's title, McCormack suggests, twisting the biblical translation of St Paul, 'through a glass darkly', may imply something similar, the twist trapping us *in* the mirror. McCormack, *Dissolute Characters*, 142. Here is the famous passage in which Alice and Tweedledum and Tweedledee come across the Red King sleeping. Tweedledee tells Alice that she's 'only a sort of thing in his dream':

> If that there King was to wake,' added Tweedledum, 'you'd go out – bang! – just like a candle!'

'I shouldn't!' Alice exclaimed indignantly. 'Besides, if *I'm* only a sort of thing in his dream, what are *you*, I should like to know?'

'Ditto,' said Tweedledum.

'Ditto, ditto!' cried Tweedledee.

He shouted this so loud that Alice couldn't help saying 'Hush! You'll be waking him, I'm afraid, if you make so much noise.'

'Well, it's no use your talking about waking him,' said Tweedledum, 'when you're only one of the things in his dream. You know very well you're not real.'

'I am real!' said Alice, and began to cry. (Gardner, *The Annotated Alice*, (London, 1960)) 238

It is bad enough to be told that you're a sort of thing, worse that you're a thing in the dream of another and could thus be extinguished; but the real anxiety comes as Alice realises the paradox that, if she *knows* that she is a thing in someone else's dream, then she knows (proof by the Cartesian *cogito*) that she is unreal. She couldn't wake him up anyway, whatever she does. This is a dreadful trap from which there is no escape. Compared to this knowledge, the fate of her imminent 'mortality', of going out like a candle, is a consolation, merely the last sputter of the tautology, so to speak. Bertrand Russell once remarked on this sequence in a radio discussion that: 'if it were not put humorously, we should find it too painful' (Gardner, op. cit., 238).

11. The source of *Through the Looking Glass* was revealed in 1938 by another Alice: Alice Raikes, a little friend of Alice Liddell, who recounts the following dialogue with Carroll in front of a mirror in their house:

'Now', he said, giving me an orange, 'first tell me which hand you have got that in.' 'The right', I said. 'Now', he said, 'go and stand before that glass, and tell me which hand the little girl you see there has got it in.' After some perplexed contemplation, I said, 'The left hand.' 'Exactly', he said, 'The left hand.' 'Exactly,' he said, 'and how do you explain that?' I couldn't explain it, but seeing that some solution was expected, I ventured, 'If I was on the *other* side of the glass, wouldn't the orange still be in my right hand?' I can remember his laugh. 'Well done, little Alice,' he said, 'The best answer I've had yet.' (Gardner, op. cit., 180, N)

Martin Gardner has shown the asymmetric nature of left–right reversals; but the striking thing here is the confidence and alacrity with which Alice goes hypothetically behind the mirror and remains herself. It is the reversed image which is the representation; the original is the same way round and thus confirms herself: right is right. In his later work *Syvlie and Bruno*, Carroll has many right–left reversals, none more potentially 'Gothic' than the anagrammatic transformation LIVE into EVIL. (Gardner, op. cit., N182)

12. Le Fanu, ibid., 259.
13. Le Fanu, ibid., 260.
14. Le Fanu, ibid., 260
15. Le Fanu, ibid., 261.
16. Le Fanu, *Best Ghost Stories*, ed. E.F. Bleiler, Dover, New York, 1964, 277.
17. Le Fanu, op. cit., 277.

18. And yet, articulates doubts at the same time, in the novel's final spate of rhetorical questions:

    Am I giving this infinite true love in vain ? I comfort myself with one vague hope. I cannot think that nature is so cynical. Does the love phantom represent nothing ? And is the fidelity that nature claims, but an infatuation and a waste? *Willing to Die*, London, 1873, III, 280.

19. The elaborate paratextual framing, added after the original publication of 'Carmilla' in *The Dark Blue*, is frequently commented on. For commentary, see Robert Tracy's notes in the Oxford edition, ed. cit. It is perhaps worth mentioning that there is a glitch, or an extra link, in the paratextual chain. Hesselius refers in the preface to his female correspondent: many readers assume this to be Laura herself. But Laura's text is addressed to a female 'You', who is never named, and who we know has died in the meantime. This is either a mistake of Le Fanu's, who had intended to frame it differently, or another (absent) witness in the chain. This is a doubtful point: but I am willing to believe it is the latter, given the elaboration of his framing devices elsewhere.
20. Le Fanu, ibid., 262.
21. Le Fanu, ibid., 277.
22. Le Fanu, ibid., 312.
23. Le Fanu, ibid., 319.
24. For an illuminating summary of which Swedenborgian ideas are powerful in Le Fanu's characters, based on the stipulations of 'Green Tea', see J. Moynahan, *Anglo-Irish: The Literary Imagination in a Hyphenated Culture*, Princeton, New Jersey, 1995, 130.
25. Le Fanu, ibid., 278.
26. Le Fanu, ibid., 311.
27. Le Fanu, ibid., 267–8.
28. Le Fanu, ibid., 268.
29. Le Fanu, ibid., 269.
30. Le Fanu, ibid., 269.
31. Le Fanu, ibid., 270.
32. *Buffon*, Otis E. Fellowes and Stephen Milliken (New York, 1994), 143.
33. Buffon, *De L'Homme* Presentation et notes de Michele Duchet (Paris, 1971), 404. One of Buffon's favourite words is 'funeste', which Le Fanu may have taken from him.
34. Le Fanu, op. cit., 271
35. Compare the observation of Marina Warner about the Bogeyman:

    Beneath the grotesque fantasmagoria of cannibal bogeymen there pulses the biological urge to perpetuate the line; the folly and horror of child murder and abuse recur alongside other violations and terrors. At its heart flourishes anxiety about generational order, the stewardship of the future by the living on behalf of the vulnerable who should inherit. (*No Go The Bogeyman* (London, 1997), 66.

36. Le Fanu, ibid., 273.

37. Le Fanu, ibid., 282

38. Compare the only other occurrence in Le Fanu of such a figure, the story 'The Child that Went with the Fairies', reprinted in ed. Bleiler, *Ghost Stories and Mysteries*, Dover, 1973, 136–43.

39. Le Fanu, ibid., 283.

Postscript

1. Le Fanu, *Willing To Die*, 3 vols, (London, 1873), I, 1

2. Roland Barthes, *The Responsibility of Forms*, translated by Richard Howard (California, 1985), 120.

Bibliography

Primary texts, by Le Fanu, Joseph Sheridan

The Cock and Anchor, Dublin, William Curry; London, Longman's; Edinburgh, Fraser, 1845

The Fortunes of Colonel Torlough O'Brien, Dublin, James McGlashen, 1847; London, William S. Orr, 1847

Ghost Stories and Tales of Mystery, Dublin, James McGlashen, 1851

The House by the Churchyard, London, Tinsley, 1863, 3 vols

Wylder's Hand, London, London, Dover, 1978

Uncle Silas, ed., with Introduction and Notes by V. Sage, Harmondsworth, Penguin Classics, 2000

Guy Deverell, London, Richard Bentley, 1865, 3 vols

All in the Dark, London, Richard Bentley, 1866, 3 vols

The Tenants of Malory, London, Tinsley Brothers, 1867, 3 vols

A Lost Name, London, Richard Bentley, 1868, 3 vols

Haunted Lives, London, Tinsley Brothers, 1868, 3 vols

The Wyvern Mystery, London, Tinsley Brothers, 1869, 3 vols

Checkmate, London, Hurst and Blackett, 1871, 3 vols

The Rose and the Key, London, Chapman and Hall, 1871

Chronicles of Golden Friars, London, Richard Bentley, 1871, 3 vols

In A Glass Darkly, ed., with an Introduction and Notes by R. Tracy, Oxford, World's Classics, 1993

Willing To Die, London, Hurst and Blackett, 1873, 3 vols

The Purcell Papers, London, Richard Bentley, 1880, 3 vols

The Poems of Joseph Sheridan Le Fanu, London, Downey, 1896

Secondary sources

[Anon], 'Joseph Sheridan Le Fanu', *Dublin University Magazine*, vol. 81 (March, 1873), 319–20.

Auerbach, Nina, *Our Vampires, Our Selves*, Chicago, 1995.

Barthes, Roland, *The Responsibility of Forms*, trans. Richard Howard, California, 1985.

Begnal, Michael, *Sheridan Le Fanu*, Lewisburg, 1971.

Bleiler, E.F., 'Introduction' to *Best Stories of J.S. Le Fanu*, New York, 1964, v–xi.

——,'Introduction' to *Ghost Stories and Mysteries*, New York, 1975, v–ix.

Botting, Fred, 'Power in the Darkness: Heterotopias, Literature and Gothic Labyrinths', *Genre*, Summer/Fall, 1993, 253–82.

Bowen, Elizabeth, *Collected Impressions*, London, 1950.

——, 'Introduction' to *The House by the Churchyard*, London, 1968, vii–ix.

Brantlinger, Patrick, 'What is "Sensational" about the "Sensation Novel"?', *Nineteenth Century Literature*, vol. 37, no. 1, (1982), 1–28.

Brantlinger, Patrick, 'Imperial Gothic: Atavism and the Occult in the British Adventure Novel, 1880–1914', *English Literature in Transition, 1880–1920*, vol. 28 (1985), 243–52.

Brooke-Rose, Christine, *The Rhetoric of the Unreal*, Cambridge, 1981.

Briggs, Julia, *Night Visitors: The Rise and Fall of the English Ghost Story*, London, 1977.

Bronfen, Elisabeth, *Over Her Dead Body: Death, Femininity, and the Aesthetic*, Manchester, 1992.

Brooke, Nicholas, ed., with an Introduction and Notes, *Macbeth*, Oxford, 1993.

Brown, Malcolm, *The Politics of Irish Literature From Thomas Davies to W.B.Yeats*, London, 1972.

Byrne, R., *Prisons and Punishments of London*, London, 1992.

Cahalan, James M., *Great Hatred, Little Room: The Irish Historical Novel*, Dublin, 1983.

Carver, Steven, *Abnormal Literature: the Early Fiction of William Harrison Ainsworth, 1827–1848*, Unpublished PhD Thesis, University of East Anglia, 2000.

Castle, Terry, 'The Spectralising of the Other in *The Mysteries of Udolpho*', in *The New Eighteenth Century*, eds Laura Brown and Felicity Nussbaum, NY and London, 1987, 231–54.

——, *The Female Thermometer*, Oxford, 1995.

Collins, Wilkie, *The Black Robe*, London, 1881.

Corkery, Daniel, *Synge and Anglo-Irish Literature*, Cork, 1966 (first published, 1931).

Coughlan, Patricia, 'Doubles, Shadows, Sedan-Chairs and the Past: the "Ghost Stories" of Sheridan Le Fanu', *Critical Approaches to Anglo-Irish Literature*, eds Michael Allen and Angela Wilson, Totwa, NJ, 1989, 17–39.

Davie, Donald, *The Heyday of Sir Walter Scott*, London, 1961.

Diskin, Patrick, 'Poe, Le Fanu and the Sealed Room Mystery', *Notes and Queries* (New Series), vol. 13 (Sept. 1966), 337–9.

Duchet, Michele, ed., Presentation et Notes, *De L'Homme, Buffon*, Paris, 1971.

Duncan, Ian, *Modern Romance and the Transformations of the Novel: The Gothic, Scott, Dickens*, Cambridge, 1992.

Eagleton, Terry, *Heathcliff and the Great Hunger*, London, 1995.

Edens, Walter C., *Sheridan Le Fanu: A Minor Victorian Novelist and his Publisher*, Unpublished PhD Thesis, University of Illinois, 1963.

Ellis, S.M., *Wilkie Collins, Le Fanu, and Others*, London, 1951 (first published, 1931).

Fellowes, Otis E., and Milliken, Stephen, eds, *Buffon*, New York, 1984.

Fielding, Penny, *Writing and Orality: Nationality, Culture and Nineteenth Century Scottish Fiction*, Oxford, 1996.

Fierobe, Claude, 'Le portrait dans le Récit Fantastique', in *Vivante Tradition, Sources et Racines*, eds Olivier Lutaud, Marie-Madeleine Martinet, Roger Lejosnes, Paris, 1982, 43–52.

Flanagan, Thomas, *The Irish Novelists 1800–1850*, New York, 1959.

Foster, Roy, *Paddy and Mr Punch*, London, 1993.

Frye, Northrop, 'Dickens and the Comedy of Humours', in Ian Watt, ed., *The Victorian Novel*, New York, 1971, 49ff.

Gardner, Martin, *The Annotated Alice*, London, 1960.

Gates, Barbara T., 'Blue Devils and Green Tea: Sheridan Le Fanu's Haunted Suicides', *Studies in Short Fiction*, vol. 24 (1987).

Genette, Gerard, *Paratexts*, trans. Jane E. Lewin, Cambridge, 1997.

Gettmann, Royal, *A Victorian Publisher: A Study of the Bentley Papers*, Cambridge, 1960.

Gilbert, Sandra and Gubar, Susan, *The Madwoman in the Attic*, New Haven, 1979.

Gordon, Jan B., 'Narrative Enclosure as Textual Ruin: An Archaeology of Gothic Consciousness', *Dickens Studies Annual*, vol. 11, (1983), 209–38.

Hall, Wayne, 'Le Fanu's House by the Marketplace', *Eire-Ireland*, vol. 21, no. 1, 1986, 55–72.

Haynes, D.A.L., *The Portland Vase*, London, 1964.

Heilman, Robert B., 'Charlotte Bronte's "New Gothic" ', in eds R.B. Rathburn and M. Steinman Jnr, *From Jane Austen to Joseph Conrad: Essays Collected in Memory of James T. Hillhouse*, Minneapolis, 1958.

Hopkins, Paul, 'An Unknown Annotated Copy of *The Tenants of Malory*, J. Sheridan Le Fanu Regrets Some Anti-Semitic Expressions', *Long Room*, vol. 30, (1985), 32–5.

Houghton, Walter E., *The Victorian Frame of Mind, 1830–1870*, New Haven, London, 1957.

Howes, Marjorie, 'Misalliance and Anglo-Irish Tradition in Le Fanu's *Uncle Silas*', *Nineteenth Century Literature*, vol. 47, (1992), 164–86.

Hughes, Winifred, *The Maniac in the Cellar*, Princeton, NJ, 1980.

Jedrejewski, Jan, ed., with an Introduction and Notes, J.S. Le Fanu, *The Cock and Anchor* (1873 text), Gerrard's Cross, 2000.

Kenton, Edna, 'A Forgotten Creator of Ghosts: Joseph Sheridan Le Fanu', *Bookman* (July, 1929), 528–34.

Kilgour, Maggie, *The Rise of the Gothic Novel*, London, Macmillan, 1994.

Lamb, Charles, 'On the Artificial Comedy of the Last Century', in Roy Park, ed., *Lamb As Critic*, London and Henley, 1980, 65–7.

Le Fanu, Thomas Philip, *Memoir of the Le Fanu Family*, Manchester, 1924.

Le Fanu, William, *Seventy Years of Irish Life*, London, 1893.

Longheed, W.E., 'An Addition to the Le Fanu Bibliography', *Notes and Queries*, June 1964, 224.

Lozes, Jean, (ed.), 'Fragment d'un journal intime de J.S. Le Fanu ... 18 May 1858', *Caliban* (Annales de l'Universite de Toulouse-Le Mirail), new series, vol. 10, no. 1 (1974), 153–64.

——, *Un Roman Gothique Irlandais: Uncle Silas de Sheridan Le Fanu*, Bordeaux, 1992.

Lukacs, Georg, *The Historical Novel*, trans. Hannah and Stanley Mitchell, London, 1962.

McCormack, W.J., *Sheridan Le Fanu and Victorian Ireland*, Oxford, 1980; revised ed., Dublin, 1991.

——, *Dissolute Characters: Irish Literary History Through Sheridan Le Fanu, Balzac, Yeats and Bowen*, Manchester, 1993.

Madoc-Jones, Enid, 'Sheridan Le Fanu and North Wales', *Anglo-Welsh Review*, vol. 17, no. 40, 167–73.

Massinger, Philip, *A New Way To Pay Old Debts*, in *The Selected Plays of Philip Massinger*, ed. Colin Gibson, Cambridge, 1978, 183–277.

Millgate, Jane, *Scott's Last Edition*, Edinburgh, 1987.

Moynahan, Julian, 'The Politics of Anglo-Irish Gothic: Maturin, Le Fanu, and the Return of the Repressed', *Studies in Anglo-Irish Literature*, ed. H. Kosok, Bonn, 1975.

——, *The Anglo-Irish: The Literary Imagination in a Hyphenated Culture*, Princeton, NJ, 1995.

Nethercott, Arthur, H., 'Coleridge's "Christabel" and Le Fanu's "Carmilla" ', *Modern Philology*, vol. 147 (Aug., 1949), 32–8.

O'Neill, Patrick J., 'German Literature and the *Dublin University Magazine* 1830–1850: a Checklist and Commentary', *Long Room*, nos 14/15 (1977), 20–31.

Orel, Harold, 'Rigid Adherence to Facts: Le Fanu's *In a Glass Darkly*', *Eire-Ireland*, Vol. 20, no. 4 (1985), 65–88.

Philips, Walter C., *Dickens, Reade, and Collins: Sensation Novelists; a Study in the Conditions and Theories of Novel Writing in Victorian England*, New York, 1919.

Pick, Daniel, 'Terrors of the Night: *Dracula* and "Degeneration" in the Late Nineteenth Century', *Critical Quarterly*, vol. 30 (1988), 71–87.

Praz, Mario, *The Romantic Agony*, Oxford, 1933; repr. 1970.

Pritchett, V.S., *The Living Novel*, London, 1946.

Punter, D. ed., *A Companion to the Gothic*, Oxford, 2000.

Rashid, Salim, 'Political Economy in the *Dublin University Magazine* 1833–1840', *Long Room*, nos 14/15 (1977), 16–19.

Ray, Gordon N., 'The Bentley Papers', *The Library* (5th Series), vol. 7, (Sept 1952), 178–200.

Robertson, Fiona, *Legitimate Histories: Scott, Gothic, and the Authorities of Fiction*, Oxford, 1994.

Roop, Kel, 'Making Light in the Shadow Box: the Artistry of Le Fanu', *Papers on Language and Literature*, vol. 21 (1985), 359–69.

Ruffles, Thomas, *Life after Death in the Cinema*, Unpublished PhD Thesis, 2001, University of East Anglia.

Sadleir, Michael, *Dublin University Magazine; its History, Contents, and Bibliography*, Dublin, 1938.

Sage, Victor, *Horror Fiction in the Protestant Tradition*, Basingstoke, 1988.

——, 'Resurrecting the Regency: Comedy and Horror in the Fiction of J.S. Le Fanu', ed., J. Wolfreys, *Victorian Gothic*, Basingstoke, 2000.

——, ed., with an Introduction and Notes, *Melmoth the Wanderer*, Charles Maturin, Harmondsworth, 2000.

——, ed., with an Introduction and Notes, *Uncle Silas*, J.S. Le Fanu, Harmondsworth; 2000.

——, 'Irish Gothic: C.R. Maturin and J.S. Le Fanu', in ed. D. Punter, *A Companion to the Gothic*, Oxford, 2000, 81–93.

Sanders, Andrew, *The Victorian Historical Novel, 1840–1880*, London, 1978.

Scott, Ken, 'Le Fanu's "The Room in the Dragon Volant" ', *Lock Haven Review*, no. 10 (1968), 25–32.

Sedgewick, Eve Kosofsky, *The Coherence of Gothic Conventions*, London, 1986.

Spence, Joseph, *The Philosophy of Anglo-Irish Toryism, 1833–1852*, 1991, Unpublished PhD Dissertation, Birkbeck College, University of London.

Sullivan, Kevin, 'The House by the Churchyard: James Joyce and Sheridan Le Fanu', *Modern Irish Literature: Essays in Honour of William York Tindall* (eds R.J. Porter and J.D. Brophy), New York, 1972, 315–34.

——, 'Sheridan Le Fanu: The Purcell Papers 1838–1840', *Irish University Review*, vol. 2, no. 1, (Spring 1972), 5–19.

Sullivan, Jack, *Elegant Nightmares: the English Ghost Story From Le Fanu to Blackwood*, Athens Oh., 1978.

Trevor, Meriol L., *Newman*, 2 vols, London, 1962.

Veeder, William, 'Carmilla: The Arts of Repression', *Texas Studies in Literature and Language*, vol. 22, no. 2, Summer 1980, 197–223.

Warner, Marina, *No Go the Bogeyman*, London, 1997.

Wauchope, Piers, *Patrick Sarsfield and the Williamite Wars*, Dublin: Irish Academic Press, 1992.

Willier, S.A., 'Madness, the Gothic, and Bellini's "Il Pirati" ', *Opera Quarterly*, vol. 6 (1989), 7–23.

Wilt, Judith, *Secret Leaves*, Chicago, 1985.

Wolff, Robert Lee, *Strange Stories and Explorations in Victorian Fiction*, Boston, 1971.

Index

Addison, Joseph, 35
Ainsworth, Harrison, 5, 43–4
Anglican, 105, 112
'anguine', 138, 167, 186
Anthony, St, 25
Anti-semitism, 36, 176
Appel, Johan, Augustus, 'Der Freischutz', 165
Arachne, 188
Athenaeum, The, 2
'attestation', 22
Auerbach, Nina, 178
Aughrim, Battle of, 31
Augustine, St, 118
Avernus, 200

Bacon, Sir Francis, 197
Barthes, Roland, 204–5
Beaumaris, 131
Beckford, William, 119
Bellini, Giovanni, 158
Belisarius, 121
Bennett (Le Fanu), Susan, 88, 89, 141
Bentham, Jeremy, 16
Blake, William, 123
Bleiler, E.F., 1
Bonaparte, Napoleon, 22
Botticelli, Sandro, 138
Bowen, Elizabeth, 1
Brontë, Charlotte, 5, 20
Brontë, Emily, 178
Buffon, 196–7
Burke's Peerage, 109
Byron, Lord George Gordon, 49, 94, 119, 124, 169

Caen, 146
Calvinism, 202
'Carmagnole, La', 122
Carroll, Lewis, 183, 205
Catholic, 11, 23, 33, 34, 35, 158
Cenci, Beatrice, 136
Cervantes, Miguel, 48, 61, 77

Christ, Jesus, 13, 64, 120
Christiana, Queen of Sweden, 196
'chiaroscuro', 23, 118
Civil War, Irish, 33
Collins, Wilkie, 1–2, 66
Cresseron, de, Charles, 47, 55, 77
Corday, Charlotte, 173
Cromwell, Oliver, 50
'Cyclopean', 52, 95, 134, 136

danse macabre, 116, 123
'Darkness', as readerly condition, 43, 46, 65, 203
Darwin, Charles, *The Descent of Man*, 190, 197
Darwin, Erasmus, 123
Darwinism, 190
Defoe, Daniel, 14
De la Tour, Georges, 115
Demeter, 123
Dickens, Charles, 3, 36, 43, 98, 103, 122, 140, 154, 161
Diderot, Denis, 197
Doges, of Venice, 94
Dublin University Magazine (*DUM*), 5, 12, 16–17, 115 (text of *Uncle Silas*), 126
Diablerie, 15
Dutch (–Irish connection), 20
    painters, 22
Douw, Gerald, 22, 25

Eagleton, Terry, 2
Edens, Walter C., 128
Eliot, George, 73
    parody of, 66
Eleusinian mysteries, 123
Elizabeth I, Queen, 158, 161, 173; Elizabethan sonneteers, 195
Enlightenment, 12, 180, 190, 192, 195
    Sadeian side of, 197
    (post-), 205

Erl King, The, 139
'explanation', suspended by narrative,
  19

Fantasmagoria, the, 40, 46, 181
Ferguson, Samuel, 11
Fielding, Henry, *Tom Jones*, 61, 129
Flaxman, John 123
Fleet prison, 168
Fouqué, Baron de la Motte, 134

Gainsborough, William (?), 119
Gordon, Jan, 6–7
Gordon riots, 158
Gospels, The, and corroborative
    witnessing, 13
  Christ's utterance, 81
  Matthew, 101
Gothic
  holding narrative at bay, 3–4
  Le Fanu's as rhetoric, 4
  as agent of textual hybridity, 5
  as cultural response, 5
  epiphanies, 12, 30
  informal manifesto for, 17
  effects and grotesque, 22
  full-blown, 29
  vocabulary of hellish darkness, 51
  mixture with sentimental, 62
  fairytale of Lady Ringdove, 90
  horror, language of and mirror-
      images, 94
  anti-Gothic feint, 103
  rhetoric of Heaven and Hell, 105
  romance and fairytale, 106, 110
  double, 129
  anti-Catholic plot, 130
  stone tablet, 144
  Romance, 158
  Old Gothic, 172
  as framing device, 174
Grand Guignol, 116

Hades, King of, 123, 200
Hoffmann, E.T.A., 26
Hogarth, William, 28
  Hogarthian brute, 68
  'Marriage a la Mode', 129
Holy Office, 95

Hume, David, 113

Ireland, as Whig-dominated House,
  32
Iscariot, Judas, 121
Ithuriel, 187

Jacobin, 12
Jacobite, 3, 12, 33, 44
James, II, King, 38
James, M.R., 37
Jedrejewski, Jan, 35
Jepthah, 124
Jewish usurer, stereotype of, 36
Jewsbury, Geraldine, 2
Job, Book of, 113
Jonson, Ben, 128
Joyce, James, 1, 170

Llangollen, Ladies of, 93
Lee, Gypsy Rose, 40
Le Fanu, Joseph Sheridan, 2
  Chronicles of Golden Friars, 2
  In a Glass Darkly, 2, 23
  Uncle Silas, 3, 5–6
  tragic death of his wife, 3
  'Carmilla', 6, 23, 178, 253
  Willing to Die, 6, 129;
      anchoritic fantasy in, 187
  and Protestant cultural nationalism,
      11ff
  'A Chapter in the History of a
      Tyrone Family', 13ff, 21
  The Wyvern Mystery, 20, 129
  'The Fortunes of Sir Robert Ardagh',
      21, 25
  'Passage in the Secret History of an
      Irish Countess', 21, 126
  'Schalken the Painter', 21; 1851
      text, 27, 44; source in 'Jan
      Schalken's Three Wishes'; 'The
      Ghost and the Bonesetter',
      21–2
  resurrection motifs and *The Purcell
      Papers*, 21, 29, 31, 36, 40
  'The Last Heir of Castle Connor', 21
  'The Drunkard's Dream', 21
  'The Bridal of Carrigvarah', 22
  'Jim Sullivan's Adventures', 22